Weapons
of
Mass Seduction

Weapons
of
Mass Seduction

Film Reviews and

Other Ravings

by Lucius Shepard

🌾 Wheatland Press

http://www.wheatlandpress.com

Published by
Wheatland Press
P. O. Box 1818
Wilsonville, OR 97070

ISBN 0-9755903-1-6
Printed in the United States of America

Contents

True Life Adventures

Ravings

Introduction:
Movies, Football and Breathing Meaningfully

SOME TIME IN THE 80S MY MOTHER, a long-time reader of SF/F started talking about this new writer who had turned up in *Asimov's* who, she insisted, I really, really ought to read. "Lucius Shepard," she said. "He writes like nobody I've ever read. You have to read his stuff."

Yeah, yeah, sure Mama, whatever you say. I was busy being a sophisticated graduate student and couldn't be bothered with science fiction.

Fast forward to the late 90s. I have time to read fiction again, and I return to the SF/F magazines. Huh, this is pretty good stuff, I say to myself. I start buying *Year's Best* volumes and sort of catching up on the field. I read a story called "The End of Life as We Know It," by this guy Lucius Shepard. Hey, isn't that the guy my mom was always talking about? So I pick up whatever collections of his I can find. Holy crap, this guy is good. Ever the completist, I start reading his film reviews as well. Some of them made me laugh, some of them singed my eyebrows.

Fast forward a bit farther. I start writing. I join a workshop. Jay Lake and I decide to try to start an anthology series (*Polyphony*). We're driving along in the workshop car pool one night talking about what Big Name Authors we might possibly get stories from and I say, Whoa, wouldn't it be great to get a story from Lucius Shepard! Do we know anyone who knows him? We realize that we do in fact: we'd both recently met Bob Kruger, who runs *Electric Story*.

I email Bob asking if he would convey an invitation to Lucius to send a story to *Polyphony*. Bob emails me back and says, Hey, I'm going to be in Portland to go to a movie with Lucius soon, why don't you meet up with us and ask him yourself. I reluctantly agree, not sure if I'm *ready* to meet my favorite writer in person. Then, I figure the worse that can happen is he'll say no.

To add to the tension, Bob emails me a few days before the appointed meeting time and says, "Oh, by the way, I'd invite you to join us for the movie, but sometimes that's not the best way to meet Lucius. If he doesn't like the movie he'll keep looking at you and *breathing meaningfully*."

Oh, good.

The appointed Saturday arrives. Bob and Lucius go to see *Y Tu Mama Tambien* and I meet them outside the theater after the show. Introductions, handshakes, and we set off for the Virginia Cafe. We sit at a table near the bar. The first thing I notice about Lucius is that he is wearing a Miami Hurricanes National Championship cap.

Here I should make a brief aside for those readers who know little and care less of sports. For football fans, passions run high, especially about college teams. I am a fan of one of the teams those Miami Hurricanes perennially abuse. Oh, the horror: My favorite writer is a *Miami* fan. Then I remember reading that he grew up in Florida. It fits. Oh, hell. But I decide I'm not going to say anything because I really, really want a story from him and I don't think mentioning my disdain for the Hurricanes is going to get me that story.

When the talk does turn to sports, we talk about *professional* football and it turns out we are both Cleveland Browns fans. Whew. Safe territory. We exchange Browns code words: Oakland, Denver, Ozzie, Baltimore, *Modell*.

All in all it's a pleasant couple of hours which ends with Lucius saying he'll see if he has something that would fit in *Polyphony*, he's pretty sure he does, and we go our separate ways.

Lucius and Bob both loathed the movie by the way.

That meeting was three years ago. Each volume of *Polyphony* has contained a story by Lucius, including, in my opinion, some of the best of his work of the past couple of years. I've even witnessed the meaningful breathing Bob Kruger warned me about in the context of football. He does it when Miami is losing, too.

Some time ago, Lucius' fans started asking (on the Night Shade Books discussion board, among other places) whether anyone was planning to do a print collection of his film reviews. The reviews appear regularly at the *Electric Story* website and often in the *Magazine of Fantasy and Science Fiction*. I jumped at the chance.

Lucius' film reviews are not for the faint of heart. In fact, after his review of the first Harry Potter film appeared at *Electric Story* he received venomous hate mail from English school girls and Bob Kruger felt moved to add a disclaimer to the effect that these reviews were intended for an adult audience. Enter at your own risk.

And it's true that you will find many recent block-busters and award-winners treated with something less than reverence in the pages that follow. But Lucius doesn't attack wounded animals. Indeed, if there is one theme running through these reviews it is a deep disgust at the waste inherent in the operations of the Hollywood Machine. Money, time, talent, all wasted. And yet, the disgust is tinged with sadness.

See, Lucius is a fan of films in the same way that he is a fan of football. He has a vision of how it could be, how the medium could be used to tell great enduring stories, or even just to entertain. He told me once that every time he goes to the theater, every time he sits down and waits for the lights to dim, he believes he is going to see something good. He's the football fan making his way to his seat in the stands knowing he's going to see a great game. He's worked in Hollywood, is well-acquainted with the system, and knows first hand how it could work.

When we started to put this book together, Lucius wanted to

include some other non-fiction pieces he'd written over the years. These you will find in the section called "Ravings." Lucius may be one of the few people to put anything sensible in print about the Columbine shootings. You'll also find a moving and thoughtful piece about Mike Tyson. They fit because they are all about the Media's twenty-first century shuck and jive.

If I was still an academic, I might launch into a boring, and probably questionable, analysis of the Theme of Loss in the Shepardian Ouevre and I would write about how that same preoccupation with loss permeates his film reviews. But I won't. Instead, I'll say this. I'm proud to be able to bring out this collection of reviews and ravings from my friend, and *still* my favorite writer, Lucius Shepard.

Deborah Layne
Portland, Oregon
March 2005

Science Fiction

SPACE REPUBLICANS

Space Cowboys
Release Date: *August 4, 2000 Wide*
Director: *Clint Eastwood*
Screenwriter: *Ken Kaufman, Howard Klausner*
Starring: *Clint Eastwood, Tommy Lee Jones, Donald Sutherland, James Garner*
Distributor: *Warner Brothers*
Review Date: *October, 2000*

HAVING RECENTLY LISTENED TO GEORGE W. Bush woodle-ing the nation from Philadelphia, my ears ringing with resounding generalities and guaranteed pre-broken promises, I asked myself, what fine cinematic product could be a more perfect complement to that feast of Gerber's Baby Food philosophy than Clint Eastwood's latest film, *Space Cowboys*? And thus it was, my fellow Americans, that I found myself standing outside the Galaxy Cinema shortly before noon on Friday last, purely convinced that this paean to the "Greatest Generation" and the geriatric institution of NASA would give glorious embodiment to the GOP's professed desire to Renew America's Promise and thereby make us all better stronger wiser richer and morally straight by ridding the free world of the Democratic Satan who had for so long perverted our children, shamed our god, and levied a multitude of oppressive taxes upon our freedom-loving oil and tobacco billionaires. Joining me by the entrance to the Galaxy on this sunny pre-apocalyptic day was a babble of senior citizens, a sprightly bunch judging by their stylish active wear. They clearly had been buoyed by Boy George's vow to eliminate the Death Tax and not even the threat of contention, offered by a spry seventy-something ex-damsel in pink slacks and matching blouse, could disturb their mood.

—Where's the line?, asked Mrs. Pink, and when informed there was no official line per se, the ticket booth not yet having opened, she replied with a significant degree of querulousness and outrage that she wished there was a line.

Immediately upon her comment, as is the tradition in our great land, a genial discussion began amongst those gathered concerning the rightness and efficacy of lines, the effects of their absence, the inability of the young to form proper ones, and—a dissenting voice—the virtues of milling about. All the while, several gentlemen were engaged in maneuvering their women-folks into appropriate positions so that the semblance of a line—not, sadly, a formally sanctioned line such as might have been hoped for—was created. Once this had been achieved, the discourse continued. Many facets of the topic were touched upon, notably an elaboration of various lines previously stood in by members of the group, lines remarkable for their length, their unmoving-ness, their historical import, et al. Though not a participant in the conversation, I was ensnared by the threads of talk and soon became numb and disoriented, as if afflicted by a nerve-deadening, conscious-altering venom. By the time I took my seat I had experienced several out-of-the-body moments, which was an apt physical condition for someone about to witness a film that, I assumed, took place for the most part in a gravityless environment.

If I may here inject a critical note—had I been the director of *Space Cowboys*, telling the story of four aged astronauts, a team of pre-NASA pioneers called upon to make an emergency shuttle flight to a Russian communications satellite that is about to fall from orbit, I would have quickly transported them out into the void and created a claustrophobic setting in which to examine the problems of age, the erosion and redefinition of friendships, and, as the men battled their own limitations, their unforgiving surroundings, secret enemies, I would have gradually and suspensefully revealed an unexpected evil force that threatened to overwhelm them. Mr. Eastwood, however, chose to spend the first hour or so of his film on Planet Earth, detailing in an unengrossing by-the-numbers style the origins of the team in the 1950s, their *Magnificent Seven*-like recruitment some forty years later, their training, etc., etc., and this stretch of time was made to seem interminable by the constant insertion of lame age jokes into the process. My attention drifted, and my thoughts returned to the speech...not the stump speech with which the man from Midlands has regaled crowds all over our Fabulous Fifty, bellowing out his simplistic yet eccentric slogans ("We got philosophy..." being my personal favorite). No, my brother and sister patriots, I am talking about The Speech, the Oration, the Mighty Verbal Sword with which George the Second slashed away the jowly, liver-spotted, squint-eyed, sneering demon mask that has for so long obscured the shining, almost completely white face of the Compassionate Conservative, a creature without an ounce of greed in its heart or a mean bone in its body. I studied the words that the president-to-be's revivalist passion had burned into my brain, trying to interpret the strange parables encysted within the corpus of the text, particularly fascinated by the story regarding a young prison inmate whom His Bushness had counseled back in Texas. I must admit to thinking that had I been the aforementioned inmate, confronted by a man who signs execution orders with the profligacy of Pete Rose signing autographs at a baseball card show, I would have been less than comforted by his interest in me. But to indulge in such negativity would have been barely a step removed from engaging in the politics of personal destruction, and so I pressed on with my analysis, believing that this apparent irony must be an indicator of a deeper, cleverly embedded truth. And perhaps, I thought, Mr. Eastwood had employed a similar technique in *Space Cowboys*. Perhaps the fact that he eliminated suspense by giving away the ending of his movie early on—I mean, when one sees a Russian general participating in classified Pentagon briefings, exchanging meaningful glances with the head of NASA, it takes no consequential intuitive leap to deduce that the Russian satellite about to fall from orbit is carrying a nuclear payload of some sort... But as I was saying, perhaps this and other anti-dramatic disclosures constituted a directorial sleight-of-hand that allowed the development of a subtler brand of suspense imperceptible to audiences but important in some revolutionary and as yet unfathomable way. It's possible that just as the new George Bush's too-obvious shallowness has proven itself a symptom of compassionate spirituality, *Space Cowboys'* patent lack of subtlety and paucity of tension were achieved by a delicately nuanced mastery of expression designed to produce effects that we will not fully comprehend for weeks or even years (rather like the eventual onset of a recession triggered by a massive, ill-considered tax cut). This theory may also shed light upon Eastwood's refusal to develop his astronaut characters, offering stereotypes instead: a toothless womanizer (Donald Sutherland); a goofy Baptist preacher named Tank (James Garner); an assholic Top Gun type named Hawk (Tommy Lee Jones), and Frank the Alpha Male (Clint his own self). And it might further call for a re-examination of the ludicrous premise that underlies the film—i.e., that of all the people in the entire world, only these four doddering American pilots are qualified to troubleshoot an outmoded technology pirated from NASA by the Russians and maintained by them in an orbital satellite ever since.

Yeah...right.

Something else must be going on, something less expressed

than emblematized by the clumsy linkages of the plot, something that would justify and allow for a reinterpretation of what seems a superfluity of the vacuous, the superficial, and the absurd.

Once again I feel compelled to inject a critical note. Someone less attuned than I to the secret mechanisms of *Space Cowboys* might suggest that Eastwood has herein attempted to make two movies in one, the first a comedy and the other a thriller, and has managed instead to make only two half-movies, neither of them especially successful. They might further suggest that the thriller half, being overly compressed, skips a number of logical steps, replacing them with a welter of pseudo-scientific jargon intended to persuade the viewer that one of our heroes ultimately must strap himself to a turbinelike section of the satellite encircled by armed nuclear missiles and blast off moonward, thereby simultaneously achieving his life's ambition and a noble end (which one of them will make the supreme sacrifice is never in doubt, since the astronaut in question has been conveniently diagnosed with a fatal illness). On the surface it would seem that these hypothetical judgments are correct, but I discovered that the boredom inspired by the lapses in Eastwood's storytelling induced me to focus the larger part of my attention upon the satellite itself, which bears the name IKON, a scary-looking-and-acting relic of the evil empire brought low by the forces of Reaganomics, still magically alive, its steel body infused with a scrap of cold Soviet villainy. It spins and rotates with martial precision, extruding radar arrays and missile bays and all manner of sinister objects, reminiscent of those children's toys that mutate from innocent robotic figures into insectile rocket launchers, and as I meditated upon this icon of our fabled victory over Communism, I was sequentially induced to contemplate once again the current of renewal abroad in the land.

(I should tell you at this point that sitting in the theater, I felt as if The Movie and The Speech were resonating with one another, sandwiching me with harmonious vibrations, causing my mind to shift back and forth between the two, not competing for my attention so much as energizing me, imbuing my thoughts with increasing momentum and spin. But I digress...)

The previous night, while basking in the afterglow of St. George's gospel spell, I had tuned my radio to a call-in show and listened as the American people responded, engaging in yet another of our grand traditions—eschewing individual opinions and parroting comments they have heard spoken by television pundits. I was enthralled to hear one man say in doltish Homer-Simpsonesque tones, "I really like Bush 'cause he's not negative." At that precise moment this characterization of W, who studied dirty tricks under the infamous Lee Atwater and himself is rumored to employ a legendary dirty tricks operator known by the code name of Turdblossom...well, it struck me as incongruous to say the least. But the following afternoon, watching the space cowboys rope in their satellite, that anonymous caller's touching, childlike offering of allegiance to a concept as elegantly sophisticated as the non-negative, with its oblique implication of cinematic relevance, suddenly made sense to me in terms both of the movie and the idiot wind blowing out of Philly. My God, it was all so simple!

If I could explain to you the illumination I then experienced, my fellow Americanauts, believe me, I would. But because the principle of absolute non-negativity that I touched—or, perhaps, that touched me—was simplicity itself; I'm afraid that explanation would fractionate it and thus act to obscure. I do, however, believe this principle can be experienced by others, that watching a videotape of the George-a-roo's big moment followed closely by a viewing of *Space Cowboys* will result in a "white light" experience similar to that cited as the central element of the world's great religions, the contact with a being so immensely itself, it is truly—like the Republican Party—all-inclusive. And once this contact has been made, everything dark will become bright, the aesthetic puzzle posed by the poignant ineptitudes of Eastwood's film will open to you like lotus blossoms, and you will be able to perceive that for all his obvious mental impairment, the man described by Ronald Reagan Jr. (who should know something about the subject) as the least qualified person ever to seek the Presidency, the George-ous One, The Non-Negative Candidate himself, is nearly Christlike in his simplicity (I say "nearly" only because of my cautious nature, not trying to deny that my heart has been filled by His Message of Hope) and that he will in the near future, I dare say, crown our 'hood with brotherhood from sea to shining sea...whatever the hell that means. My American friends, my precious family of ideologically pure patriot saints, usurers, good buddies, ladies bimbos religious devotees, priests nuns out-of-work lounge singers, violent children homeless schizos migrant workers, disgusting yuppies, just plain folks extraordinary talents, rappers trappers bitch slappers and drug addicted overweight race haters, I am so blissfully persuaded of the blessings conveyed by this magic cocktail of film and oratory, I am delighted to offer you a videotape containing both a reproduction of The Speech and an uncut bootleg of *Space Cowboys* including full frontal shots of both Tommie Lee and Donald Sutherland. The cost of this tape is not, as you might expect, $39.99. Nor is it a ridiculously cheap $29.99. Nope, I am making a one-time offer of both products for a mere $19.99. That's right, folks! For only 19 dollars and 99 centavos, you can experience the light of the burning Bush, the satori of space flight, decryptify the hidden meaning of any movie mystery, and inoculate yourself permanently against the examined life. But you must act now! Just dial 1-800-GET HELP or 1-800-SHOOTME. If you call within the next half-hour I will also include a collector's-edition troll doll of Dick Cheney in full-on grimace, complete with a plastic replica of the War Room, where you can pose Dick with his finger on the button. And just because you're you and you and you, I will throw in an autographed copy of Dirty Harry's Geriatric Hunks, the hottest calendar of the new millennium.

But you Must. Act. Now.

Well, I have a business to run, and I'd best get back to it. But before I join my fellow Americans, none of whom—to the best of my recollection—have ever seen me snort coke or womanize or commit any misdeed that might sully the sanctity of marriage or put a frown on Miss Liberty's face...before I join them in their relentless quest for equal justice and human rights, I have one final comment. I noticed yesterday that in their review of *Space Cowboys*, the *New York Times* proclaimed it to be the best movie of the summer. I was initially nonplussed by this seemingly unwarranted hyperbole, but then, casting my mind back to films like *The Patriot*, *The Nutty Professor II*, *Gladiator*, *Battlefield Earth*, *Gone in 60 Seconds*, and the like, I realized that the *Times* was damning with faint praise, and I said, Hey, why the hell not? *Space Cowboys* certainly wasn't any worse than most of the schlock I'd seen, and the blue-haired, electrolysis-loving set appeared happy as they exited the theater, formed into single file and marched smartly off to their appointed parking slots. Indeed, as Mrs. Pink tottered giddily heavenwards, I heard her say in an oddly uninflected voice, "That sure was some movie," a statement that might someday serve as her exit line from the theater of life and with whose generic character and neutral level of affirmation I cannot help but concur.

AI YAI-YAI-YAI-YAI!
(*AI* PREDICTION)

AI
Release Date: *June 29, 2001*
Director: *Steven Spielberg*
Screenwriter: *Ian Watson, Steven Spielberg*
Starring: *Haley Joel Osmint, Jude Law, Frances O'Connor, Sam Robards*
Distributor: *Warner Brothers*
Review Date: *June 17, 2001*

WORD HAS IT THAT PRIOR TO ITS general release, Steven Spielberg premiered his new mega-glop wad of saccharine and special effects, *AI,* for an audience of MIT students and professors, many of them involved with machine intelligence. Apparently Spielberg's ego remains unsatisfied by the adulation of the dull-eyed millions who munch and gape their way through his sentimental epics, and thus he requires the validation of those whom the movie's subject matter most concerns. So it was that in a highly publicized noble gesture, he donated prints of his slavery-era film, *Amistad,* to California high schools with student populations dominated by Afro-Americans, perhaps feeling that these young folks might derive poignant insights from his deep, heartfelt understanding of negritude, rather than—as was the case—causing them to go "Huh?," slip on their headphones, and get real with a joint by Tupac or Notorious B.I.G.

According to reliable sources, the reaction of the machine-intelligence people was even less kind, ranging from scathing comments on the film's implausibility to outright derisive laughter.

Poor Steve.

Nobody knows the trouble he's seen.

Denied a Best Director nomination for *The Color Purple*, in which he turned Alice Walker's delicate novel of poor blacks in the South into a cloying load of zippety-doodah featuring the godawful acting debut of Oprah Winfrey; shunned by the youth of South Central; and now his latest Spielburger must suffer the slings and arrows of the pocket-protector set.

AI, inspired by Brian Aldiss' vignette "Supertoys Last All Summer Long," began its cinematic life as a project of the late Stanley Kubrick, who decided—against Aldiss' advice—to transform the story of an artificially intelligent child unloved by its mum into a retelling of "Pinocchio." In the hands of a great filmmaker, especially one of Kubrick's cold, meticulous sensibility, the movie might have avoided the excess of sentimentality inherent in the idea; but when Spielberg—who never met a button he failed to push—inherited the project and then rewrote the script, it was pre-ordained that the spirit of cutesy-poo would be invoked to the max, and some big-eyed waif like a Keane child come to life would be chosen to embody The Machine Who Wants To Be A Real Boy, and that at some point said big-eyed waif would be depicted staring with "Aw, goshes!" awe up into white Jesuslight, and everybody in the theater would be either sobbing or spewing stomach acid and liquefied popcorn into the aisles.

Pray to be among the latter. To weep during a film by St. Spielberg, to surrender to the entirely unsubtle manipulations of the most crassly commercial, hanky-drenching, family values-humping faux-auteur in the history of the universe...Well, it's just not a good sign.

Apart from a smattering of cuddly robots and computers with

sexy voices, machines generally have been cloaked with menace by Hollywood, perceived as agents of chaos or evil. Exemplary of this are the horny computer of the *Demon Seed* that impregnated Julie Christie; the sinister computer of *The Forbin Project* that sought to become humanity's master; the unforgettable Hal of Kubrick's *2001*; etc., etc., these etceteras inclusive of a small army of movies and TV shows concerning computer-run buildings that attempt to kill their tenants. There has been at least one previous film that treated of a machine intelligence who had the urge to be—or rather, harbored delusions of being—a real boy, this the uninspired *D.A.R.Y.L.* But neither one bad film, nor even several, should detract from the scope and dramatic simplicity of the basic concept.

Choosing big stories with broad appeal has always been a Spielberg strength, and early in his career, it appeared that this along with his technical imagination might produce that rarest of breeds, a commercial director capable of making films of a certain quality. But somewhere along the way, Spielberg's artistic instincts went soft, his epic sensibility betrayed him, and he began to make films in which easy sentiment was penciled in for honest, earned emotion. Commercially speaking, this was a canny decision, and there is nothing intrinsically wrong with making commercial movies. There's a place for all of them...even Adam Sandler films. My guilty pleasures include a number of calorie-less comedies and ultraviolent actioners. But Spielberg's movies have achieved such a potent level of commerciality, he now bestrides the world of the studios like a vast, rather goatlike colossus, having become both figurehead and the leading exponent of a machine that churns out tasty-looking, brain-deadening garbage masquerading as art and funnels it down the throats of a burgeoning race of Homer Simpsons who—having been nourished on such sewage—have predictably grown increasingly brain-dead and eager for more donuts. Why Spielberg threw away his abilities as an artist and evolved into the pope of professional pandering, the titan of tear-jerking, the Mister

Please-Please-Please-the-Lowest-Common-Denominator Himself, I have no idea. Some will tell you it was due to the fit of pique he suffered after Close Encounters was shunned by the Academy. Shamed and reviled, unloved, he wandered the streets of lower Hollywood for days, preaching the gospel to whoever would listen, targeted by brickbats and the laughter of whores, until at last, despairing, he stood on a sewer grating with rank steam rising up around him, muttered a Kabalistic spell, and was subsumed into the lower orders of the Damned. Now I don't altogether buy into this story—I've also heard it was his mother's cousin, Max, who advised Stevie to forget all that dreck about quality and go for the loot. But whatever the case, a close examination of his recent films testifies that some degrading influence is at work. I submit as evidence the regrettable *Amistad*, being Steven's filmic assertion that slavery was very likely immoral, and containing one of the worst casting decisions in the history of cinema, that of signing to the role of a Pre-Revolutionary lawyer Matthew MacConaughey, an actor who may one day be known as the Matt Damon of the late 90s; *Saving Private Ryan*, which is basically an episode of the old TV show Combat with an okay Grand Guignol beginning and a mawkish framing device, and features the Mister Potato Head of contemporary thespians, Tom Hanks; the ludicrously over-hyped *Schindler's List*, which should be on no one's list of decent Holocaust movies, a Grade C picture with Grade A cinematography, another mawkish framing device, and little sad kiddies staring up into light, a film to which we owe an eternal debt of hatred for giving us yet another half-baked British ham whose acting is all accent and wan looks, the loathsome and completely one-dimensional Ralph Fiennes, who stands to become the incessantly dewy-eyed cinematic successor to the unrelentingly dewy-eyed Omar Sharif...

I started this review well prior to the release of *AI*, even before watching any trailers for the film (in one of which, I should add, Hayley Joel does that staring-up-into-white-light thing), and I will finish it three weeks before the release date, because I do not believe it's necessary to see it (though at some point, after loading up on happy pills, I will doubtless drag myself off to the multiplex for a matinee, if for no other reason than to test my endurance). I can tell you right now that the money will be on the screen as regards the production values, and that between that every highly paid critical pimp that ever there was will be screeching "Oscar, Oscar!" for the waiflike Hayley Joel Osment (*The Sixth Sense*), and that the film will be lauded for its many virtues by the clones of Joel Siegel, and that none of this will have any meaning whatsoever, because *AI* will have all the illuminative value of a neon suppository. As far as entertainment value goes...well, picture a waffle made of styrofoam inundated in a gallon of heavy syrup. If I am wrong, I will retract these unkind words. But that's a serious long shot.

One clue to the film's quality is the idiotic tag line attached to all promos:

HIS LOVE IS REAL BUT HE IS NOT

Hmmm, I thought on first seeing this, Spielberg may be offering an ontological argument here, i.e., God is dead, but his legacy lives in us as love, blah blah blah... But upon further deliberation I have decided that, No, alas, it's not even that swift—Steve was being literal. Which presents a problem, Like, okay...I get he means that Haley Joel's character is a machine, thus unreal (I personally think that machines ARE real; however, Stevie had a bad experience with a mechanical shark and may still be in denial). But how the hell is his love real? Because his program is uploaded from a human mind, and thus real? How real is that? Having not seen the film, I'm left to ponder, for all the sense the copy makes, it might as well read:

HIS CRUD IS TEAL SO'S HIS SNOT

Tag lines aside, what this film is about, really, is not whether Haley Joel the cute machine lad is or ever will be a genuwine boy. Naw, it's about combining the right mix of mushy strings with a sad wittle pookie guy and a harsh cold unfriendly world and then just when you think it's all so mean and nothin's fair... Whammo! A bullshit transcendent ending and a soaring theme that will send a kazillion or so tear-stained hairless monkeys streaming toward the exits believing they have thought something, when actually all that has happened is that they have paid eight-to-twelve bucks to take another foreign object up the yin-yang.

It may seem that I'm being too hard on America's most talented billionaire, and maybe I am. I'm sure that Steve's love is real, equally sure that he is not, and that he's a prince of a guy with a Cinemascope-sized heart who doubtless spoonfeeds his children the same vitaminless pap he feeds the world. So fucking what? He's no less a schlockmeister for all that, and to anyone with a living brain who believes the radical notion that entertainment should not be absent of intelligence and should have at its core a soul, a passion, and not a happy face painted on a balloon, and that stories can be told in which the noble and the inspiring are expressed honestly, vigorously, in terms of the common measure of the human spirit, without resorting to the Welch Men's Chorus humming a glorioso passage in the background to cue our tears... To anyone who feels this way, Spielberg must be considered the high priest of Moloch or whatever god it is that has risen from the ashes of literature and art to inundate civilization with its vomitus. Every cretinoid producer and director in Hollywood who worships at the Mel Gibson Memorial Blockbuster Temple of Explosive Faith has a statue of Spielberg on his or her mantle and each night sacrifices a virgin cockroach in hopes that someday they may become a demiurge like Him. In other words, He (along with His chief minions, Robert Zemeckis, the perpetrator of *Forrest Gump*, and Chris Columbus, the artiste behind *Mrs. Doubtfire* and *The Bicentennial Man*) is spawning others like himself. I know I'm only talking about a lousy film director guy, an ordinary guy named Steven, but seriously, folks, if you care about maintaining literacy or having your grandkids grow up in a society where books can be found outside museums, or even if you merely want to take up rational thought as a hobby, for all intents and purposes, His name might just as well be Legion.

AIEEEEEEEEEEEEE!

AI
Release Date: *June 29, 2001*
Director: *Steven Spielberg*
Screenwriter: *Ian Watson, Steven Spielberg*
Starring: *Haley Joel Osmint, Jude Law, Frances O'Connor, Sam Robards*
Distributor: *Warner Brothers*
Review Date: *June 17, 2001*

AT THE END OF AI, STEVEN SPIELBERG'S filmic molestation of the Pinocchio story, after the credits have rolled, there is a final black frame on which the words "For Stanley Kubrick" are imprinted. If this exercise in manipulative ineptitude is to be viewed as a tribute to Kubrick, we must then consider every beer fart ever loosed to be a tribute to the Big Bang. True, Spielberg does incorporate elements of Kubrick's original script, and these are nice to look at. But they stand out like islands in a river of pink ooze, and serve merely to point up the overall impotence of the piece.

The most astonishing thing about *AI* is how uninvolving it is. Spielberg's work generally achieves a level of competence that enlists tearful reactions even from those who have no sympathy for what he is trying to do. But *AI*'s characters are so crudely drawn, so ploddingly stated, it is impossible to identify with them, despite Spielberg's thoroughly unsubtle use of somber light and misted eyes and a multitude of other tricks designed to pluck at our heartstrings. The situation of the film is this: Martin (Jake Thomas), the only son of Monica and Henry Swinton (Frances O'Connor and Sam Robards), has been afflicted with an incurable disease and is now in cryo-sleep awaiting a cure that may never come. To ameliorate Monica's despondency, Henry brings home a robot child, David (Haley Joel Osment), who is the first robot ever programmed to love, the creation of Professor Alan Hobby (William Hurt). Monica is at first horrified, but gradually comes to love David. However, when a miracle cure is found for Martin's affliction and he returns home, he becomes jealous of David and through lies and subterfuge manages to convince Henry that David is dangerous and must be returned to the manufacturer, where he will be destroyed. Monica, unable to bring herself to kill her ersatz son, drops David off in the woods along with his teddy bear, a Supertoy capable of movement, speech, and a wisdom more soulful and profound than that of any human being (or robot, for that matter) in the movie. David almost immediately is captured by the agents of a Flesh Fair—an entertainment spectacle in which robots are destroyed in a variety of colorful ways all in the name of human supremacy. After a thoroughly unlikely escape, off David goes in the company of another escapee, Gigolo Joe (Jude Law), a love robot who has been framed for murder by the husband of one of the women he services.

To this point, Spielberg has been rather ineffectually aping Kubrick's cold style of cinematography, but once Joe and David get together, we're in another movie, a very familiar one—it's *The Wizard of Oz*, with Joe playing Tin Man to David's Dorothy, as they and the teddy bear search for the Blue Fairy who—according to the *Pinocchio* text David has read—will make him a real boy. Their journey leads them to Rouge City, a future Las Vegas which seems somewhat less futuristic in design than its 21st Century counterpart.

There David consults Dr. Know, a cartoonish hologram that represents a data bank, and is told that he must journey "to the end of the world where the lions weep." He and Joe steal a police jetcopter and off they go to a nearly submerged Manhattan (the ice caps have melted and the stone lions in Fun City do, indeed, weep), where David learns that the information he gained from Dr. Know was planted by his creator, Professor Hobby, in order to lure him back (why they didn't simply retrieve him themselves is not quite clear). Depressed on learning from Professor Hobby that there is no Blue Fairy, David throws himself into the sea and winds up in the submerged ruins of Coney Island. He is rescued by Joe, who is subsequently captured by the police and whisked away to his judgment. David thereupon takes the copter and, with Teddy in the passenger seat, goes back down underwater and eventually finds a statue of the Blue Fairy. Shortly after he comes upon the statue, David and Teddy are trapped when a submerged steel structure collapses, pinning the copter.

If Spielberg had chosen to end the movie at this point, with David staring gloomily at his eidolon, his dream of real boyhood forever unattainable and his hoped-for miracle maker a few feet away, I would be inclined to rate *AI* as just another lame sci-fi movie with wonderful special effects (courtesy of Stan Winston). But in his wisdom, our boy Steve has tacked on a thirty-four-minute-long ending involving the freezing-over of the entire planet in 2000 years, the extinction of humanity, a visitation of saintly elongated aliens who love love love our music and our art (Sheesh!), resurrection for David and his moms, and a denouement whose maudlin excess is so execrable that it nearly blinds one to its underlying message, which appears to be a resounding endorsement of child suicide. "Lame" does not apply here. Nor does bad, shitty, unpalatable, disgusting, excremental, or any other deprecating word or term of which I can think. *AI* demands an entire new vocabulary of vilification to adequately sum up its primal lousiness. One wonders how even cheerleader-type review services such as *Sixty Second Previews* could lap up this puddle of Technicolor barf and spit forth a nugget of praise. One has to wonder even more what could possibly have induced relatively credible critics in national publications to lavish praise upon it. Perhaps the studio arranged for happy dust to be slipped into their popcorn.

Or something.

Over the next months we will have two further offerings from Le Gran Steve to consider, two more tasteless pasteurizations of the human experience. Steve's take on Harry Potter will be out before Christmas—the mind quails when presented with the prospect of the rampant cuteness that will eventuate from this union of giants. And following that, the Stevenator will perform yet another cinematic autopsy on the life's work of Philip K. Dick and thereafter spread some thin pink residue of the man's creativity over a two-hour-long flimsy contrived of explosions and the nonpareil acting talent of Tom Cruise, who—now that he has slipped the surly bonds of Nicole Kidman—is free to bob for apples anywhere he chooses along Gender Boulevard. With the release of these two future classics, Spielberg's name will take its place (if it hasn't already done) not with those of the great American directors—Welles, Huston, and so on—but rather alongside names such as Velveeta, McDonald's, Jello, Swansons, and all the other great purveyors of bland processed cheapness, products designed to fill a void, to (perhaps) sustain life though certainly not to enrich it.

As horrible as it is, when you look at *AI* in context with the other summer movies that have thus far flickered across American screens, it seems only slightly substandard. Take *Pearl Harbor*, wherein Michael Bay transforms geopolitical tragedy into a video game and a love story involving the indescribably affectless Ben Affleck; or *Swordfish*, John Travolta's latest step downward from his career peak; or any number of other instantly forgettable films with eight- and nine-figure budgets. I have long resisted the temptation to hop on board the bandwagon of those who seek to impose restraints on Hollywood, because I believe that the things targeted by these folks—excessive violence and too-explicit sex—are minor symptoms of the real disease. The corporate recognition that packaging is everything, that the multi-billion-eyed beast of the consumer will buy anything if they are told to do so with sufficient persuasiveness and repetitiveness... this recognition and its manifestation in every form of entertainment has come to hang cloudlike over the culture and threatens never to leave, but to grow denser, darker, until it succeeds in bringing about an intellectual nuclear winter. There seems to be no contrary force that will dispel it short of an extinction event.

Violence and sex have always been the subject of art, and even of good movies. Polanksi's *Chinatown*, for instance. If this film were remade today, *Chinatown 2001* would feature a detective who, unlike Jack Nicholson's character Jake Gittes, would not be in any way ambivalent about his career or his goals and instead of using his wits would be busting down walls and breaking bones and engaging in car chases with Schwarzeneggerian abandon in his pursuit of a villain who would sit like the head of Spectre behind a wall of pony-tailed assassins armed with Uzis, and project a far-less-menacing figure than did John Huston's perverted old man. He, the detective, would engage in hot monkey love with the Faye Dunaway character and have an amusing sidekick (Tom Arnold? Rob Schneider?). The ending, of course, would have to go. Can't have the bad guys win, no sir! That might strike the groundings as being too negative, it might make them uneasy and thus they wouldn't consume as many packets of Goobers as otherwise they might. Naturally we would have to change the title, throw out all those less-than-politically-correct references to Chinatown and the Chinese. And who the hell would care about a film concerning a battle over water rights? Naw, what we need is something sexy. Nuclear triggers. Stolen plutonium. A magical computer chip. There you go. We'll call it *Silicon Jake*, attach Matt Damon and Sarah Michelle Gellar ("in her first dramatic role"), and funnel it down the throats of enough clots of flesh to bring in a thirty-million-buck opening. If you doubt the accuracy of this presumption, I refer you to the remakes of *Get Carter* starring Sly Stallone and *Point Blank*, which was turned into *Payback* starring Mel Gibson. Both originals were excellent gangster films with interesting leads played respectively by Michael Caine and Lee Marvin. The leads in the remakes were modeled after Schwarzenegger's *Terminator* character, unfaceted, single-minded men who ate steel and crapped bullets and shtupped a few blondes along the way. The process is one of simplification, of erasing every least deviation from the formulaic, and—to put it bluntly—that process is killing our minds, reducing us from being an actual audience to organs that require frequent pyrotechnic doses of crude visual stimuli. Though Spielberg is not entirely responsible for this state of affairs, it will nonetheless determine the shape of his legacy.

When at life's end Steven Spielberg looks back upon his days of nature, I'm quite certain he will be pleased with what he has wrought. He will see no admirable films but a long line of bloated highly colored visions before which billions of ex-people have genuflected and that they have celebrated with uncounted trillions of wasted breaths. He will see shelves of trophies bestowed in the name of artistic achievement but given in the hyperbolic spirit of financial success. And he will very likely see a world in which functional literacy is defined by whether or not one can read the big print on a Kellogg's box. He will then smile and allow the technicians who surround his bed to assist him into a cryogenic unit where he will gaze up yearningly into white light for a moment before he begins to sleep away the centuries. Thousands of years hence he will wake to find himself surrounded by saintly elongated aliens who love love love our art and music, and who think his work is the acme of human achievement (like most aliens we have known, they are not terribly bright). But rebirth and the adulation of these godlike beings will not be sufficient for little Steven. His heart's wish will not have been granted, and in order to pursue that wish, he will escape the aliens' loving confine and journey to the ends of the earth, prone to the vicissitudes of a harsh unfeeling world. He will be accompanied by an amusing sidekick, perhaps a little animatronic buddy. Together they will steal an ancient jetcopter and sink beneath the waters of a submerged LA and search the drowned city until at last they will happen upon the ruins of a film museum. They will explore the ruins and eventually reach the display for which they have been searching. But just as they reach it, a steel structure will collapse, pinning the copter, and so Stevie will sit there for a long, long time, a period that will seem every bit as unending as those final thirty-four minutes of *AI*, staring out at the pantheon of great men, at statues of Kurosawa and Huston and da Sica and Welles and all the rest, his dream of being a real director just out of reach, forever unattainable.

This is, at least, my fond hope.

DARK, DARKER, DARKO

Donnie Darko
Release Date: *January 19, 2001 Sundance '01; October 26, 2001 Limited*
Director: *Richard Kelly*
Screenwriter: *Richard Kelly*
Starring: *Jake Gyllenhaal, Jena Malone, Patrick Swayze, Drew Barrymore*
Distributor: *IFC Films*
Review Date: *November 1, 2001*

THE WAY I SEE IT, AN UNHERALDED film named *Donnie Darko* is hands-down the best science fiction movie in quite a few years.

Granted, this verges on damning with faint praise, but actually it's quite a good picture and deserves a much wider audience than it has received.

Darko was not blessed with a massive budget, and features neither spaceships nor ethnically stereotyped aliens nor a comic-book plot nor actors in ape makeup, as have the recent top grossers in the genre; but it does possess qualities its rivals lack, i.e., a good script, a complicated and compelling story, and excellent acting. Admittedly, these qualities do not normally translate into box-office clout, and the genre's focus being what it is, the Best Film Hugo and Best Script Nebula will doubtless be awarded to some marketer's wet dream of an FX-laden movie featuring an elf or two thousand. But my personal awards, which I believe are no more meaningless than those others, go to Richard Kelly, *Darko*'s first-time director and scriptwriter.

Like the word "irony," which is habitually and wrongly used to characterize mere coincidence, the nature and meaning of the term "black comedy" is often misapprehended. Thus it is that *American Beauty*, perhaps the most self-congratulatory film in the history of the motion picture, a pompous art-statement made by folks who wouldn't recognize art if it stuck its tongue down their throat, has been labeled a black comedy, whereas it is in actuality a tired and pretentious social satire that launches a labored attack on the wages of consumerism (a blatant hypocrisy, considering its origin at Dreamworks) and concludes with a voiceover narrated by a dead man telling us how he wouldn't change a thing about his life, which included alienation from his wife, the contempt of his child, a joyless job, a self-destructive infatuation with a cheerleader, and his subsequent murder at the hands of a deranged homophobe/homosexual. The imperatives of black comedy demand a less deluded resolution and permit no such sappy epiphanies. By any definition, however, *Donnie Darko* is a black comedy, albeit a most unconventional one that juxtaposes concerns with mental problems, troubled teenagers, families, the 80s, time travel, and the institutions of self-help, high school, and psychiatry, and somehow manages to juggle all this material and achieve an allusive beauty. And unlike most black comedies, *Darko* is hilariously funny.

The title character, played by Jake Gyllenhaal (Homer Hickham in *October Sky*), is a bright suburban teenager currently on medication and undergoing therapy for undefined psychological problems that manifest in sleepwalking and the occasional act of arson. He also receives visits from an imaginary (or perhaps not so imaginary) friend named Frank who wears the dirt-smeared costume of a heavy-metal Easter Bunny with pupilless eyes, ferocious teeth, and antlerlike ears. One night after being summoned from his dreams by Frank, Donnie sleepwalks, and Frank tells him that he has traveled back from the future to warn him that the world will end in slightly more than twenty-eight days. After sleeping until morning on a golf course, Donnie returns home to find that a jet engine has fallen out of the sky (yet no plane reports one missing) and crashed into his bedroom—Frank has, in effect, saved his life. From this point on, Frank returns every so often to remind Donnie that time is running out and instructs him to commit a number of increasingly violent crimes that appear to be unrelated, but eventually are seen to be elements of a larger and more mysterious event. Donnie soon begins to observe strange distortions in reality. For one, he sees transparent liquid entities that emerge from the chests of his friends and family and precede them as they move through their days, almost as if these creatures were leading their human hosts along predestined paths. How Donnie interprets these phenomena and learns what he must do in order to spare the people he loves (a new girlfriend, parents, et al) from mortal danger and a more punishing variety of grief than they otherwise might suffer forms the basis of the plot.

Of the smallish tradition of American black comedies that have utilized a high school setting—*Heathers, Rushmore, Election, The Faculty* (I insist it's a comedy), none has done so more effectively than *Darko*. Donnie's school, Middlesex, is lorded over by a grotesque bronze mascot, half-man, half-bulldog, known as the Mongrel, and this bizarre piece of statuary informs the character of the school, a place where self-help guru Jim Cunningham (a perfectly cast Patrick Swayze) is regaled by half the faculty, reviled by the other half, and whose student body has the paranoid cohesion of patients on a mental ward. Donnie constantly gets himself in trouble by challenging the school's short-sighted authority figures, but finds a sympathetic ear in the person of an English teacher played nicely by Drew Barrymore, who also served as the film's executive producer (God bless you, Ms. Barrymore! I take back every nasty thing I ever said about you, except for the stuff about *Charlie's Angels*) and a physics teacher who nourishes Donnie's interest in time travel by giving him a book on the subject written by a former Middlesex faculty member—she has since devolved into a creepy old neighborhood lady known by the kids as Grandma Death.

The most astonishing thing about Darko is its level of ambition and the degree to which it succeeds in doing what it seeks to accomplish. Not only is it a black comedy, it is also an effective period piece—the story unfolds against the backdrop of the Bush-Dukakis election—and a poignant family drama. Generally films that attempt this much, especially first films, wind up being complete messes; the problem of creating characters that are at the same time real and funny usually proves too much to overcome. But while some of *Darko*'s characters are wrought with broad strokes, the accuracy of Kelly's dialog inspirits other of his creations to stand and breathe with authentic power. I've seen the movie twice now, and I'm still not quite certain how Kelly manages to pull his complex materials together. But pull them together he does, and in a manner that is both startling and intensely moving. Gyllenhaal, by turns menacing, vulnerable, and funny, brilliantly assists his director in conveying the emotional substance of the film, and the remainder of the cast—notably Katherine Ross as Donnie's psychiatrist, and Mary MacDonald and Alex Greenwald as his well-intentioned but bewildered parents—complements his performance. If *Darko* had been better distributed and given a sufficient advertising budget, I'm convinced that Gyllenhaal would have a chance for an Oscar nomination.

Those who have read this column may have concluded that I have no affection for the tropes of traditional science fiction, but this is not the case. I would love to see a science fictional *Lawrence of Arabia*, an epic space opera replete with explosions and aliens and so forth, and that also is gifted with vital characters and a story that aspires to do more than update a fairy tale or repackage a western. But given the state of the industry, I'm not so sure such a film is possible. Having endured almost every genre movie released this year, from the putrescence that was *Mission to Mars*, through the faux-Kubrickian puffery of *AI*, to *Planet of the Apes*, a laughably incompetent film that Tim Burton appears to have assembled from spare parts fallen out of Charleton Heston's brain, it's become apparent that there is a formula at work here: the bigger the budget, the dumber the movie. Perhaps this process has some economic validity, though the box-office performance of such films as I have mentioned—one-week-wonders all—seems to imply that there is plenty of room for refinement. Give a director eight or nine figures to play with, and you are flat guaranteed a mediocre-at-best product with a great look and way-cool FX and the intellectual content of a Saturday morning cartoon. Much of this is due to the fact that studio heads, paranoid about their massive investments, cannot stop tinkering, and assign writer after writer to perform serial hack jobs on what once may have been decent scripts, the idea being that this employment of multiple incompetents will transform the script into something accessible to the lowest common denominator, thus making it appeal to a wider audience. Indie films, once the refuge of the auteur, have become little more than a farm system for Hollywood. Films by new directors such as Kelly are essentially job applications. The odds are good that *Darko* will not be merely Kelly's first film, but his only good film, and like his immediate predecessors Daniel Aronofsky (*Requiem for a Dream*), now assigned to *Batman Beyond*, and Chris Moran (*Memento*), currently filming a remake of the Danish film *Insomnia* starring the gag-and-shudder pairing of mugger Robin Williams and shouter Al Pacino, and like dozens of others before them, he will be gobbled up by the studios and assigned to a project that pays him a seven-figure director's fee and has no chance whatsoever of being worth mule spit.

Is there a remedy for this?

In a better world, where punishment and reward were fairly apportioned out by Hollywood, a director like Martin Scorsese, say, would be called into the office after producing several losers in a row and told, "Marty, we're sending you down to the minors. Let's see what you can do with a five-million-dollar budget. Reacquaint yourself with story values, and then maybe we'll bring you back up."

Or let's suppose that Hollywood was run like the NBA, with a rookie salary cap. Every new director brought into the system, instead of one moment being in charge of a film he made on credit cards, faith, and cheap take-out, and the next moment driving down the highway in a 100-million-dollar star vehicle, so intimidated by the experience that he permits himself to be dictated to by Armani-clad bozos whose idea of a good time is sitting around a table talking concept with twelve guys named "Hey, you!"—instead of that, if they were moved along slowly, given a few smallish vehicles to prove their worth before handing them the keys to the stretch limo, if Hollywood were run like any ordinary business, then we might actually get to see a big-budget science fiction movie that's aimed at an audience who have stopped measuring their rate of growth with marks on a doorframe.

But that day will likely never come.

Hollywood, stoned on the fumes of ego and power, perceives a different reality than most of us and operates with a lurid dysfunctionality that, though horribly inefficient, manages to survive in a celebrity-driven environment. Should that environment change, however, a thousand blackly clad lizards will scurry from the studio lots, squeaking that the sky is falling, seeking to avoid being crushed by the fall of the fabulous edifice that protected them from the killing light of truth and beauty, and the laws of Karma.

The Sky Is Falling.

A disaster flick starring every lame-o actor whose career expired in this industry ELE.

Now that would be a dumb big-budget movie I'd like to see.

For now, those who yearn for adult science fiction films are stuck with little pictures like *Donnie Darko* and Aronofsky's *Pi*. It's not such a bad place to be stuck, really. There's a considerable joy to be had in discovering such films, in wandering into a theater and watching something completely unexpected on the screen, something that hasn't been denatured, castrated, and covered in a thin candy shell.

At any rate, it'll have to do until something better happens along.

VANILLA GUYS

Vanilla Sky
Release Date: *December 14, 2001*
Director: *Cameron Crowe*
Screenwriter: *Alejandro Amenábar, Cameron Crowe, Mateo Gil*
Starring: *Tom Cruise, Penelope Cruz, Cameron Diaz, Jason Lee, Kurt Russell*
Distributor: *Paramount Pictures*
Review Date: *December 16, 2001*

TO RAIL AGAINST TOM CRUISE THE ACTOR (a petty crime I admit to indulging in) is rather like protesting the existence of pudding. He's ubiquitous, not in the least nourishing, but essentially harmless—so what's the point? As a dress-up doll, Cruise is fine. See Tom the Master Spy in shades and black leather. See Tom the dread vampire Lestat in what appears to be Adam Ant's cast-off wardrobe. See Tom the Crippled Vet in camo jacket and jeans (wheelchair accessory not included). Put him a romantic comedy and he'll be serviceably shallow, but cast him in an actual dramatic role and you're likely going to wind up with something on the order of his Little Lost Boy take on the mid-life crisis in *Eyes Wide Shut*.

When I learned that Cruise's production company had bought the rights to Spanish director Alejandro Amenábar's outstanding science fiction thriller *Open Your Eyes* (*Abre Los Ojos*), my reaction was one of dismay. The protagonist of Amenábar's film is a pitifully self-involved, narcissistic twenty-something, a fact crucial to the denouement of the plot. I did not believe Cruise would allow himself to play such an unsympathetic character (few Hollywood stars will), and this caused me to suspect that the remake would involve said protagonist in some sort of heart-warming redemptive transformation, thereby neutering the sinister perversity of the original. When I further learned that the director of the remake, *Vanilla Sky*, was to be Cameron Crowe, who had heretofore specialized in making romantic comedies and whose previous film, *Almost Famous*, unforgivably sanitized early 70s rock and roll, transforming that milieu into a kind of summer camp experience, populating it with wise, compassionate groupies and sensitive guitarists who smoked the occasional doobie but never touched the hard stuff . . . well, this pairing of the Vanilla Ice of the acting world with the Vanilla Fudge of directors promised a bland mediocrity of surpassing vanilla-ness.

Hollywood remakes of foreign films rarely succeed in creating even a competent version of their source materials. The 90s were rife with unspeakably bad examples of this artistic malpractice, mostly remakes of French pictures, a surprising percentage of these rendered hors du Hollywood by the presence of either Robin Williams or Martin Short, surely our two most Gallic actors. A few examples? *La Femme Nikita*, a movie driven by its style and the sensual appeal of Anne Parillaud was morphed into the thoroughly unstylish *Point of No Return*, featuring the marginally appealing Bridget Fonda. The classic thriller *Les Diaboliques*, a showcase for the great Simone Signoret, became a forgettable Sharon Stone vehicle *Diabolique*. The Dutch suspensor *The Vanishing*, one of the most harrowing films in recent memory, was given a ludicrous happy ending and a Jeff Bridges villain who seemed inspired by heavy dose of Quaaludes. *La Chevre*, a brisk little comedy, devolved into *Pure Luck*, one of Martin Short's many undistinguished flops.

La Cage aux Folles lost all its glitzy panache when passed into the hands of Robin Williams and Nathan Lane in *The Birdcage*. The elegant period piece, *Le Retour du Martin Guerre*, was recast with a gray-haired marionette (Richard Gere) and reduced to the soporific *Sommersby*. The classic romantic comedy *Cousin, Cousine* was reincarnated as *Cousins*, starring the immortal Ted Danson, and the sterling British mini-series, *Traffik*, was compressed into a civics lecture (*Traffic*) that played like an ABC After-School Special.

All this said, *Vanilla Sky* exceeded my expectations by not providing an easy redemptive out to its protagonist, and although it failed to equal *Open Your Eyes*, it was not without its pleasures. For one, Oscar-winning cinematographer John Toll (*The Thin Red Line*) has shot the film beautifully, infusing every frame with a glowing artificiality that is entirely appropriate to the subject matter. Cameron Diaz turns in a wickedly edgy performance as an obsessed femme fatale that should earn her a shot at more substantial roles in the future, and there are some excellent performances in smaller roles, notably by Noah Taylor and Tilda Swinton. Most significantly, the picture is faithful to the densely plotted, intricately non-linear structure of the original—a number of scenes are reconstructed shot by shot, the dialogue being rendered in almost literal translation.

Cruise plays David Aames, a callow, wealthy Manhattan media prince who, as he puts it, is "living the dream," is up to his dimples in power, and has a penchant for using beautiful women, one of whom, Julia (Diaz), has developed an unhealthy attraction for him. But when his best friend Brian (Jason Lee) brings a date to David's birthday bash, love (or is it only lust elevated to a gothic intensity?) rocks David's world. The date, Sofia (Penelope Cruz, essentially reprising her part in the original movie), is a dancer—she's even prettier than David, much more soulful, and he just has to get next to her. In his pursuit of Sofia, he neglects Julia, who grows increasingly disturbed and finally wreaks a terrible vengeance by driving herself and David off an embankment, killing herself and disfiguring him. For long months thereafter, agonized, ashamed of his horribly scarred face, grieving his lost beauty, David imprisons himself in his home, all while a hostile takeover threatens his publishing empire.

Yet all is not quite as it appears.

As the narrative jumps back and forth, we learn that David is being refreshed as to the details of his life by a psychiatrist (Kurt Russell), who visits him in a prison where he has been incarcerated for murder; he tries to persuade David to confront what he has done. But what exactly has he done? Can we be sure who he has killed? Or that he has killed anyone at all? Is the psychiatrist simply another element of the conspiracy that David claims has been mounted against him? The more we are told about what David thinks has happened, the less certain the truth of his situation becomes. Is he insane? Is he, as he believes himself to be, scarred, or—as the psychiatrist insists—have his scars been healed? Is there an actual conspiracy to drive him mad? Who is the little man who keeps popping up and trying to explain things to him? The answers to these questions comprise the substance of the twisty plot, of the puzzle that David must solve in order to ferret out the real nature and extent of his dilemma.

While Crowe strives to do justice to this dark puzzle at the heart of the story, he seems at times uncertain in his handling of the thriller genre. His cleverly rewritten dialogue, though apt in its evocation of David's shallowness, is too sprightly and slogan-ish by half to articulate the trauma and confusion that come to beset him. Cruise also tries hard, but his often histrionic reading of David is ultimately unconvincing. Spending most of the movie hidden behind a mask (or, as the script calls it, an "aesthetic-regeneration shield"), unable to use his best acting weapon, that trademark boyish charm and jauntiness, he simply does not have the imaginative or physical resources to convey what Eduardo Noriega managed to bring across in the same role in *Open Your Eyes*—the shell-shocked, spasmodic awakening and Catholic terror of a man who becomes aware of his failings too late to change his fate, who deserves what has befallen him and yet somehow manages to enlist our interest and, to a degree, our sympathy, because we perceive in him our own failings, our own shallowness.

It would be easy to dismiss *Vanilla Sky* as being a flawed yet sincerely crafted remake of a somewhat less flawed and far more depthy Spanish thriller, a textbook example of what happens to an intelligent, low-budget film when it is elephantized by a Hollywood process that specializes in technical embellishment and glib polish, thereby creating a movie that is more pretentious than artistically successful, one marred by the unsteadiness of its direction and the inadequacy of its leads (Cruz is an attractive but not a skilled actress, and her purported off-screen relationship with Cruise does not translate into any noteworthy chemistry). That much it certainly is. But something else is going on here, for it becomes apparent that *Sky* was for Cruise his most personal project to date. Early in the film, the superficiality of David's existence, his breezy charm and masculine potency, the perfect dream of his life—this is all painted with such brio, we have an apprehension that it may well be Cruise's movie star life that is being depicted. Later on, when David is deformed and tormented by inner demons, we are given ample reason to believe that this turn of events may reflect Cruise's view of himself. Ever since 1994, when he played Lestat in *Interview with a Vampire*, he has shown a tendency to take on roles that disguise his good looks in one way or another. In several other of these films—the two *Missions Impossible*, *Eyes Wide Shut*—he has also worn masks. *Sky* seems the summing up of this trend. It might be said that Cruise is merely attempting to stretch as an actor, but this stretch has maintained such a consistent character in its evolution over the past eight years, it's difficult to believe that he is not, for whatever reason, offering us a pathological confession, a wormy vision of the self-doubt and self-loathing that attend celebrity. The suspicion that such is the case lends *Sky* a profound creepiness that serves to outstrip the Dickian paranoia of *Open Your Eyes*, achieving its effect not in the way of a good artwork but rather as might a peek into a private psychiatric file, and this makes the experience of watching it a fascinating if not an aesthetically satisfying one.

The convulsed post-modernity of the idea that a celebrity would find a project that speaks to him so deeply as to motivate him to use it as a lens through which he reveals his private demons to the extent that Cruise appears to do—that in itself might be a fit subject for an even more convulsed and post-modern film. The concept of celebrity has come to emblematize our age, and for all its artistic shortcomings, *Vanilla Sky* stands as an odd memorial to and a relic of the *fin de siecle* culture that produced it. It speaks to our bizarre absorption with Great Identities who rise from our midst, archetypal schmucks whose public posturing and incessant foibles, drug rehabs, religious conversions, shoplifting busts, marriages, divorces, sexual peccadilloes and et al, come to represent and perhaps to validate the dread muddle and insignificance of our own inglorious existences, providing us with an ersatz connection to the transcendent, the divine—all the divinity, at any rate, that we are capable of embracing. Perhaps *Sky* marks a passage from one time to another; perhaps Cruise, consciously or unconsciously anticipating an imminent revolution in digital film and an end to the age of celebrity, has attempted to contrive an Ozymandias-like monument to himself that will cast a shadow beyond the end of the studio system and movie stars and the media priesthood who so devoutly report on and prophesy their movements. This being the circumstance, then *Sky* is undoubtedly a more important film than its original and might be worth your attention, if only as a curiosity. It's not terrible (not by the standard of remakes, anyway), and at the very least you have to give Tom Cruise credit for the overarching purity of his egomania, for turning self-love into something of a fabulist artifact. But if it's a good movie you're interested in, a literate and suspenseful psychological thriller that has passion at the core of its ultra clever construction, then I would advise you to skip the vanilla and check out the richer, more human flavor of *Open Your Eyes*.

THE TIMEX MACHINE

The Time Machine
Release Date: *March 8, 2002*
Director: *Simon Wells*
Screenwriter: *Simon Wells, John Logan, H.G. Wells*
Source Writer: *H. G. Wells*
Starring: *Guy Pearce, Mark Addy, Samantha Mumba, Jeremy Irons*
Distributor: *Warner Brothers, DreamWorks SKG*
Review Date: *April 2, 2002*

IT WAS WITH SOME TREPIDATION that I, Herbert George Wells, set forth once again into the future, this time in order to view a motion picture based upon my novel *The Time Machine* and directed by my great-grandson Simon. I had, during a previous visit, viewed Mr. George Pal's spirited but trashy attempt at filming my little book, and there was a correspondence between the two productions that gave me pause—the casting of an Australian actor in the lead. I had found Mr. Pal's choice for the role, Rod Taylor, to have the emotive capacity of mutton, and I feared that this new Australian incarnation, Guy Pearce, would also prove unequal to my conception of the character. Why this insistence on a colonial? I wondered. Why not an Englishman to play an Englishman (or an American, for it turns out that the Time Traveler has been recast as a resident of New York City)? It seems one should expect this much regard for one's work from a relation, no matter how distant and devoid of traditional values he may be.

I prefer to use the time machine for serious business, but I must confess that on my several journeys to the late 20th and early 21st centuries, I have developed a fondness for the motion picture, especially for those films treating of time travel. This is not to say that I have thought many worthwhile. Of them all, only *Time After Time*, whose conceit was to detail one of my earliest temporal expeditions, featuring the excellent Malcolm McDowell, possessed the least verisimilitude and charm; though even this film roused in me no little revulsion with its insistence that my dear friend, the late Dr. _____, a gentle, inquiring soul, was none other than Jack the Ripper. *Time and Again* was, I suppose, a harmless enough love story, poignant in an overly sugared fashion, but its lack of scientific rigor was dismaying. As for the rest, my God!, the idea of a simple tale told well appears to have eluded those who dictate the policies that command the industry responsible for these gaudy idiocies. Still, I cannot deny a certain admiration for the technical aspects of such films. Judging by the size of the explosions they generate, a studio such as DreamWorks might well be capable, should they effect a journey back to the 19th century, of conquering a considerable portion of the globe.

In relating my experience of my great-grandson's film, I must first state that I understand this century's expectations of its entertainments are not those of my own. Every age demands certain elements designed to appease the public mind, just as in the Elizabethan era the Bard himself was induced to leaven his masterpieces with low comedy so as to delight the groundlings; and thus I assumed what I was about to see would not be a faithful rendering of my book, but rather a different work entirely, one infused with the spirit of the thing. I did not expect, however, the amalgam of illogic and hyper-kinetic foolishness with which my eye was met. Even for those who have read my book, it will be necessary to recount the plot of the motion picture, for it differs widely from that of my quiet story.

Andrew Hardegen (Pearce) is a college professor whose attention is given over to two interests: the nature of time and the romantic pursuit of a young woman, Emma (Sienna Guillory). When Emma is killed by a thief in Central Park, Hardegen becomes obsessed with building a time machine so he can travel into the past and prevent her death. After four years of maniacal work, he succeeds in his objective, returns to the moment when he met Emma in the park, and steers her away from the place, only to have her killed by a runaway hansom cab. At this juncture Hardegen decides that the past is unalterable. Having been in love on several occasions, most notably with the director's great-grandmother, I insist that obsession should be made of sterner stuff. Had I been in Hardegen's shoes, I would have tried in the service of love to alter the past at least a few more times; in fact, I likely would have exhausted myself in the process (it occurs to me that such an exhaustive process, Hardegen attempting again to again to save Emma, ludicrous though it might appear, would have made a more compelling film than the one I saw). But Hardegen, obeying a hastily conceived logic, determines that it would be best to travel into the future in hopes of finding a solution to the problem. During a stopover in the 21st Century, he discovers that the moon has been destroyed by subsurface excavation and debris is pelting down upon New York City. In his haste to escape emergency workers who want to take him to a place of safety, he is rendered unconscious as he throws himself into the time machine and inadvertently sends it forward into the distant future.

My great-grandson's redefinition of the lotus-eating Eloi and the feral subterranean-dwelling Morlocks, those two strains into which I imagined the human race might diverge by the year 802,007, does not reflect my intention that they emblematize the class struggle between the poor and the wealthy. Stripped of symbolic weight, lacking the gravity of social speculation, this division now strikes me as somewhat arbitrary. Beyond that, the Eloi are scarcely the childlike, docile creatures I imagined. On the contrary, they are exceptionally athletic and well-muscled, in aspect rather like a thriving tribe of South Sea Islanders. Further they are skilled with primitive weapons and have constructed an aesthetically spectacular village that clings to the cliff sides of a gorge, protected from the elements by shell-like canopies. That my great-grandson's conception of the Eloi differs from my own does not of itself perturb me, but the Morlocks . . . there is another story. Though for the most part appropriately bestial, they are led by an über -Morlock portrayed by Jeremy Irons, who, done up as an albino with an augmented spinal cord protruding from his skin, has now added an inglorious footnote to a generally illustrious career. It is this addition to my story that utterly derailed the reasonable progress of the film. When Hardegen invades the Morlocks' underground complex to rescue Mara (Samantha Mumba), the lovely Eloi woman who befriended him and who has since been captured, Irons informs him that the Morlocks live beneath the ground because they cannot endure the light of the sun (this flying in the face of the fact that Morlock hunting parties routinely go out during the day to kill and enslave the Eloi). He goes on to say that he can control the thoughts of both Eloi and Morlocks alike, and that while the majority of the Eloi are eaten by their captors, women such as the beauteous Mara are utilized for breeding purposes. Upon hearing this, I wondered why—if the über-Morlock possessed such powers—he simply did not summon the Eloi to their fate rather than sending his minions to hunt them down. Did they need the exercise? Just for fun? I also wondered where were the Morlock women? Could my great-grandson be so degraded in his intellect as to conceive of a sub-species without females? Was this ridiculous conclusion the narrative justification for the kidnapping of comely Eloi women? It must be so, for otherwise a Morlock would probably not consider such women attractive . . . unless some Morlock advertising agency had so distorted these poor monsters' sense of self-esteem that their notion of beauty disincluded their own kind.

Even greater gaps of logic were at hand. After engaging in an absurd fight with the über -Morlock, during which Irons hangs half-in, half-out of the bubble of force enclosing the time machine as it accelerates into the future, a circumstance that would likely have substantially impeded its operation, Hardegen travels to an age in which the Morlocks have gained absolute dominance. As if they had not already done so. There he decides that while he cannot change the past, he can change the future. This judgment, made while in the future concerning the past, meets no rational standard with which I am familiar. I would hazard to guess that from whichever direction one approaches it, time is either unalterable or it is not. Nevertheless, Hardegen returns to rescue Mara from the caverns, leaving behind the time machine—which he has set to explode—and they escape into the surrounding hills. This hitherto unhinted-at explosive capacity is a wondrous thing, for not only does the machine produce a considerable pyrotechnic display, but—as if it had a mind of its own—the explosion manages with surgical precision to annihilate the Morlock caverns without spreading destruction to any other precinct.

Every work of the imagination, my own not excepted, is afflicted with logical imperfections. It is the job of the craftsman to direct the reader's or the viewer's attention away from these flaws by dint of his skill at narration. One of the tools that can effect such a sleight-of-hand is pacing, and if *The Time Machine* had been well paced, its logical gaffes might not have seemed so glaring. But under my great-grandson's aimless direction, the story does not build so much as it drearily accumulates. Nor does the acting distract from the film's relentless stupidity. Though Mr. Pearce has previously turned in admirable performances in *L.A. Confidential* and *Memento*, I must now infer that these performances were extracted from him by talented directors, an asset with which he was not blessed while making *The Time Machine*. Rather than acting, he appears to be doing a series of impressions, all of them inept. His evocation of a man in love is particularly grotesque—bug-eyed, gaping, as if the emotion were no more than a kind of inflamed earnestness. Special effects, too, tend to gloss over logical errors, but *Machine*'s special effects were of uneven quality. Rumour has it that following a number of unenthusiastically received test screenings, 20 million dollars worth of extra effects were added at the last moment—as a result they are not up to the standard set by various other recent films.

As I stood in the lobby afterward, observing the streams of children exiting the theatre, idly wondering which of them might— should my scenario of the future come to pass—become the ancestors of Eloi and which might produce Morlocks, I grew irate at this perversion of my work. Not only had one of my descendants savaged my book, but he had created a work of such joyless and debased intelligence, it might well add some crucial bit of momentum to the flow of history and assist in the creation of a world like that I had envisioned, one in which the human mind has been rendered useless for anything except the most rudimentary of gratifications. Thus it was I determined that on my return to the past I will not seek to consummate my relationship with Simon Wells' great-grandmother. Though my feelings for the woman remain strong, the attraction has been dimmed by my recent experience, and the loss of her affections is not too great a sacrifice if I can expunge this excrescence from the record of history. Should the fabric of time prove resistant to alteration, I will refuse to submit so easily to that rule as did Andrew Hardegen. And if I should fail, well, perhaps the record of my failure will work some small benefit. But then it may be too late for action. Intellects cool and vast may already be watching us from afar, preparing to strike so as to prevent my great-grandson from ransacking the remainder of my legacy. Even Martians, I believe, would prefer an ultimate anonymity to enduring the puerile re-imagining that he might visit upon them.

ATTACK OF THE CLOONEYS

Solaris
Release Date: *November 27, 2002*
Director: *Steven Soderbergh*
Screenwriter: *Steven Soderbergh*
Source Writer: *Stanislaw Lem*
Starring: *George Clooney, Natascha McElhone, Jeremy Davies, Viola Davis*
Distributor: *20th Century Fox, Focus/USA Films*
Review Date: *December 1, 2002*

I ONCE TOLD A HOLLYWOOD AGENT it struck me as odd that a studio had decided to change a character in a screenplay based on a novel of mine from a 19-year-old raw recruit into a middle-aged top sergeant. Her response was, "You're lucky they didn't turn him into a black grandmother." The point my agent was in essence making was that when you sell a piece of intellectual property to Hollywood, you often come to wonder why they bothered to buy it at all, because they have modified your work to such a degree that they could easily have circumvented the copyright laws and produced their own variant work without paying you a nickel. Which leads me to consider the question of Steven Soderbergh's *Solaris*. If it was Soderbergh's intent to turn Stanislaw Lem's novel of ideas into a romance, why not just hack out a screenplay, slap a more pertinent title on the puppy—*Astronaut Love Crud* or some such—and avoid paying a substantial sum for the rights? What's left of the story might be tweaked to bear no copyrightable resemblance to Lem's book and the original title surely has no great resonance in the public mind. While the novel is considered a minor classic within the bounds of the genre, I assume that, prior to the movie's release, were you to ask an average sampling of the populace what *Solaris* was, they would likely have responded by saying it was a brand of sun block or a new model Chevrolet.

In 1972 Russian filmmaker Andrei Tarkovsky made a version of the Lem novel that ran for approximately three hours, a movie that some critics have called a work of art and others describe as tedious and pretentious. (I tend to straddle the fence on the issue and think of Tarkovsky's movie as a tedious and pretentious work of art.) The most remarkable thing about this new version is that Soderbergh's picture—essentially a distillation of the Russian film—runs a mere 98 minutes but feels as though it lasts every bit as long as Tarkovsky's. The story is set in a future that appears to differ from our present in only a few ways—men's suits have no lapels, it rains all the time, they have really cool TVs set in plastic panels, and the space program has unaccountably bounded forward and established a station orbiting a remote poem of a planet called Solaris, a globe done all in swirling indigos, electric blues and greens, replete with thready electric thingys designed to resemble synaptic transmissions—the whole deal looks very much like a high-end Lava Lamp such as one might find in The Sharper Image catalog. Psychiatrist Kris Kelvin (George Clooney) receives a message from his friend, Dr. Gibarian, aboard the station asking him to come and help unravel a mysterious problem. On his arrival he discovers that Dr. Gibarian has killed himself. Indeed, everyone on the station is dead except for Dr. Gordon (Viola Davis) and science wonk Snow (Jeremy Davies), both of whom are displaying symptoms of psychoses. Unable to make any sense of the situation, exhausted,

Kelvin goes to sleep in his quarters and wakes to find his wife Reya (Natascha McElhone), who committed suicide several years before, giving him a hug. Freaked by her presence, suspecting she is—well, we're not really sure what he suspects at this point—he leads her into an escape pod and jettisons her into space; but when next Kelvin falls asleep, Reya reappears and this time he becomes reconciled to her presence and sets about attempting to understand what she and the "visitors" who have attached themselves to Snow and Gordon are, and further to determine what should be done about them.

Though it is the consensus among Snow, Gordon, and Kelvin that the "visitors" are somehow being manufactured from their memories by Solaris itself, none of them appear to be in the least concerned with how this is being achieved. Of the planet we are told, "it reacts as if it knows it's being observed," and that is all. No further mention is made of the Solaris' possible sentience—the idea that occupies the heart of Lem's novel—and thus the planet's potentials come to seem those of an enormous magic bean that grants wishes whether you want it to or not. Soderbergh seems chiefly interested in the love story between Kelvin and Reya, and for the first part of the movie this suffices. Rapidly intercut flashbacks fill the audience in on Reya's mental difficulties and the marital problems that drove her to suicide, and we soon learn that her present incarnation, configured solely from Kelvin's memories of her, is as confused and unhappy as was her original, albeit for slightly different reasons. But as the movie progresses we discover that while Soderbergh is less than engaged by the scientific aspects of the story, he finds the metaphysical shadings downright fascinating and rather than emulating the poetic melancholy that infuses the Tarkovsky film, the script devolves into a sophomoric speculation on the nature of identity, with snatches of dialog that one might expect to run across in a *Classic Comics* rendering of Herman Hesse novel, often given a ludicrously portentous weight by

Chris Martinez's overbearing score, and a happy ending that is entirely inappropriate both to the sterile feel of the film and to the bloody events that precede it. An unwitting complicitor in this downward spiral is the leading man. George Clooney has proved himself to be a serviceable comedic actor, but though he appears to be giving the part of Kris Kelvin his best shot, he lacks the chops to do drama. When called upon to project fear or existential confusion, he merely succeeds in looking as if he has eaten some bad clams. But the true architect of his failure—and of the film's—is Steven Soderbergh.

Technically, for the most part, *Solaris* is state of the art, its editing and cinematography top notch, but it's evident that Soderbergh is not overly conversant with science fiction. Lately he has directed a series of remakes (*Oceans 11, Traffic*), and it may be that, mistaking the commercial success of these films for a proof of genius, he has come to look upon himself as able to do a quick study and thus become the master of each and every genre. Judging by the set design in *Solaris*, it would seem that the only science fiction film to have made an impression on him is Kubrick's *2001: A Space Odyssey*. The docking sequence in *Solaris* is almost a quote from that film and throughout there are sequences that reflect Kubrick's influence. Yet while this is somewhat annoying, it is his refocusing of the story that stands as his most egregious error. The sentient ocean of Lem's novel, an entity capable of replicating not only people but cities, would—in this age of CGI effects—have made a memorable centerpiece for a movie that lacks any memorable centrality. Without this underpinning, Kelvin's interaction with Reya seems less redolent of cosmic mystery than of pure idiocy. I mean, one would think that after a bad marriage to a mentally disturbed woman who kills herself after a quarrel, after a subsequent liaison with her—let's say—clone who kills herself by drinking liquid oxygen (only to be reborn), even an unreasonably smitten man would find this a cure for obsession. Had there been, however, some scientific promise in her origin, some hint that this new Reya offered Kelvin at least a scant hope of fulfillment, a portrayal of that relationship would have not only made more sense, it might have created a magical sense of wonder, a quality the film possesses in short supply. Soderbergh's decision to concentrate on the question of identity strikes me as an almost equally myopic choice. The recognition of Philip K. Dick's work as a source for cinematic stories appears to have exercised a deadening effect upon whatever remained of the Hollywood imagination. What is reality? What is life? Do clones have souls? Does George Clooney? Variants of these questions, simplistically stated, have informed the thematic structure of a veritable deluge of recent films, including a mainly regrettable batch treating of Dick's own properties, most recently *Imposter* and *The Sixth Day*. It is as if Hollywood has decided that science fiction is either a monster-disaster genre or else should be invested with the intellectual content such as might be gathered from sitting in one evening on a Survey of Contemporary Philosophy course at an especially non-descript community college. Given the staleness of the thematic material, the stilted dialogue in the second half of the film, its derivative setting and under-equipped leading man, *Solaris* ultimately weighs in neither as an entertainment nor as a serious film, but rather as the latest in a line of movies (a la *American Beauty, AI, Road to Perdition*) in which the studios have taken a ponderous stab at doing art and produced instead a series of pompous, self-important, expensively mounted Technicolor belches.

As the saying goes, the third time is a charm. It's easy to see what a great genre film Soderbergh could have made from Lem's novel, and since this Solaris falls so far short of realizing its source materials, it's tempting to hope that another director will pick up the torch and shoot a film that actually dares to tell Lem's story rather than "making it more accessible," "tuning it to the present," "updating it," or any one of a number of popular studio strategies that every one translate to "screwing it up" or "removing all the individuality." Considering what directors like Darren Aronofsky and Christopher Nolan and various others might do with the project . . . It's an alluring prospect. But the chances are, given the necessarily high investment, the multiplicity of voices that would badger the director, whoever he turned out to be, into broadening the picture's appeal, it's probably not worth the effort. For my part, I would prefer to skip another remake, to revisit the novel, close my eyes and imagine what might have been.

NO ID, NO SERVICE

Identity
Release Date: *April 25th, 2003 (wide)*
Director: *James Mangold*
Screenwriter: *Michael Cooney, James Mangold*
Starring: *John Cusack, Jake Busey, Rebecca DeMornay, Clea Duvall, Ray Liota*
Distributor: *Columbia Pictures*
Review Date: *May 16, 2003*

28 Days Later
Release Date: *June 27, 2003*
Director: *Danny Boyle*
Screenwriter: *Alex Garland*
Starring: *Cillian Murphy, Naomie Harris, Megan Burns, Christopher Eccelston, Brendan Gleeson*
Distributor: *Fox Searchlight*
Review Date: *May 16, 2003*

IN 1995 DIRECTOR JAMES MANGOLD MADE his first feature film, *Heavy*, a quiet, poignant study of an overweight chef coping with unrequited love and the death of his mother, a role played with wonderfully, painfully stated inarticulateness by Pruitt Taylor Vince. The movie earned Mangold a Hollywood gig and since then it's been all downhill. His first Hollywood feature, *Copland*, turned what started out to be an interesting psychological portrait into a bloody shoot-'em-up. Next came *Girl Interrupted*, essentially a clumsily mounted pity party for rich-girl neurotics. This was followed by the eminently forgettable Meg Ryan-Hugh Jackman romantic comedy, *Kate and Leopold*. Now we have *Identity*, an overwrought slasher flick that works a riff on Agatha Christie's *Ten Little Indians*, then devolves into a bad horror movie, and then devolves further into something that many reviewers are loathe to discuss, fearing it would be a spoiler. Why their reticence, I have no idea. Unless you had to retake shop in high school, after viewing the opening sequence, which details the pathology of spree killer Malcolm Rivers (an older, heavier Pruitt Taylor Vince) and details his slaughter of a number of guests at a motel, there's truly little left to figure out . . . though I did have a few questions concerning the picture.

Like how come Ray Liotta's wearing so much eyeliner?

If Amanda Peet's character is always so cold, why doesn't she put on a jacket?

Jake Busey's enormous teeth are on constant display in a grin that would not be out of place on a Kentucky Derby winner . . . I guess that's not really a question, but all through the film I kept imagining him wearing a horseshoe of roses.

The movie opens with River's psychiatrist and lawyer rousting a judge out of his bed on a dark and stormy night (the mother of all dark and stormy nights, actually), claiming they can prove that their client, Rivers, who is due to receive a lethal injection in twenty-four hours, was insane when he committed the murders and thus cannot legally be executed. As they wait for the judge, Mangold switches story tracks to a ruinous desert motel that makes the Bates Motel look like a Hyatt Regency, where ten people are in process of being stranded by a flash flood. Joining the motel manager, a creepy woman-hating, knife-carrying individual named Larry (John Hawkes), in this less-than-splendid isolation are Ed (Jon Cusack), a burnt-out ex-cop turned chauffeur who is driving a faded ex-movie star of the '80s, Caroline Suzanne (played appropriately enough by faded ex-movie star of the '80s Rebecca de Mornay), to LA. Distracted by Ms. Suzanne's strident complaints, Ed runs over the wife of George York (John C. McGinley)—George, wifey, and their son have stopped to repair a flat tire improbably caused by running over a spike-heeled shoe that has fallen out of a suitcase belonging to Paris (Amanda Peet), a hooker who has quit the life and is heading to Florida to live her dream of owning an orange grove. Next to arrive are Ginny (Clea Duval) and Lou (William Scott Lee), newlyweds who are already having marital problems, and, finally, along comes Rhodes (Liotta), a hard-charging cop and his prisoner, serial killer Robert Maine (Busey), whom Rhodes is conveying to prison.

Scarcely have the principals assembled, when they begin to die gruesomely. One's head is discovered tumbling in a drier; another has a baseball bat jammed down his throat. To generate tension surrounding the murders, Mangold introduces them with ineptly contrived zoom shots and loud swooshes—it seems our director believes that maniac killers are prone to make such windy noises when perpetrating their foul deeds. With each body a room key is found, numbering from one up in consecutive order, and this leads the survivors to speculate that one of them may be the killer.

Gee, ya think?

In an attempt to cloud the issue, Mangold and screenwriter Michael Cooney (*Jack Frost*) throw out a number of red herrings. Turns out Motel Hell is built atop an Indian burial ground. You've seen *Poltergeist*, so you know what that portends. Then there's the fact that Robert Maine has escaped. Serial killer on the loose. Oh-oh. Then there's the other fact that John C. McGinley has made a career out of playing dangerous whackos—he can't be as normal here as he seems, can he? And then there's Larry and his penchant for sharp pointy objects. But Mangold defuses his own fishbombs by casting in the role of George York's son a little boy whose sinister fleshiness puts one in mind of Laird Cregar, the porcine villain of *The Lodger*, a '40s Jack the Ripper film, and, coincidentally, also brings to mind the jowly face of Pruitt Taylor Vince.

After a couple or three murders, one of the characters opines that this all seems a whole lot like a movie she saw once in which ten people were stranded at some rich guy's mansion on an island and were picked off one by one. Maybe, she suggests, we have something in common, something that connects us, and that will explain why the killer is picking on us. Shortly thereafter they discover that they were all born on May 10. It was at this point I began to realize I was watching a movie that was going to rival *Dreamcatcher* for stupidity. Which is odd. Because it's apparent that what Mangold intended was to turn the horror genre on its ear, to smarten it up, to make it cool and post-modern and all that neat stuff, whereas he ended up making a picture that conjures memories of that awful TV show *Dallas*, on which everything that happened during one season proved to be a dream. When I caught *Identity*, those in the audience who hadn't figured out what was going on greeted the picture's ultimate revelation with groans and laughter and "Oh-my-Gods." It turns out there's an honest-to-Jesus reason that the characters are uniformly unconvincing and the plot devices are ridiculous, but you just don't care about anything in the movie to be swayed by this cleveresque development. And though the Big Twist at movie's end manages to make some sense of the plot, it falls far short of explaining everything. For instance, if you've been paying close attention here, you may have tumbled to the idea that said Big Twist involves Multiple Personality Syndrome. Well, I've never heard of anyone with MPS whose personalities were so evolved as to have wildly different and particularized career tracks like, for instance, an ex-cop-turned-chauffeur, an aging movie actress, a normal family man and his normal wife, their freako kid, two arguing newlyweds, and so on. . . . If my giving this away annoys you, just remember I'm doing my best to spare you my experience.

The lesson to be learned from this mess is that the best way to smarten up a horror movie is to forget clever and make it scary, a lesson Mangold failed to acknowledge, but one that Danny Boyle, the director of *Trainspotting, Shallow Grave,* and of the upcoming zombie (they're sort-of zombies, anyway) movie *28 Days Later,* has clearly taken to heart. Shooting on digital video, armed with a fraction of the budget available to Mangold and actors who—albeit talented—cannot be considered A-list, Boyle has made the best horror film I've seen in years. Working from an excellent script by Alex Garland, author of the novel *The Beach,* Boyles opens his picture with animal-rights activists breaking into a laboratory with the idea of liberating the animals used for experimentation. There they encounter a group of chimps infected with a kind of super-rabies that has come to be called "The Rage" and inspires in its victims an incessant and uncontrollable urge to kill. Twenty-eight days later, a bike messenger, Jim (Cillian Murphy), wakes up in a hospital from a coma incurred during a traffic mishap to find the place deserted, ransacked, littered with debris, implying that something dreadful has happened while he was unconscious. The city appears as ravaged as the hospital. Wreckage everywhere. Newspapers lying about sporting headlines that scream EVACUATION and tell of martial law. The scenes of his wandering across a deserted Westminster Bridge and thence into an empty Trafalgar Square are unrelentingly chilling, stunning in their impact. Not long after his emergence, while sheltering at night in a church, Jim is attacked by a foaming, red-eyed creature, once human, and is chased out into the street, where he is rescued by two of the uninfected, Selena (Naomie Harris) and Mark (Noah Huntley), who instruct him on the rules of survival in this terrifying new world. Don't travel at night. Don't interact with anyone unless absolutely necessary. If someone you're with becomes infected, you have less than a minute to kill them or else they will kill and eat you. It's not long before this last rule is put to the test—Mark becomes infected and Selena is forced to execute him.

There's nothing astonishingly new here, no ground that *Outbreak* and *The Stand* and George Romero haven't already covered, though the speed and agility of "Rage" victims make a nice contrast to the sluggish, bungling creatures of *Night of the Living Dead*. *28 Days Later* is essentially a genre B-movie, fraught with certain unsatisfying resolutions common to the form, yet it all seems worthwhile and fresh thanks to the wit and intellect of the screenwriter and director and cinematographer. Moving across the post-apocalyptic London landscape, Jim and Selena do battle with hordes of the infected, and eventually hook up with Frank (Brendan Gleeson) and his teenage daughter, Hanna (Megan Burns). When they hear a recorded broadcast urging uninfected citizens to make for the security of a military base near Manchester, they decide to risk what will surely be a perilous journey. Perilous, and incredibly suspenseful—a chase through a tunnel system is nearly unbearable in its tension. On reaching the base they discover that the army unit led by Major West (Christopher Eccleston) has its own sinister agenda.

Gritty, unendingly suspenseful, with several wonderful set pieces and a skillfully directed ensemble cast from among whom Naomie Harris is likely to break out as a legitimate star, *28 Days Later* succeeds, by straying true to its genre roots, by treating them with a passionate respect, in doing everything that *Identity* tried to do by more-or-less abandoning them. You'd do well to save that ten-spot you've earmarked for *Identity* and use it this summer when *28 Days Later* hits the theaters. Seeing it may not make you any wiser, but it'll scare the bejesus out of you . . . and what more could you ask of a horror movie? James Mangold doesn't know.

LUCKING OUT

Intacto
Release Date: *December 13th, 2002 (NY)*
Director: *Juan Carlos Fresnadillo*
Screenwriter: *Andres Koppel, Juan Carlos Fresnadillo*
Starring: *Leonardo Sbaraglia, Eusebio Poncela. Monica Lopez, Antonio Dechent*
Distributor: *Lions Gate Films (picked up at the 2002 Sundance Film Festival)*
Review Date: *September 16, 2003*

EVERY YEAR I SAY THE SAME THING: This is the worst year yet for movies. The year 2003 is no exception. Here we are (at the time I write) in September and I can't think of single studio picture that merits Oscar consideration ... though I'm certain the Christmas season will bring a surfeit of contenders every bit the equal of the fabulous Richard Gere-Catherine Zeta-Jones vehicle that won last year's accolade, a musical extravaganza that set my toes to tap, tap, tapping and my stomach to up, chuck, chucking. It's been an especially gruesome year for the English-language genre film, a year dominated by comic-book adaptations that have ranged from the execrable *League of Extraordinary Gentleman*, which features Sean Connery's woefully inept Sean Connery impression, to the unrelentingly dimwitted *Daredevil*, which offers the latest proof of

Ben Affleck's flat affect, and—a moderate high point—to the merely tolerable *X2*. The most palatable among the year's various horror films has been *28 Days Later*, a tarted-up British B-picture whose evocative mise-en-scene obscures to a degree its debt to George Romero's zombie movies and provides a particularly stirring first hour, but is nothing to shout about.

Then, of course, there are the *Matrix* sequels, for those who care to endure them.

The remainder of the year, with the possible exception of Peter Jackson's final chapter of Tolkien's *Lord of the Rings* trilogy and *Gothika*, a supernatural thriller featuring an interesting cast and helmed by talented French director Mathieu Kassovitz, promises very little: werewolves versus vampires; macho Roman Catholic priests confronting supernatural terrors with crosses and prayers; the usual gaggle of haunted houses, assorted less-than-creepy CGI monsters, and sequels documenting the evisceration of attractive young sexually active people. And in years to come we can look forward to cinematic treats that will doubtless embody all the intelligence and imagination that informs the remake of *The Texas Chainsaw Massacre*, a picture produced by that noted auteur Michael Bay, perpetrator of the twin horrors *Pearl Harbor* and *Armageddon*, who tells us with full-on sanctimony that his version of *Chainsaw*—will not have any of the gore that made the original so yucky.

As you may recall, Tobe Hooper's version, while disturbing, contained nary a drop of gore.

While Hollywood continues unabashed and unabated on its dumb and dumber course, filmmakers in various other countries are busy developing a strong genre tradition. Korea, Thailand, and Japan spring immediately to mind in this regard. As does Spain. It could be argued that in recent years, led by directors such as Alejandro Amenábar (*Open Your Eyes*) and Jaume Balagueró (*Los Sin Nombre*, an adaptation of Ramsey Campbell's *The Nameless*),

Spain has produced the most interesting and well-crafted thrillers of any nation in Europe, movies that confront complicated philosophical questions as well as generating suspense. To that list must now be added the name of first-time director Juan Carlos Fresnadillo, whose film *Intacto* is the most original thriller of recent vintage made in any country or language, a stylish mixture of magical realism and hard-boiled mystery that might have been co-authored by Jorge Luis Borges and James M. Cain.

The idea underlying *Intacto* is that luck is not the operation of chance, but rather is itself a force, an energy, that resides in every man, woman, and child to one degree or another. This force is so tangible a thing, it can stolen by a certain people, who themselves constitute an underworld—indeed, a subculture—of gamblers whose games are somewhat untraditional. Luck for them is the coin they wager as they compete against one another for the ultimate prize: the opportunity to engage in a duel to the death with Samuel Berg, known as "The Jew," a Nazi death camp survivor who is the self-proclaimed luckiest man alive—essentially, the god of luck. Berg, played with immense gravitas by Max Von Sydow, resides in a bunkerlike apartment beneath his casino, which is situated amid a lava flow somewhere in the Canary Islands, a lunar landscape that echoes the bleakness of the gamblers' lives. Their ability to steal luck, you see, is both a gift and an affliction, for in times of great peril they—inadvertently or otherwise—steal the luck of those around them and thus cause their deaths.

The movie opens with Berg sitting in his apartment, his head covered by a black cloth, waiting for a man who was won the right to challenge him. When the man enters, he's given a handgun that holds five bullets and one empty chamber. He aims at Berg's head and fires. Click. The cylinder is spun; the gun is handed to Berg. He fires and the man falls dead. The corpse is then wrapped in a plastic sheet and removed. Thus end all challenges to Berg, but he derives no great pleasure from victory. Indeed, he seems to yearn for death.

Over the years, the cost attendant upon the gift that allowed him to survive the Nazis has caused him to rethink the advisability of remaining alive.

The chief duty of Berg's protégé and assistant, Federico (Eusebio Poncela), is to steal the luck of big winners at the casino's tables—this he accomplishes merely by touching them. It's a pretty soft sinecure, but Federico wants to go out on his own and when Berg discovers this, he seizes Federico's wrist and steals his luck. The film jumps ahead seven years and we discover that Federico has become a sort of talent scout, seeking out gifted players for the underground gambling circuit. In his search, he stumbles across Tomás (Leonard Sbaraglia), a man whom he believes may become the instrument of his vengeance against Berg. Thomas is the sole survivor of a plane crash in which over two hundred people died. He is also a bank robber. When we first see him, sitting in the wreckage of the plane, he has dozens of packets of currency taped to his torso. On waking in his hospital room, he finds a police detective, Sara (Monica Lopez), waiting to arrest him. Sara is herself blessed/cursed with the ability to steal luck and is scarred both physically and emotionally as a result of a car wreck that she survived by draining the luck of her husband and child during the moment of impact. (Plotwise, her appearance may seem a bit pat, but Fresnadillo, employing a darkly eloquent visual style and an elliptical narration reminiscent of his countryman Amenábar, manages to obscure such tactics of convenience.) Federico helps Tomás escape Sara's clutches and thereafter begins to school him in the game, honing his weapon against Berg by entering him in competition after competition against other gifted luck-thieves. As with M. Night Shyamalan's *Unbreakable*, a film with which it shares more than thematic content, *Intacto* concerns itself on one level with survivor guilt. Sara's pursuit of Tomás and Federico not only serves to create suspense, but also generates an atmosphere of grief-stricken obsession that seems to cling to all the gamblers. Of their number, only Alejandro (Antonio Dechent), a matador who no longer finds the bull ring a challenge, plays for the thrill. The rest appear motivated, to one degree or another, by the desire to rejoin those whom they have survived, and view their survival as less a product of good fortune than as a cosmic joke. Luck has corrupted them, poisoned their souls, and, like Berg, their icon, though they may not yet be prepared to die, they have forgotten how to live.

If it's Sara's compulsiveness that infuses *Intacto* with its noirish moodiness and grit, it's the games themselves that provide the picture's exotic element. The first competition that Tomás enters involves having his hair brushed with water that has been steeped in molasses, then being placed in a room with two other players and a large molasses-loving stick insect. The lights are switched off and the bug flies about the room, eventually settling on the head of the winner. In the film's best set piece, a number of contestants are blindfolded and then induced to run full-out through a dense forest, the winner being the one who does not head-on into a tree. Each contest is played for high stakes—luxurious houses and so forth—but of course the true purpose of all the competitions is to winnow the competitors down to one who will challenge Berg for the highest stakes of all in his amped-up version of Russian Roulette.

For all its virtues, *Intacto* may prove ultimately disappointing to those viewers accustomed to the more hyper-emotive narrative style of Hollywood movies; but since the remake rights have been snapped up, it's likely that they will soon be able to see the story done in an overblown, multiplex-friendly manner, with Tom Cruise, perhaps, as Thomas and Berg played by the increasingly somnolent Anthony Hopkins. As it is, the ultra-sleek visuals and the single-mindedness of *Intacto*'s characters combine to enforce an overarching mood of detachment. Fresnadillo, it seems, does not want us to connect with his characters as much as to understand their detachment, to feel their separation from the human herd, and so he seeks to engender a certain detachment in his audience. A middle ground allowing for some slight empathetic audience reaction—using Sara's tragedy, say, to affect us emotionally—might have broadened the film's appeal. And yet, being so detached, the viewer is enabled to better appreciate the perversity and cruelty of the milieu Fresnadillo is presenting, and, by association, to recognize that perversity and cruelty is the ocean in which most of us swim, protected from its zero temperature only by a thin clothing of illusion and luck.

I've spent a good bit of verbiage in this and previous columns ranking on Hollywood—as time-wasting a pursuit as lecturing a gerbil on table manners. Yet whenever I see a movie like *Intacto*, I'm always amazed that we didn't make it first, that we haven't mined the story-rich environments of our own casino landscape and come up with films that bear a stamp of originality, rather than churning out sludge of caper flicks. Not long ago, there were far more American films remade by foreign production companies than the reverse. Now that trend has turned around and it's Spain, France, Korea, et al, who are leading the way. Greed and stupidity have fostered this lack of adventurousness—that's not hard to understand. But it's harder to understand why those who direct and produce American remakes of foreign films tend to scrub away the qualities that made them attractive to the studios in the first place. It's as if they're kids who've planned a really cool trick, grown afraid nobody will get it, and so they explain it to everyone in advance, thus spoiling the effect. Usually when I see a movie that provokes such thoughts, I don't dwell on the subject. However, *Intacto* seems such an American story, so American in its compulsions (though given a Spanish accent), and there have been so many foreign movies recently that play like American movies overdubbed in a foreign language (*Open Your Eyes, City of God, Amores Perros , et al*), I began to wonder if creativity, like luck, might not be a tangible force, and rather than having it stolen from us, we were yielding it up, just letting it waft away, infecting the world not only with the worst of our culture, but also the best of it, and as a result our country was becoming the true cultural victim, growing gray and inert and sparkless . . . Throw in a plotline and you might be able to transform that notion into a decent movie.

Maybe some Spanish director will make it. . .

FORGET ABOUT IT

Eternal Sunshine of the Spotless Mind
Release Date: *March 19, 2004*
Director: *Michel Gondry*
Screenwriter: *Charlie Kaufman, Michel Gondry*
Starring: *Jim Carrey, Kate Winslet, Kirsten Dunst, Mark Ruffalo, Elijah Wood*
Distributor: *Focus*
Review Date: *March 11, 2004*

I ALMOST ALWAYS ENTER A THEATER expecting to enjoy the movie I've been assigned to review; however, I must admit that in certain instances my objectivity has been trashed by the fear that I'm about to suffer a flashback to the last awful thing that happened to me during a film featuring some of the same actors, the director, or a scriptwriter whose work I've come to see. Thus it follows that having experienced *Human Nature*, the previous genre picture directed by Michel Gondry and scripted by Charlie Kaufman (*Being John Malkovich* and *Adaptation*), being yet haunted by the memory of Patricia Arquette covered in fur, I was nearly devoid of hope as regarded their latest excursion into the genre, *Eternal Sunshine of the Spotless Mind*. Even had Gondry and Kaufman not been involved, the odd cinematic coupling of co-stars Jim Carrey and Kate Winslet would have caused me some anxiety, being reminiscent of that cosmically unfortunate pairing of physical comedian Adam Sandler and dramatic actress Emily Watson in Paul Anderson's *Punchdrunk Love*.

The movie derives its title from an Alexander Pope quatrain:

How happy is the blameless vestal's lot!
The world forgetting, by the world forgot.
Eternal sunshine of the spotless mind!
Each pray'r accepted, and each wish resign'd.

I'm not sure how the "blameless vestal" fits in, but the rest of the quote seems appropriate to the theme. *Spotless Mind* is yet another entry in the burgeoning science fiction sub-genre of movies either directly based upon or inspired by concepts exploited in the work of Philip K. Dick (though it could be argued that John Varley's work has somewhat more relation to this particular film), the majority of which deal to one degree or another with the problematic aspects of technologically altered memory. The most recent film to reference this material, John Woo's *Paycheck*, starring the less talented half of the late Bennifer, was perhaps the stalest and most unimaginatively mounted science fiction thriller in recent memory, a category that includes some remarkably stale and unimaginatively mounted attempts at simulating Dickian paranoia. Few of the films that preceded it have done much to establish a grand tradition, and the forthcoming September release, *The Final Cut*, a Robin Williams thriller treating of similar subject matter, promises no better. In spite of this record of artistic and (for the most part) box office failure, Hollywood has become so enamored of this sub-genre, it causes me to wonder if somewhere in Los Angeles there does not live a madman with an editing machine modified to perform delicate mnemonic cuts who delights in tampering with the memories of studio executives and watching them endlessly repeat their mistakes. Of course if such a man exists, he is doubtless extremely frustrated by his redundancy.

Spotless Mind is not, like the majority of its predecessors, a garden-variety action film that treats the human condition as an aspect of high concept; it actually seeks to illuminate that condition through an examination of the love relationship between geeky introvert Joel Barish (Carrey) and the hyperkinetically eccentric Clementine Kruczynski (Winslet), two mutually attracted opposites who, as the movie opens, meet for the second time at the beach in Montauk on Long Island, the same exact spot where they met for the first time many months before, an event that neither of them now remembers. These are fragmented people, impaired from having had their memories of one another excised (when Joel asks if there's a danger of brain damage from the memory wipe, he's told ". . . the process is brain damage") and bewildered by the shadows of love and anger. Their fumbling stabs at reconnecting, their inept expressions of the residue of the attraction that initially brought them together, seem despairing and childishly confused, and they try to reject those feelings. But something, some undeniable trace of what they were, continues to tug at them. As they ride the train back from Montauk, sitting separately, peeking at each other, their flirting takes on an awkward desperation that calls to mind the tragedies of junior high. We are influenced to believe that whatever happens to Joel and Clementine, it will not be good.

At this point the script conveys us seamlessly back into the past, to the morning when Joel discovers that Clementine has had her memories of him erased after a terrible argument. Broken-hearted, unable to cope with loss, further motivated by a petulant desire for revenge, he decides to have his memories of her deleted. To that end he hies himself to Lacuna, a business situated in a shabby office wherein the inventor of the process, Dr. Howard Mierzwiak (Tom Wilkinson), a doofus-y middle-aged sort with the hint of a dark side, instructs Joel to clear his apartment of every item that may remind him of Clementine. After Joel complies, delivering the treasures and detritus of the relationship stuffed into garbage bags to the Lacuna office, he's drugged, placed in his own bed wearing pajamas and a silvery metal hood that markedly resembles the headdress of the Sphinx, and the memory wipe begins.

Spanning a leisurely procession of cleverly written and emotionally honest scenes, *Spotless Mind* has by this juncture established itself as a quirky, affecting relationship movie driven by the performances of its co-stars. Unless you've seen certain of Carrey's TV and film work from the late 80s and early 90s, films like *Doing Time on Maple Drive*, it's conceivable you don't believe that he's capable of doing drama, but here he's thoroughly persuasive in his low-key depiction of a lonely, inarticulate man who's more comfortable hunched over his journal, drawing cartoons of women, than he is in talking to one. As the flaky Clementine, whose moods shift as drastically as do her day-glo hair colors, Winslet hasn't been this energized since her debut in Peter Jackson's *Heavenly Creatures*. Though they're an ill-matched couple, a combination that ensures volatility and promises emotional disaster, as actors they play off one another astonishingly well. We like these characters and, more importantly, we believe in them. We would be quite happy with an ordinary narrative detailing their passionate ascendancy and decline. However, once Mierzwiak's sloppy, irresponsible assistants, Patrick (Elijah Wood, in a sharp departure from his wholesome alpha-hobbit role) and Stan (Mark Ruffalo), set up shop in Joel's bedroom, tracking down and eliminating Joel's memories of Clementine, the pace of the picture accelerates and comes to verge on the horrific. Utilizing techniques honed in his hallucinated videos, most notably with Bjork, Gondry veers his style from the drear naturalism of the early scenes. Splashy camera work draws us into a surreal chase across the memory map of the relationship. Joel, you see, is having second thoughts. He has recalled the reasons why he loved Clementine and is now trying to hang on to his imperiled memories and, in essence, to her. He begins to flee with Clementine (or rather with his central image of her) across a landscape composed of their days and nights, a landscape that's being dismantled as they pass through it. They leap forward and backward across the timeline of the relationship, moving through rooms with pulsing walls; gray spaces from which the detail is being scrubbed, peopled by faceless figures out of a Francis Bacon nightmare; snowy beaches that morph into frozen rivers; with now and then a sudden detour into Joel's infancy and to incidences of childhood humiliation and trauma.

While Joel is engaged in this doomed struggle, Stan and his girlfriend Mary (Kirsten Dunst), Lacuna's receptionist, party beside their sleeping subject, drinking, smoking pot, and finally having sex on the bed next to him. Patrick has excused himself in order to see his own girlfriend through a crisis—the girlfriend turns out to be Clementine. It's soon disclosed that when Patrick performed her memory wipe, he became infatuated and, in order to win her, has stolen Joel's mementos of the relationship (in addition to a pair of Clementine's panties), thereby becoming expert in manipulating her. The juxtaposition of these three frantic actions, interposed by jump cuts and featuring boozy hand-held camera passages, form a giddy collage that is perfectly mated to the subject matter, but more than a little disorienting—indeed, there are times when the frenzied pacing and idiosyncratic imagery create a feeling in the viewer that borders on vertigo. This vertiginous feeling is provided with an intellectual equivalent when it's discovered that one of Mierzwiak's employees has been memory wiped and was part of an office love triangle, a revelation that ultimately serves as a crucial plot point and causes us to suspect that the reason underlying the curious behavior of all the characters may be that they, too, are impaired. And perhaps it's all a touch too vertiginous, because it's during this section that the movie's focus blurs and its energy begins to dissipate. Eventually, inevitably, Joel's last memory of Clementine— their initial meeting—is erased and he is returned to a painfully blank solitude, while Clementine inhabits an isolation no less painful, albeit heavily populated with meaningless relationships. But of course this is simply the end of their first story. The story that began with their second meeting still has to play out, and it's here that the movie falls apart.

The denouement of one of the earliest and most successful films dealing with technologically altered memories, *Blade Runner* (I'm speaking of the version that received theatrical release), consists not of footage shot by Ridley Scott, but of outtake footage culled from another film (reportedly Kubrick's *The Shining*) that shows a road passing alongside the wheels of a car, while Harrison Ford's voiceover narrates a far more optimistic result than that conceived by Scott. Apparently the studio considered the original ending a downer and therefore not accessible to the mass audience to whom they wished to appeal. It may be that something similar has occurred with *Spotless Mind*. I can't be certain who dictated that changes be made, but it's clear that there were changes, since late drafts of the Kaufman script show the characters in old age returning for yet another memory wipe at film's end, suggesting that they have become habituated to the process, relying on it as a panacea for all their emotional difficulties. The much less bleak ending imposed upon the script by agencies unknown makes a certain glib, hazy sense, but feels tonally disconnected from what has preceded it and, since it's equally as leisurely paced as the opening, gives the impression that rather than reaching a conclusion, the movie is running out of gas.

At this moment, Charlie Kaufman is one of the few scriptwriters in Hollywood whose name creates an audience expectation of a certain attitude and style, the type of expectation generally reserved for directors. The hallmark of his scripts is a post-modern cleverness, and that cleverness often seems both their greatest strength and greatest weakness. There's no doubt that this is Kaufman's most human script—unlike his previous ones, its chief concerns are its characters, not the ideas they may represent. That being so, dialing back on the cleverness might have been in order, because as things stand, the archness of the writing frequently distracts from a story that had the potential to be a contemporary tragedy with the darkly comic weight of Kafka or Celine. Despite these weaknesses, *Spotless Mind* outstrips its sub-genre by constructing a low-fi take on high concept, treating peripherally the notion of what it means to be human and, more centrally, examining the hearts of two particular humans within the frame of that philosophical context. That it falls short of achieving its ambition inspires a poignant dissatisfaction of the sort we would not feel in relation to the failure of a film with less ambition. And so the most profound tragedy here is that what might have been an important film, perhaps even a landmark film, has been reduced to a merely interesting and, in sum, forgettable two hours in the dark.

MULTIPLEXITY

The Chronicles of Riddick
Release Date: *June 11th, 2004 (wide)*
Director: *David Twohy*
Screenwriter: *David Twohy, Akiva Goldsman, David Hayter*
Starring: *Vin Diesel, Colm Feore, Judi Dench, Alexa Davalos*
Distributor: *Universal*
Review Date: *July 19, 2004*

I RECENTLY HAPPENED UPON A book entitled *Multiplexity: Why Bad Movies Taste Good and Good Taste Bites*, written by a person known as the Author, an anonymous writer once reputed to have been a harsh critic of the American film industry, but who, after years of therapy following severe head trauma incurred during an assault by an enraged scriptwriter, experienced a series of illuminations that, in their printed form, are invaluable to anyone who approaches the viewing of a summer movie with a certain trepidation. The book's rather zen premise is that if a movie appears to be awful, to make no sense, it's not the movie's fault, but rather that you have failed the movie by imposing your terms upon its creative order. The last section of the book offers a number of exercises (only a few dependent upon the use of anti-depressants) that allow those who suffer from such an impairment to relax their overly rigorous standards and sit back and enjoy the fruits of American cinematic genius. Thus, though I refrained from doing my exercises before entering the theater where *The Chronicles of Riddick* was playing, I did feel less anxious than usual when the opening scene faded in.

Prior to directing *The Chronicles of Riddick*, David Twohy had gone a long ways toward establishing himself as the new John Carpenter . . . and considering the quality of Mr. Carpenter's recent films, God knows we need a new one. In his four previous movies, *Disaster in Time* (based upon a Henry Kuttner-C.L. Moore novel), *The Arrival*, the excellent haunted-submarine flick *Below*, and *Pitch Black* (the film to which *The Chronicles of Riddick* stands as a sort of uber-sequel), Twohy demonstrated that he understood the fantasy and science fiction genres well enough to play with their tropes on a creative level apparently inaccessible to many of his more celebrated and/or successful peers, and, operating with limited budgets and second-line actors, he also demonstrated that, like Carpenter, he could create character-driven B-pictures that were more entertaining, more conceptually sophisticated, and considerably less pretentious than the majority of the mega-budgeted, FX-laden films in whose shadow they existed. In other words, smallish movies that delivered a bit more than they seemed to promise. *The Chronicles of Riddick* serves to reinforce the similarity between the two directors, for when handed big budgets to work with, Carpenter made the worst two films of the prime of his career: the gruesome-sappy *Starman* and the intolerable Chevy Chase vehicle *Memoirs of an Invisible Man*. In accordance with this tradition, handed a budget roughly equivalent to the Paraguayan national debt, Twohy has now made what many consider to be his worst film.

The strength of *Pitch Black* lay in the fact that it was not primarily about a single character, Riddick (Vin Diesel), but was about the various characters of its ensemble cast—they were sketched well enough so that if we did not deeply care what happened to them, we were at least interested in learning their fates, despite the fact that we more-or-less knew, thanks to the formulaic circumstance, what those fates would be. Drawing Riddick as an irredeemable criminal whose retinas have been polished to allow him to see in the prison dark from which he has escaped, Twohy's script gradually revealed that his protagonist might not be as primitive a soul as he appeared, yet stopped short of redeeming him completely, a development that roughly mirrors the arc of Arnold Schwarzenegger's character over the span of the first two *Terminator* films, passing from nemesis to ally, from soulless evil to rudimentary humanity. In *The Chronicles of Riddick*, however, Twohy eschews the muscular simplicity and claustrophobic enclosure of the original film (a planet soon to be darkened by a total eclipse during which flocks of predators will descend upon the survivors of a crashed spaceship), supplanting it with a lavish overdose of plot and a variety of settings—an ice planet, a civilized world, a triple max-security prison on a hell planet, the sumptuous gaud of enormous sarcophagi-shaped spaceships—and, by ladling an extra helping of mystery over Riddick's character (could it be that, like various other science fiction protagonists these days, he is the One?), he reduces our hero to, well, our hero, casting aside the more intriguing interstellar misanthrope. As the film opens, Riddick is running across an ice field, fleeing bounty hunters chasing him in a spacecraft—not only does he evade his pursuers, he captures their ship, persuades them to identify the people who put a price on his head (one being a mullah whom he saved from predation in the original movie), and then forces the bounty hunters to take him to the planet Helion Prime, where those folks live. At this point we understand there will be no further arc to Riddick's character. He is destined for great things and the only mystery attaching to him is how many people he will have to kill in order to achieve them.

Shortly after Riddick arrives on Helion Prime, after hooking up with the mullah, he learns that a being known as Aereon (Dame Judi Dench) has announced that he is civilization's last best hope against the Necromongers, a vast, remorseless army traveling in those aforementioned enormous ships toward the Underverse, a paradise that purportedly awaits them at the edge of creation—judging by the Necromongers' funky black centurion-like costumes, I'm thinking Goth nirvana, or maybe it's a place where all the little angels wear Underoos. Along the way, they happily destroy every planet in their path, and they also happily murdelize anyone who will not convert to their cause. According to Aereon, who is an Elemental (this means that every so often, provoked by no apparent stimuli, she tends to wax wraith-like and transparent, and is then capable of shifting like a ghost from place to place), Riddick is the last surviving Furyan, a race of bad motor scooters who were thoroughly Necromongered some time back, but put up one hell of a fight. It seems there's a prophecy, uh-huh, you betcha!, that only a Furyan can kill the leader of the Necromongers, the Lord Marshall (Colm Feore, who played a much scarier villain, Andre Linoge, in Stephen King's *Storm of the Century*). If you think that gives the ending away . . . Wow! You've seen this, haven't you? Before Riddick can generate much of a reaction to Aereon's announcement, here come the Necromongers laying waste to Helion Prime. At about the same time, Riddick discovers that the other person he saved from death in Pitch Black, Krya (Alexa Davolos), a teenage girl who hero-worshipped him, now bloomed into a supermodel look-alike who loves him, has followed in his footsteps along the path of criminality and is currently imprisoned in an underground maximum security facility on a planet known as Crematoria. It should be clear by this juncture that in Twohy's universe, the thing is the name, the name is the thing, and thus it's a solid bet that Crematoria is going to be a tad on the warm side. Putting the Necromonger problem on hold—and it's a fairly urgent problem, since they're preparing to turn Helion Prime into space junk—Riddick lets himself be hauled off to Crematoria by the bounty hunters, who plan to sell him to the prison.

(Perhaps I wasn't paying close enough attention, but the rationale underlying the practice of prisons buying their prisoners eluded me, and thus I decided it was time to put into practice the exercises I had learned from reading *Multiplexity*. As a result, though not completely successful in penetrating *The Chronicles of Riddick*'s mysteries, I did manage to comprehend much of what followed.)

The Crematoria segment, embodying the pulp crunchiness of Twohy's previous films, is the best part of *The Chronicles of Riddick*. Watching Riddick interact ultra violently with his fellow prisoners, reconnect with Kyra, and tame two ferocious mutant pangolins (the prison's guard dogs) all makes for good genre fun. But then, after busting out of the underground complex, Jack, Riddick, and a small group of convicts flee across the planetary surface, seeking to outrun the sunrise, which on Crematoria brings 700-plus degrees of heat, and . . . Well, if not for the puissant wisdom of *Multiplexity*, I might have been unwarrantedly dismissive when our hero and heroine manage to avoid cremation by hiding behind a rock. Newly confident in the movie's genius, however, I assumed this to be no ordinary rock, but one that emitted cool rays. Once back on Helion Prime, when the evil Necromongers imprison Aereon by clipping a ball and chain to her leg, not once did I believe that this might prove ineffective, like chaining fog—I understood that a special metal must be involved. Why does Riddick's dialogue consist entirely of tough-guy one-liners? Ritual Furyan warrior-speak. Why do Necromongers sound like actors reciting lines from a draft of a bad Shakespearean play? Bad Shakespeare is a pop culture item on planet Necro (if you've watched enough Star Trek, you'll likely tumble to this), and that may also explain the popularity among the Necromongers of armor that looks to have been scavenged from a Cinecitta dumpster, and the use of swords and axes for dueling in a high-tech culture. Continuity errors, the random, pointless appearances of Dame Judi; the pagan-temple-meets-Terry Gilliam design of the Necromongers' decor of Riddick and technology—it all makes elegant sense when you utilize the proper comic-book logic.

I will admit that there were spots when I lapsed into the mode of ordinary human being and was baffled by all I heard and saw. For instance, when one of the Necromongers says, "Take him back to the ship for mind regression," I (a) thought that the comment might have been directed toward me and (b) felt that the instruction was somewhat redundant. Once in a while, as I watched Diesel grunt and swagger, I had the impression that the survival of mankind was dependent upon the efficacy of the steroids abused by a grumpy personal trainer. And I had trouble understanding the purpose that informed Twohy's quotes from various other genre films. To list but a few: storm troopers in *Star Wars* armor; quaintly retrofitted, begoggled human hound dogs called "sniffers," who bring to mind *Twelve Monkeys* and *Brazil*; the ending of *Conan the Barbarian*. According to *Multiplexity*, the reason for my lack of understanding—I did not come sufficiently pure to the experience.

The final scenes, most of them onboard the Necromonger flagship, are enlivened by Thandie Newton's performance as Lady MacBeth-ish Dame Vaako, who throughout the movie manipulates and motivates her husband, Lord Vaako (Karl Urban, Eomer in *Lord of the Rings*), to initiate regime change and make a move on the Lord Marshall. But that's easier said than done. For one thing, Lord Vaako, a man sporting maybe the worst mullet ever, is not the sharpest tack in the box. For another, the Lord Marshall, alone of all the Necromongers, has traveled to the Underverse and there gained the power to snatch a person's soul out of their flesh (which may explain why it's so compelling a tourist attraction). You might think that this power makes him a heavy betting favorite when the time for the big showdown with Riddick arrives, but my *Multiplexity* exercises helped me to understand that the souls of Furyans come equipped with extra stickum and, though the Lord Marshall can yank a regular ol' soul from the body easy as pulling a tissue from a box of Kleenex, I knew that when he grabbed hold of Riddick's animating principle, it was going to be more like tweezing a rattler out of a steam pipe.

Thanks to *Multiplexity*, I've come not only to enjoy the summer movies, but to have learned to open myself to their simple profundities. And when understanding is not possible, as happens with the greatest of these films, films whose potency is beyond articulation, I heed the Author's advice, perform a certain muscular ritual that is only slightly painful and removes all desire for decent dialogue or continuity, and just let the pretty pictures crush my skull. As for my take on Twohy's latest, well, it's no *Battlefield Earth*. We can't hope for that until Travolta pulls off his long-promised sequel. But in the meantime, no movie is going to get you closer to that particular slice of heaven than *The Chronicles of Riddick*.

Comic Books
and Super Heroes

EXCREMENT

X-Men
Release Date: *July 14, 2000 Nationwide*
Director: *Bryan Singer*
Screenwriter: *David Hayter, Christopher McQuarrie, Joss Whedon, Tom DeSanto, Bryan Singer*
Story: *Bryan Singer, Tom DeSanto*
Starring: *Hugh Jackman, Patrick Stewart, Ian McKellen, Halle Berry, Anna Paquin, James Marsden*
Distributor: *Twentieth Century Fox*
Review Date: *September 2000*

WE HAVE REACHED A POINT IN THE American journey where it is plain to see that the millennium was the approximate moment when both the idea and reality of populist art became extinct, when the intellectual environment of the culture sank beneath a level necessary to sustain the life of the public mind, when an evolution—a mutation, if you will—in the efficiency of marketing made the entire concept of product irrelevant. This should not come as news except to those who will not understand it, those whom the marketers have lobotomized or those who were of diminished capacity to begin with. There is no going back from this moment. The consumerist religion whose roots found purchase in the previous century, whose first unwitting prophets are the unheralded shapers of our present, has sounded its evangel and like a great wave has washed over every shore, immersing all but a few unreceptive souls in the Day-Glo colors and unsubtle music of its innocuous paradise vision. We sit side by side in darkened temples and worship visual displays of litany that are as childlike in their formulae as stories told in bible schools. We are ensnared in glittering webs woven of merchandise streams and celebrity. The world is afflicted by plague, famine, genocide, instability of every sort, and our next president will be a mannequin programmed to utter a carefully scripted sermon of platitudes and assurances. Our only hope is that intelligent machines will come to save us. We are surrounded by idiots.

That these fundamental observations should be expressed in a review of a film apparently targeted at a junior-high-and-younger audience may strike some as irrelevant snobbery—why focus even the most trivial of existential lenses upon a project that aspires to neither artistic nor intellectual credential? It's a comic book, for Christ's sake!, one might say. Chew your Milk Duds and shut the hell up! Yet as I sat in the theater watching Bryan Singer's latest film, *X-Men*, listening to the audience chuckle over the inane dialog, exclaiming at the second-rate special effects, such was the nature of my thoughts, and it occurred to me that not only was the film an exemplar of cultural decline, but a parable that might be interpreted as an illumination of our essential dilemma.

In the "not-so-distant future," when the incidence of human mutation is on the increase, producing men and women with uncanny powers of mind and body, the mutants have separated into two opposing groups, one led by the telepathic Professor X (Patrick Stewart), the other by Magneto (Ian McKellen). X runs a school for young mutants, one of whom bears a startling resemblance to the celebrated student Harry Potter. He is determined to mainstream mutants, to bring them into human society, despite the fact that humanity fears and loathes them. Magneto, a survivor of the

Warsaw ghetto who can control electromagnetic fields, has darker designs. Into this circumstance comes a newly awakened teenage mutant named Rogue (Ana Paquin), whose ability to drain the life force and personalities of others proves an allure to Magneto—he wants to let her drain a portion of his electromagnetic power, then use her as a battery to energize a machine that will—he believes—change all normal humans into mutants. Aligned with Magneto are the shapeshifter Mystique (latex-clad supermodel Rebecca Romjin-Stamos); a mesomorphic lionman, Sabretooth (wrestler Tyler Mane); and Toad (Ray Park), whose rather pornographic powers include a whiplike tongue and the capacity to give slimy, suffocating facials. On the side of goodness and niceness are Storm (Halle Berry), who controls the weather, redirecting lightning, snow, hail, and—I suppose—the humidity in order to confound her enemies; telepathic and telekinetic Jean Grey (Famke Janssen), who functions as a healer; and Cyclops (James Marsden), who has to wear Raybans or else his optic blasts will incinerate whatever he sees. Standing with them, but not truly part of the team, is Wolverine, a mutant surgically altered by the mysterious hooded figures who haunt his dreams; he is invulnerable to injury and sprouts a nasty set of adamantine claws in times of stress.

After the first twenty minutes or so, *X-Men* slumps into a predictable sequence of action scenes mixed in with campy dialogue and mutant soap opera, much of this aimed at promoting the film's simplistic message (Just because people are different doesn't mean they're bad), as the X-Men battle not only Magneto and his minions, but also a right-wing Senator (Bruce Davison) intent upon Hitlerizing the situation and forcing mutants to register with the government. All this has been done before with far more deftness and style, yet just as I was on the verge of losing interest, I came to notice a more significant message embedded in the film's subtext.

Our culture generally perceives the upper-class English accent to be an indicator of erudition, intellect, refined sensibility, and I found it curious that both Professor X and Magneto spoke with this accent, that in the *X-Men* universe these qualities were associated with both good and evil. But soon I realized that Professor X and Magneto were only superficially representative of good and evil. Magneto's intention to supersize human potential might well be seen as a desire to elevate, to improve, to brighten the senses—the same goals attributed to great art, to any profound intellectual endeavor.

On the other hand, Professor X maintains a purely reactionary stance and voices no positive goals; his sole intention is to thwart Magneto and maintain the status quo. He is, in effect, a kind of intellectual quisling. This infant metaphor can be extended when one examines the opposing mutant teams. Cyclops, with his frat boy looks and glibness; Jean Grey, the all-American mom, the sexy nurturer; Storm, the white-haired, light-skinned black woman who expresses almost no personality and is used, rather slavishly, as a weapon—they are all conservative emblems, symbols frequently employed (whether cynically or sincerely) to denote the forces of restrictiveness, to make the state of restriction seem cozy and attractive. Magneto's team, however, seems emblematic of the messiness of art, the risk of intellectual experiment: the unhouse-trained Toad with his quick, vicious tongue, itself a symbol of verbal acuity; Sabretooth, the untamed natural man, his uncontrollable violences contrasting with those of the leash-trained Storm; and Mystique, the image of sexual danger, embodying the ephemeral, the mercurial, the transforming power of the mind. And of course these two groups are contending for the heart and mind of Wolverine, the prototypical blue-collar guy, conflicted, angry, confused, soulful, manipulated by mysterious forces beyond his control—the man with whom the audience most identifies.

Was it possible, I asked myself, that the Orwellian message stated in the opening paragraph of this review was buried in the script of *X-Men*, that some capybara-skin-booted, Hugo-Boss-clad producer had this much clever self-consciousness? Or had Brian Singer, years removed from his one good film (*The Usual Suspects*), teetering on the precipice of hackdom, decided to incorporate a hidden statement, a final subversive bleat, before toppling into the abyss of the once-promising? Whatever the case, the more closely I examined the film, the more certain I became that the message was there. The metaphor was consistent on every level. For instance, the X-Men's stealth vertijet, the high-tech machinery that enhanced the Professor's telepathic skill, the precise geometries of lightning and snow and so forth generated by Storm's and Cyclops' surgical laser strikes, redolent of our military adventure in Kuwait—these were the nifty, sterile weapons of Ronald Reagan's wet dream American Paradise that helped bring about the New World Order, whereas Magneto's foaming, chaotic tide of electromagnetic plasma might be taken as the ultimate expression of unbridled creativity. I wondered—no, I suspected—that if I were to go back for a second viewing of any of the summer's apparently unending string of unaccomplished movies, *Gone in 60 Seconds*, *The Patriot*, *Shaft*, and etc., I might find a similar message embedded in each.

The film raced toward conclusion, the X-Men triumphed in a battle fought atop the Statue of Liberty—that matronly French insult to the Land of the Free that we've adopted as irrefutable proof of our long-fled compassion—and Magneto was locked away in a prison of white plastic where there was no metal that would enable him to use his power. (Are we not all so locked away from the wild desires of our natures by the plastic bonds of culture, kept separate from the necessary metal of our individual potencies?) With visions of a sequel dancing in their heads, the audience began filing out. The majority of them were considerably older than junior-high age, and most were unsmiling, gaping—they had been filled and dulled by what they'd consumed, and were now headed home to practice other varieties of consumption. And I saw that this was good.

It certainly made my job easier. I'd planned to analyze the

acting, the direction, the writing, to discuss *X-Men* in context of more artistically successful comic book treatments, movies such as *The Crow, The Matrix, Batman,* and to cite the film's few interesting moments, most of which occurred at the mutant school, an environment Singer would have been smart to mine further. But I realized now that these things were of no consequence—indeed, they did not really exist the way they once had. Actors had morphed into fashion statements, directors mutated into crafts-morons, and scriptwriters...well, soon there would be no scriptwriters, only directors with a beautiful dream and a Scriptomatic Story Program for their PCs (if you want a preview of this reality, check out *The Phantom Menace*). Quality was no longer an issue, or more precisely, the old critical standards had been abolished, and an entirely new range of judgments was required. Thus in the interests of the new cinematic order, I have decided to review all future Hollywood films as though they were fast food. *X-Men*, I believe, is best looked at in terms of pizza.

The film is not a top-of-the-line pie, not the well-seasoned, cheesy, crisp-crusted food item you might find at Pagliacci's in Seattle or Patty's in Brooklyn. Yet neither is it the slimy cardboard with orange sauce you buy by the slice on the streets of Newark. It's a step up from the average Domino's offering, spicier and with mushrooms that do not appear to have been lying on a countertop for most of the day. However, the toppings are sliced wafer-thin, the crust is on the doughy side, and the sauce contains far too much oregano. Pizza Hut, I think. Nothing out of the ordinary. A medium mushroom and pepperoni. It won't come back on you, you will likely not be exposed to E. coli or any infectious diseases, but you probably won't want to hang on to the leftovers. If you need a nosh, hey, go for it. If not, you might just as well wait for Paul Verhoeven's upcoming *Hollow Man*, which, I'm told, promises to be a Pizza One large bacon and pineapple with extra cheese.

MORE BITING COMMENTARY

Wes Craven Presents: Dracula 2000
Release Date: *December 22, 2000 Nationwide*
Director: *Patrick Lussier*
Screenwriter: *Joel Soisson*
Starring: *Jonny Lee Miller, Justine Waddell, Gerard Butler, Vitamin C, Christopher Plummer, Omar Epps*
Distributor: *Dimension Films*
Review Date: *March 2001*

Shadow of the Vampire
Release Date: *December 29, 2000 LA/NY; January 19, 2001 Limited; January 26, 2001 Wide*
Director: *E. Elias Merhige*
Screenwriter: *Steven Katz*
Starring: *John Malkovich, Willem Dafoe, Aiden Gillett, Cary Elwes*
Distributor: *Lions Gate Films*
Review Date: *March 2001*

EVER THINK HOW IT WOULD BE IF things sounded in life as they do in the movies?

A dog barking would sound like Godzilla with a toothache. Handguns would use amplifiers, not silencers, and folks like

Brittany Spears and N'Sync would have to be summarily executed.

But not even Dolby Digital Reality could prepare you for the sonic excesses of *Dracula 2000*. When this Dracula hisses, it's like somebody released the air brake on an 18-wheeler. When he farts, it's like a rip in the space-time continuum (though breaking wind would have been fitting in context, the count doesn't actually do so in the film. I'm extrapolating here). If magnificently inappropriate noise were a criterion of filmic excellence, *Dracula 2000* would be the greatest vampire movie of all time, and not a bad video game, a babe-rich environment designed for 11-year-olds whose notion of female perfection is the thought of Jeri Ryan dressed in Underalls.

Hmm . . .

Of course you know going in that any movie with a date attached to the title is going to be product. We're probably going to see lots more of this. Like for instance:

HAMLET 2012

The Man in Black Is Back . . .

. . . this time he's strapped . . .

Loathsome as this may sound, it would nonetheless be preferable to Ethan Hawke's recent ninety-minute version of the play, a project that only serves to cement young Hawke's position as Hollywood's resident arts idiot.

The reason for these digressions is that I have little to say about *Dracula 2000* apart from, "I went to see it and I am ashamed." But a few words about the story would, I suppose, not be out of place. Years ago the original vampire hunter Van Helsing (Christopher Plummer) bagged the evil count and for some dumbass reason locked him away in a vault that occupies the basement of a London book store now belonging to his great grand-something (also Christopher Plummer). Burglars come ("What you reckon's in that coffin, Alf?") and free the Bitemeister, who then goes off to search for Van Helsing's daughter. . . .

Okay. That's enough.

You have to feel for Christopher Plummer. The guy must have serious tax problems.

Responsible for the direction is one Patrick Lussier, who—judging by his breast fixation and gaudy post-rock style—comes from the spawning ground of MTV, which previously has given us such auteurs as Tardem Singh (*The Cell*), Antoine Fuqua (*Replacement Killers*), and Michael Bay (*Con Air, The Rock, Pearl Harbor*).

A list to conjure with.

I was once accosted in a bar by a drunken pre-med student who proceeded to tell me the truth about vampires. He'd figured it all out. I don't recall a great deal of what he said—I'm not terribly interested in the metabolisms of fictional creatures (personal note to my stalker: Stay calm. I believe in *your* vampire). But I do remember him saying that given the fact vampires spend half their time in a vegetative state, half in an accelerated condition that affords them inhuman strength and inspires the fiercest of appetites, their digestive processes would likely be a gross parody of the human, producing incredibly vile liquefied wastes and ghastly breath. He went on to extend this chain of logic *ad nauseum*, but I had already gotten his point: the undead are a skanky bunch. The original cinematic vampire, *Nosferatu*, conformed to the pre-med student's model, but Bela Lugosi's poetic Valentino-esque take on Count Dracula—elegant pomaded blood junkie in white tie and tails—was a complete departure. These seminal images have developed over the years into two sharply divergent filmic strains, the latter incarnated by Anne Rice's tortured decadents, the former by the seedy Darwinism of Kathryn Bigelow's *Near Dark*, with its lowlife vampire "family" living like murderous cockroaches in the contemporary Southwest.

Like most things—like the economy, our chances for survival as a species, and Madonna's bust line—Hollywood vampire flicks have suffered a decline. In recent years, only *Blade* with its comic-book smarts and high-octane pacing made a respectable entry. One would have to look back to the aforementioned *Near Dark* to find a classic of the genre; and before that we would have to return to the 60s and George Romero's horrifyingly mundane *Martin*, which treats of a teenage vampire without fangs forced to chloroform and then cut open his victims. Francis Ford Coppola's attempt to revive the gothic form, *Bram Stoker's Dracula*, would have benefited had Mr. Coppola understood that at least half of the Nineteenth Century did not look as if it were set dressed by Rembrandt, and that a gothic atmosphere is best achieved by understated dramatics and a subdued, even crepuscular palette. John Carpenter's *Vampires* . . . Faugh! A total waste of Thomas Ian Griffith. *Interview with a Vampire*? Two words—Tom Cruise. Then we have the also-rans: *Vampire's Kiss* with Anne Parillard; *A Vampire in Brooklyn* with Eddie Murphy; *Modern Vampires* (Caspar Van Dien on a blood rampage); *Children of the Night*, in which redneck vampire Karen Black in all her voluptuous decay is kept chained in the attic by her husband and whines, "Gettin' little tired of eating leeches!" I'm certain I'm overlooking loads of gory trash, but who cares. The Future? More of the same. Though I must admit to having some nostalgia-driven interest in *The Omega Man* remake (despite Arnold's Schwarzen-presence), and I'm intrigued by the forthcoming *Teething*, which supposes a vampire baby born to normal parents.

At least day care will be no problem.

Last year while I was taking part in a discussion about *Blair Witch 2* on a web chat (I had an hour free, okay?), *Shadow of a Vampire* was mentioned as a film some hoped might bring new vitality to the genre, and I looked forward to seeing it. I eventually watched the movie in the company of a friend, and afterward she turned to me and said, "Boring shitty pretentious." Well, I simply could not agree. To be considered truly pretentious, a film director must overindulge his vision and sense of style; since *Shadow*'s director M. Elias Erige is sadly lacking these qualities, I think it more accurate to say that his film aspires to pretension. "Boring" and "shitty," I'm all right with. I note that *Shadow* was awarded the Bronze Horse at the Stockholm Film Festival, which is impressive on the face of it; but I have sufficient respect for audiences in Sweden to make me wonder if this isn't some sort of booby prize.

Technically, the film is a mess. The cutting verges on the professional, some of the worst I've seen, and the cinematography . . . It's as if Erige tried in the main to limit himself to techniques available in the 1920s. If that's the case, then maybe I'm wrong about the pretension thing (I believe an analysis of the film would reveal this is not the case, yet the camera work has such a static character, the result is the same as if it were). It's hard to recall a movie with this much art-house juice that was so ineptly crafted. It's equally hard to recall a script with so much wasted dramatic potential. The focus of all this incompetence is the shooting of F. W. Murnau's silent classic *Nosferatu*, and that choice of focus was a serious mistake.

Gods and Monsters worked because the emphasis was not on Frankenstein but on the man who directed the film. Moviemaking involves a good bit of tedium, and instead of ranging peaks and valleys of tension and release, Erige's story kerflop kerflops along just like the film in Murnau's rickety camera. Most of the mayhem occurs off-camera, a strategy both inoffensive and ineffectual.

The best thing about *Shadow* is its premise that Max Shreck, the lead in *Nosferatu*, was an actual vampire. Great start. But Erige does nothing with it. His approach to narration is that of a man who tells a successful joke at a party and then spends the next 90 minutes explaining why it was funny. Characters are stated, not developed. Most of the cast are there to carry spears or be eaten. Of Murnau

(John Malkovich) we know only that he is arrogant, a sexual omnivore, and shoots dope. Of Shreck (Willem Dafoe) we know even less—he's a vampire who has a prior relationship with Murnau. Shreck should have been the focus of the film, its real subject. When he peers intently at the grainy black and white raw footage of a sunrise, we want to understand everything he is feeling; but Erige's interests apparently lay elsewhere, and Shreck remains for the most part unexploited, unexplored, and unexplained.

Willem Dafoe is a terrific actor with excellent range, and I have no quarrel with him receiving awards; but if truth be told, this is not an awards-caliber performance. He does an accent, he makes Mandarin gestures, he mugs. The make-up, which is outstanding, does the rest. Had Gilbert and Sullivan done a vampire operetta, Dafoe's Shreck would be right at home. As for Malkovich, one of the finest actors of his generation, this is not a shining moment. His accent wanders, and his devotion to the role seems shaky—which is understandable, since it appears to be designed solely as a commentary on the megalomania of all directors, another joke that grows tiresome. The upshot of this woeful mismatch of talent and material is that I had more fun hating *Dracula 2000* than I did staring dully as *Shadow of a Vampire* bellywhomped and went splat.

It's conceivable that another great vampire film may yet be made. I'd like to see one that eschewed the rococo and did without door closings that sound like guillotines and footsteps like the Tread o' Doom, and concentrated on the dark animal aspects of a solitary monster, showing us his biological requirements and some of the small moments of his life. A figure not altogether deromanticized. Defrocked of his cool cape or shades or whatever, but not—not entirely, at least—of his human sensibilities. A character who must change as he lives. Generally speaking, though, vampires may be a played-out proposition. They've done a prolonged term as the romantic emblem of our fears concerning the afterlife, and the new millennium offers replacement terrors more relevant to the contemporary nightmare. However, vampires may retain value as satiric devices. A corporate vampire would be fun, humorous in its implicit redundancy. A vampire on Ecstasy would be a trip, and *Vampire on Ecstasy* isn't a bad title. Then there's my own vampire script, which has the working title *Dark Pretender*. Or maybe *The Pretender* would be classier. (I know there was a TV show with a similar name, but that's so over!).

Here's how it goes.

A powerful vampire runs for president and wins by turning a plurality of voters. The nation thrives. Private negotiations with world leaders, they're a snap now. Just one little bite and those ol' trade agreements get signed tout suite. Economy's rosy, world peace is starting to happen, and there's a bright golden haze on the meadow.

So the Pres knocks off an intern now and again . . .

What the hey!

But-then-it's-discovered-the-Pres-is-really-evil-with-a-plan-to-pardon-the-hellspawn-and-release-them-from-exile.

And what if that plan succeeds?

Wellsir, along comes another vampire president out of the great Southwest, and he's got a new vision for America. Aided by his loyal minions in Florida, he'll take care of them hellspawns. Imagine this digital poster. The White House superimposed over a bone-white full moon. Then the whole thing washes red.

Very sexy.

This could get green-lighted. No lie. It's got enough sizzle to attract a major star, and is sufficiently generic to please the bean counters. And it's got an important message, too. One that speaks to the heart of all our problems, and makes plain the only thing we know for certain about real vampires:

They rule.

PICKING APART A PECK OF PETER PARKERS

Spiderman
Release Date: *May 3, 2002 Nationwide*
Director: *Sam Raimi*
Screenwriter: *Alvin Sargent, David Koepp, Sam Raimi, Scot Rosenberg, Neil Ruttenberg*
Source Writer: *Stan Lee*
Starring: *Tobey McGuire, Kirsten Dunst, Willem Dafoe, James Franco*
Distributor: *Columbia Tristar*
Review Date: *June 3, 2002*

IN THE MIDST OF VIEWING SAM RAIMI'S *Spiderman* I became concerned that I'd misplaced a Safeway coupon guaranteeing fifty cents off on a Healthy Choice dinner, but after a thorough search I found it crumpled in my shirt pocket and glanced up in time to catch another shot of Spidey (Tobey Maguire) swinging off through digital Manhattan. This might indicate that I was uninvolved with the film, and I admit such is the case; but then unless you are—for whatever reason—still given to thumb-sucking, *Spiderman* is not a movie that requires concentrated attention, since the large majority of its audience are familiar with the story and familiar also with its brand of visual pyrotechnics, its generic style of narration, and, indeed, with its every particular. One does not attend such a movie with any greater expectations than that one will see what one anticipates seeing. The entertainment industry, publishing included, has retooled itself so as to provide us with an infinite feast of comfort food, and Hollywood, its most conservative arm, has decided that by churning out remakes, rehashes, and franchise properties, they expose themselves to less financial risk than were they to offer their audience even a feeble intellectual challenge. Dozens of comic books are currently in development. *Wonder Woman, Aquaman, The Fantastic Four, Superman, Batman, Daredevil* (starring Ben Affleck—can anyone explain why this guy has a career?), *Iron Man,* and others more obscure, projects that range from the intriguing— Ang Lee's *The Hulk,* featuring the fine Australian actor Eric Bana— to the off-putting—*Hellblazer,* with Nicolas Cage slated to portray the cool, cynical anti-hero John Constantine, a casting choice that's rather like trying to pass off a pound of pork sausage as filet of sole.

Thanks to this policy of intellectual debasement, genre film fails to reflect the rich potentials embodied by the science fiction field. Despite occasional Great Leaps Forward like Kubrick's *2001,* the status quo is God. So it is that franchises like *Star Wars* and *The Matrix* (both, in essence, comic books) will continue, as will the strip-mining of Philip K. Dick's legacy, the extraction of his basic ideas and the tossing aside of the unique sensibility that made his work valuable. The latest of these pictures, Spielberg's *Minority Report* with Tom Cruise, appears to transform a clever albeit minor Dick story into a higher tech version of *Logan's Run.* Inimical space travelers will proliferate—*Predator* types and big-eyed Roswellian grays a la James Cameron's upcoming *Brother Termite* —and so will creepy space relics and disasters precipitated by extraterrestrial sources. We'll have the odd low-budget film that strays from these parameters, but basically that's what lies in the filmic future, even though the actual future promises to be so much more complex.

With the development of computer graphic imaging, all that

prevents the studios from tackling stories previously deemed unfilmable, like *Ringworld* and *Rendezvous with Rama*, are their greed and stupidity, qualities that, however docile the audience, will eventually sabotage their marketing tactics. There are some terrific properties languishing in development, but it's probably a blessing that many of these—an example, Tom Hanks as Gulliver Foyle in *The Stars My Destination* —die aborning. It may be that Bester's story could not be sufficiently dumbed down to make its filming feasible. The dumbing down of character and story, you see, has become a requisite for most green-lighted projects. It's been brought to my attention that a major selling point written into a treatment for a film based on a Disneyworld ride, *Pirates of the Caribbean*, was the assurance that the picture would contain no subplots and no depth of characterization. Thus it is that we are doomed to endure at least another decade of George Lucas' dotage, Stephen Spielberg's crass, simplistic humanism, Cameron's megalomania, Ridley Scott's opulent vacancy, and the like. But the day is coming when a kid with a credit card will be able to walk around carrying a movie studio on his back, and when that day arrives, it's probable that some of the great science fiction stories will be filmed imaginatively and lovingly by young men and women outside the system. Perhaps then we will see a movie version of, among various possibilities, *Neuromancer*. I suspect the idea of filming Gibson's book is low priority for whoever owns the rights. After all, they might say, the high concept trappings of the book have been done to death in dozens of films, most of them trashy. That whole Cyberpunk thing . . . it's so last millennium! They don't get that what makes Gibson's book compelling is the storytelling, the dark energy that illuminates his setting. But given the advent of new technology, I'm certain someone will get it, and they will make the movie and it will be markedly more successful than any of the imitations that have already been mounted before the cameras.

Think about the stories the studios are capable of telling

nowadays. At the top of my list would be Le Guin's *The Left Hand of Darkness*. Then Disch's *Camp Concentration*; Stephenson's *Snow Crash*; Effinger's *When Gravity Fails*; Aldiss' *Helliconia Spring*; Zelazny's *Lords of Light*; Bear's *Blood Music*; Wolfe's *Shadow of the Torturer*; Simmons' *Hyperion*. Anyone reading this could in a few minutes generate an entirely different list that would be every bit as worthwhile. Of course when you think about whom the studios might cast in these movies—Afflecks and Cruises ad nauseum— perhaps it's better to wait for that kid carrying the studio on his or her back.

In the meantime, we have George Clooney remaking *Solaris*, Mel Gibson staring aghast at a crop circle, and the endless Sequel-O-Rama.

As an exemplar of the contemporary genre film, *Spiderman* is not so bad. In fact, the first hour is quite entertaining, detailing the origin of Peter Parker's arachnoid powers via mutant spider bite, his difficulty in coming to terms with said powers, his unspoken love for the girl next door, Mary Jane (Kirsten Dunst), and the simultaneous evolution (by means of self-testing performance-enhancement drugs) of industrialist Norman Osborn (Willem Dafoe) into the Green Goblin. Sam Raimi, who reached his creative peak during his *Evil Dead* period, does an outstanding job with the action sequences, handling the acrobatic ineptitude of the Webcrawler's first swings through Manhattan with a sure-handed comedic touch. Especially effective is the scene during which Parker, clad in a shabby prototype of his costume, challenges a professional wrestler (Randy Savage) in order to win money to buy a car with which he can impress Mary Jane. Tobey Maguire's greatest asset as an actor is his ability to project internalized discomfort, and though he seems incapable of much more than this, that quality alone suits him for the lead. Dafoe, in full-on scenery-chewing mode, cackles and grimaces with persuasive élan and invests the gradual change of Osborn into the Goblin with more subtlety than might be expected, and Dunst, a better actress than her role deserves, portrays a damsel in nearly constant distress with appropriate sweetness and vulnerability.

The second hour, however, is less successful. As often happens in the comic book, Parker's sad-sack emotional stammering grows tiresome and the predictability of the plot—the Goblin discovering Spidey's identity, his kidnapping of Mary Jane to draw Parker into his clutches, and the final battle between them—overwhelms the film's energy. Growing disaffected, I found myself hoping for *Spiderman* to encounter Spiderwoman, that we might witness Peter Parker plucked apart by purple pincers, his legs chewed off, eggs laid in his flesh. On a more practical level, things would have been improved had tabloid editor Jonah Jameson (a perfectly cast J.K. Simmons), for whom Parker works as a free-lancer, been more than an afterthought in the movie. In the source material Jameson provides *Spiderman* with comic grounding for his frustration that contrasts well with his woman trouble and the unending stream of super villains. The addition of a couple more scenes featuring Jameson might have blunted the drippy effect of Maguire's wet-eyed stare.

The problem with *Spiderman* is more-or-less the same that afflicted the *Harry Potter* movie: it was given into the hands of a caretaker director, a man who would take no risks, whose intent was to transfer the source materials onto the screen instead of translating them. A superhero who shares our insecurities is an attractive idea, yet though Spiderman becomes braver, faster, stronger, famous, a veritable icon, though he does gain a moral purchase, his personality essentially remains that of a teenage nerd. This illogical continuity of character may suffice in a commercial comic book, but the more vital process of a film—even one based on a comic—demands something deeper. A spot of creepiness would have served the film well. It stands to reason that Parker might develop an obsession with arachnids, and it would have added a layer to have him communing with his loathsome genetic kin on a cobwebbed rooftop. In both the comic book and the movie, Parker experiences bitterness, but it's always an ineffectual, petulant bitterness, not the more volatile and dangerous emotion of a young man. Giving Spiderman some potentially destructive issues might juice him up a notch. There is, for instance, his iffy relationship with the public, many of whom consider him a villain. His reaction to this is also petulant, but I would think that sooner or later this might mature into a seriously mean-spirited attitude. A few touches of the sort would have generated a more pronounced character arc and thus increased dramatic tension . . . and perhaps Raimi has this in mind for the sequels; but come 2006, I bet we'll find Parker still mooning over Dunst, as he does at the end of this movie. Or else they'll live happily ever after, displaying nary a trace of the emotional damage attendant upon such a prolonged separation.

Somewhere along the line—and this is true of both writing and film—the notion of what is artful and what is entertaining became separated. Gradually writers and directors considered by the critics at the top of their field came to be viewed as limited in their appeal, and writers and directors who had been viewed (be it rightly or wrongly) as journeymen came to be seen as populists. Storytellers. As if Gene Wolfe, for example, were not a storyteller. Back in the 30s and 40s, men like Hemingway and Orson Welles had great commercial success; but it's tough these days to point to a critic's darling who is also the author of a best-seller or the director of a blockbuster movie. Whatever the cause of this separation, be it the evolving science of marketing alone or in tandem with a decline in educational standards and reading levels, the reaction of most Hollywood directors has been to dumb it down, and as a result we're being force-fed a diet of increasingly simplified stories. Franchises, comic books, remakes. I've heard it said that *Spiderman* is the best superhero movie yet, and maybe it is. I don't know. Myself, I have a fondness for Donner's *Superman*, but making judgments about this type of film is basically a case of which do you like better, chocolate or strawberry? For my part, I had a good time. As all the chubby TV reviewers will tell you in their shilly little voices, it's a freaking thrill ride, a roller-coaster experience. Like *Pirates of the Caribbean*, it's fun for the whole family, a simple, splashy passage without depth or subplot. And that's cool. Nothing wrong with fun. But I wish once in a while they'd serve it up with a side of truth and beauty, because it's my feeling that fun is not merely—as the folks at MGM, Fox, and Dreamworks would have you believe—something vacuous, bright, and feel-goodish, something that goes good with Raisinettes and a Coke, something even an idiot can understand.

FLAT AFFLECK

Daredevil
Release Date: *February 14th, 2003*
Director: *Mark Steven Johnson*
Screenwriter: *Mark Steven Johnson*
Starring: *Ben Affleck, Michael Clarke Duncan, Jennifer Garner, Colin Farrell*
Distributor: *Twentieth Century Fox*
Review Date: *September 26, 2002*

YOU CAN ACTUALLY FEEL YOURSELF growing stupider while you watch *Daredevil*. As the bright and dark flicker-flickers on the screen, you have a growing sense of vacancy and agitation such as a chicken might endure when it realizes its legs are bound, it's on a moving conveyer belt, and something sharp up ahead is flashing down and doing truly creepy things to other chickens. You're not suggesting here that seeing *Daredevil* would prove fatal, but the vagueness and frail apprehensiveness that come after suffering through it seem redolent of—at the least—a Near-Death Experience.

Ben Affleck, the World's Sexiest Man according to *People Magazine*, and don't you have to wonder who's on that selection committee, because in most circles, excluding that of necrophiliacs, sexiness is generally associated with vitality of some sort . . . Ben is having a really bad career day. Dressed in a scarlet leather rig that's surely the envy of every fetishist, emblazed with a double D that makes you think he might work as a stock boy at some sort of Chains n' Things franchise. Having to upchuck dialog like, "Can one make a difference? There are some days I believe."

Whoa!

But then Ben is not only the World's Sexiest Man, he's also the World's Most Vapid Actor (note to every other actor: you want Affleck's agent, because the guy's got to be an ace!), so he may well belong in the World's Lamest Superhero movie.

When you arrive at the theater and settle into your seat, you have some hope for the picture because it's based on Frank Miller's *Elektra Saga*, one of the better comic book runs of the 80s, and you don't yet know that director Mark Steven Johnson is Ed Wood with a budget and his looks-like-a-movie-but-really-isn't plays more like an episode of *Celebrity Mismatch*, that show in which just for yucks we try to put together two Hollywood stars and see how little chemistry they can generate while surrounded by popular brands of candy, soft drinks, and toothpaste . . . His "movie," then, is an idiotic, crass, overstuffed jumble of story lines held together by vacuous characters and ineptly conceived scenes (many lifted from other somewhat less awful superhero flicks), all dressed up in the usual post-*Matrix* camera tricks and some of the most abysmal CGI effects to date, larded with spasmodic bouts of brainless violence and lapses into sophomoric humor. Nevertheless, you're still hanging onto that little scrap of hope when the opening shot fades up. A rat scurries down the street. You understand this is Johnson's subtle way of telling you, it's going to be a dark ride.

Oh my God.

Ben's doing a voiceover, telling us about his life.

Let's listen, shall we?

Daredevil, aka Matt Murdock, is another of the *Marvel* stable of tormented, alienated heroes. Orphaned by hoodlums who slew his daddy, prizefighter Jack "The Devil" Murdock; blinded in a tragic childhood accident for which fate compensates by bestowing upon him incredibly heightened senses and a brooding, tormented nature that's tailored for wreaking vengeance. As you sit there, you wonder how Ben's going to handle the role. Smug and self-satisfied? No problem. Bored and dumbstruck? A snap. Dazed, listless, pouting? All within the Sexiest Man's repertoire. But brooding and tormented . . . ? The answer is, sometimes he winces and at other times he furrows his brow and looks down. Down, you suppose, is the direction of brooding and torment. Up, then, must be where fulfilled and happy lies.

Okay. You've got it.

The first time you see Daredevil in action, while cruising for a little vigilante justice, he follows a rapist into a packed bar and proceeds to beat the living doo-doo out of everyone in the place while they fire their pistols non-stop, loosing maybe three, four hundred rounds, and, miraculously, nobody gets hit.

Just the thing to inspire the kiddies—they've been wondering how fun it would be to play with daddy's gun.

Turns out Daredevil's day job is attorney-at-law. Got a nice little practice. Only defends innocent people with no money, yet he's obviously making a killing at it, given all his fine clothes and gadgets and stuff. Nights, he goes after the bad guys who slip through the cracks of the judicial system. He loves his work . . . and he's a lover, too. It isn't long before he meets and mates the World's Sexiest Woman, Jennifer Garner. She's playing Elektra Natchios, who in the Miller comic was an assassin, but in Mr. Johnson's world is a supermodel or something who just happens to know a mess of martial arts. Their foreplay consists of a kung fu battle that's more than vaguely reminiscent of that heinous rape thing our hero so deplores. Then comes the chemistry part. Watching Bennifer and Jen make love arouses in you the same stuporous feelings you get when watching bacon drippings congeal after drinking a few too many brewskis the night before.

Dum de dum de dum . . .

Did you leave the door to your apartment unlocked? Maybe you should pick up some of that new Pepsi Twist on your way home.

As you've been watching, bits of dialogue come to your ears.

"I didn't catch your name."

"I didn't drop it."

To your immediate left, several skinny, wan-looking young boys accompanied by a pudgy middle-aged man with Coke-bottle specs seem glued to the screen by this edgy exchange.

"Does everybody have to go through this to get your name?"

"Try asking for my number?"

To your right, three popcorn-munching pre-teen girls giggle at the brisk repartee.

It's hard to keep track of the "movie," because Johnson is determined to cram around a hundred issues-worth of Daredevilish information into an hour forty minutes or thereabouts. The whole thing's like the digest version of a novel, a trilogy with the second book left out. It's more fun watching the audience drool and gibber. No wonder, you think, George Bush won the election.

A few inconsistencies appear. Daredevil, not gifted with superpowers, is capable of keeping pace on foot with a car. He can leap from a skyscraper, fall a tenth of a mile and catch hold of a wire without ripping his hand off. He can avoid machine-gun fire. Hmm.

The man seems pretty darned healthy for a guy who guzzles pain pills and takes downers to sleep. Oh, well.

Villains materialize from the Johnsonian chaos. There's Bullseye (Colin Farrell), an unerring marksman who hits everything he aims at . . . except one. He's got his grouch on for Double D because Daredevil once made him miss. Talk about pique. Bullseye has about 8-10 minutes of screen time, much of which he spends donning his cool leather coat—it goes Whoosh! each time he puts it on, whirling it like a matador's cape. You consider obtaining your own sound effect. A cigarette lighter that sounds like a nuclear explosion. A cell phone that sounds like the whack of a guillotine blade severing bone when you flip it open. Bullseye's head is shaved, and he has a telescopic range-finding display tattooed on his forehead. He looks, you think, like Andre Agassi turned S&M party animal.

The interest of Mr. Pudgy Guy and his pet children peaks whenever Bullseye makes an appearance. They hunch forward and rest their chins on the seats in front of them. You begin to have suspicious thoughts regarding their relationship.

Then there's Kingpin. In the Miller comic, Wilson "Kingpin" Fisk (Michael Clarke Duncan) is an enormous white man who is mad for evil and capable of tossing cars around. Duncan is appropriately enormous. My God, the man is his own CGI effect. But he plays the role with all of the dread panache of Urkle on steroids. He's responsible for several murders and lots of other evil stuff, and this has something to do with the plot.

Even the pre-teen popcorn munchers are beginning to look disengaged, but they're going to go to school tomorrow morning and tell everyone how cool *Daredevil* is, because it wouldn't make them look cool to have seen an uncool movie.

Maybe this also helps explain George Bush.

All the big fight scenes, you observe, have been edited into incoherence. Jennifer Garner is the most physically incompetent female action actress since Geena Davis tried her hand at swashbuckling in the gloriously, albeit unintentionally, funny *Cutthroat Island*. Thinking about how frightened Geena looked each time she whipped out her sword makes you laugh, something that Daredevil does not. It's a hell of a lot darker ride than you expected. The film may not end. You may be stuck here forever with the popcorn munchers and Mr. Potential Child Molester and his sickly brood, watching Jennifer worry about her motivation and Ben practice his scowl. There are worse fates. You pass the time enumerating them. There are seven in all, you decide. Eight, if you believe that an Iraqi invasion is not beyond the realm of probability.

But it does end, it really does ... though "end" is perhaps not the term you'd use. It collapses. Finally deflates. Finishes dissolving into a puddle of Johnsonesque putrescence. You stagger up and head along the aisle. You feel collapsed, deflated, dissolving. The popcorn munchers brush past you—their giggles sound muted and joyless, squiggles of random girl noise more than expressions of delight. Glancing back at the screen, you catch the announcement that there'll be a sequel. Your step falters, you reel. Something's wrong inside you. The aisle seems to go on forever, angling up and up, a long dark tunnel at whose end people are waving, silhouetted against the light, a beautiful, soft white radiance. Your old friends and relatives, waiting to welcome you into an environment wherein there is no pain, no worry, no *Daredevil*. You hope that's what's happening because ... Jesus! A sequel. You just can't wait.

AIN'T HE UNGLAMOROUS?

The Hulk
Release Date: *June 20th, 2003*
Director: *Ang Lee*
Screenwriter: *David Hayter, James Schamus, Michael France, John Turman, Michael Tolkin*
Source Writer: *James Schamus*
Starring: *Eric Bana, Jennifer Connelly, Sam Elliott, Nick Nolte*
Distributor: *Universal Pictures*
Review Date: *July 8, 2003*

BACK IN THE DAY WHEN MOVIES WERE movies and Humphrey Bogart loved Lauren Bacall and cartoons were less than ten minutes long and ran before the feature, the appearance of comic-book/strip characters on film was generally limited to Saturday-morning serials that played to audiences of children. Now that a large majority of the American audience have, for all intents and purposes, been reduced to children, their critical faculties nearly obliterated by decades of real good blow-up and cartoonish scenarios, comic-book heroes and villains zoom across the screens of the nation's theaters a half-dozen times a year in films with nine-figure budgets and scripts churned out by an assembly-line process that might be as well served by the employment of chimpanzees as the doubtless far more impeccably tailored—yet no more gifted—writing "talent" that in fact does the actual typing. If there exists a comic book not currently in development, then surely it must be under option. We are already beginning to see remakes of comic-book movies, the next in line being next year's *The Punisher*, which will likely be a better film than the 1989 version starring Dolph Lundgren . . . but probably only marginally better and ten times more expensive to make. This year's comic feast has thus far included such ghastly menu items as *Daredevil* and *The League of Extraordinary Gentlemen*, a relatively palatable *X-Men* sequel, and several overdone slabs of deafening Dolby-ized grunge (*T3, The Matrix: Reloaded, et al*) that, while not directly derived from comics, reference the comic-book tradition. The difficulty with most such films, at least to my mind, has been that those charged with adapting these simplistic, violent stories have not taken into account the dynamics and demands of the medium to which they are being adapted. Instead of seeking to translate the stories, to imbue them with the heightened complexity and depth that would allow them to be cinematically compelling (as, most notably, Tim Burton did with *Batman*), their main goal has been to transfer them to film and thus preserve the materials as inked upon the page so as not to annoy the title character's fan base. This may or may not be a wise marketing decision, but it has certainly proved to be, generally speaking, a horrid artistic choice. So it was that when I learned Ang Lee (*Crouching Tiger, Hidden Dragon*) had signed on to direct *The Hulk*, and that the part of Bruce Banner would be played by Eric Bana, whose striking debut in the Australian film *Chopper* marked him as an actor to watch, I thought this combination of directorial and acting talent might be capable of creating a comic-book film that would satisfy on every level.

I find it amusing that one of the more frequently voiced complaints about *The Hulk* is that the Hulk himself does not look real. The celluloid version of Doc Bruce Banner's inner child seems considerably more real to me than does the print version, and I can't help but think that were a fifteen-foot-tall, green-skinned humanoid figure with limbs like oak trunks to materialize in the parking lot adjacent to my building and begin tossing cars about, or whatever suited his pleasure, he would look distinctly unreal by any standard. If truth be told, the Hulk is the most realistic element of Ang Lee's movie. Though the effects do not achieve the uniform brilliance of those in *Crouching Tiger, Hidden Dragon*, several sequences capture an equivalent magic—in particular, a long chase scene during which the Hulk, having escaped from captivity on a secret army base, is hunted through the desert by fighter jets and choppers, and, while running, discovers that he has a prodigious ability to leap. This scene and others are enhanced by split-screen effects designed to give the frames the look of comic-book pages and are themselves enhanced by a variety of digital zooms, wipes, and dissolves. Images are spun, split, letter-boxed, shunted to one side, etc.—this is one busy, busy motion picture. The overall effect is like having opened a comic book whose pages then come to life—though sometimes confusing, on the whole it's a stimulating and beautifully managed device. If they had used these techniques in Operation Iraqi Freedom, it would have been even more popular a mini-series.

The origin story of the Hulk has been scientifically upgraded, lent a smidgen more plausibility, by attributing Doc Bruce Banner's Hulking-out not merely to being belted by gamma rays, but mainly to self-experimentation done by his father, David Banner, while working on a military project dealing with regeneration. When the gamma rays finally strike Banner the Younger, they activate mutated genetic material that has been passed down to him from his father, and they further serve to amplify a rage born of childhood trauma, this stemming from a terrible domestic event involving his mother that Bruce has blacked out and that is fragmentarily revealed during the course of the film. Said trauma has made Bruce, according to his ex-girlfriend Betty Ross, "emotionally distant," a charge that strikes an odd note given the emotionally distant fashion in which Jennifer

Connelly establishes the role—she displays throughout a gloomy stupefaction overlaid by what seems a Valium-induced calm. For the most part, Bana offers little contrast; only when he's beginning to change into the Hulk does he exhibit strong emotion. Sam Eliot, as Betty's father, General "Thunderbolt" Ross, is appropriately, gruffly martial. He was the head of the project on which David Banner worked and knows something of Bruce's secret. Nick Nolte, as the elder incarnation of David Banner, who returns into his son's life after more than twenty years' incarceration, is not to blame for the unevenness of his performance—that blame and, indeed, blame for the majority of the movie's significant problems, must be attributed to the script, to writers of record John Turman, Michael France, and James Schamus, and to the god-knows-how-many-other trade rats who took their turn gnawing at its edges. As it's written, Nolte's character alternates between that of a deeply troubled obsessive and that of a ham-fisted evil guy, and no substantial logical support is given for either condition. As a result, it's tough to discern the path that led David Banner from his misguided scientist phase to the cosmically demented super villain—the Absorbing Man—whom he ultimately becomes. Not that such a road is required by the dictates of the basic story, but Ang Lee, by virtue of both his reputation and his leisurely approach, seems to promise us one, and thus its absence comes as something of a letdown.

There is nothing intrinsically wrong in beginning what is essentially an action picture with forty minutes of character development; but if you're hoping to please an action audience—any audience, for that matter—you'd best make said development good and dramatic. The lugubrious exchanges of dialogue between Bana and Connelly that dominate the first third of the film are marked by a flatness that makes the Mojave look like a mountain range. For the life of me, I can't remember a thing they talked about; not a single line had sufficient pungency to linger in my memory. The interjection of a minor-league villain/potential romantic rival, a smarmy corporate pirate played with an Oil Can Harry-ish lack of shading by Josh Lucas (last seen smirking at Reese Witherspoon in *Sweet Home Alabama*), does absolutely nothing in the way of striking a spark, even though it's his unrelenting no-goodness that eventually pushes Bruce's badass button. By the time Bana morphed into the Grumpy Green Giant, I was reduced to wondering whether Jennifer Connelly's moist-eyed somnolence was a directorial choice or the result of mild flu; to hope that the mountain-bike-riding Bruce would hit the mother of all gopher holes, take a terrible spill, and subsequently lay green-fisted waste to all the little forest creatures; and to speculate that Ang Lee might have decided to do a Zen thing and film the first superhero movie in which the central figure was merely thought about and never seen.

Once the Hulk puts in an appearance, the pace of the movie switches gears with alarming suddenness. It's rather like watching a car that's been idling at a stoplight for the better part of an hour, while its occupants chat about interesting topics like their favorite brand of paint thinner, abruptly peel away from the intersection, downshifting, swerving, ramming into garbage cans, roaring past plot points, whoosh, with only Jennifer Connelly gazing out the passenger side window with her lovely gray eyes and dovelike gray composure to remind us, I suppose, that it's all so very sad and slow and we're really going nowhere, don't you know . . . A gradual build would have been preferable, but once the film gets up to speed, there are plenty of good moments as the Hulk is captured, escapes, smashes stuff, gets recaptured, all leading to his final battle with the Absorbing Nick Nolte, looking here as ratty and forlorn as he did in his famous mug shot. Special mention should be made of the scene in which the Hulk hitches a ride on the rear of a fighter jet, whose pilot flies up into the troposphere in hopes of rendering the Big Green Guy unconscious. As they fly higher and higher, the Hulk's monstrous visage grows to fill the canopy above the pilot's head and that face, barely conscious, eyebrows frosted, registers with us in the cool and poignant way that only great comic-book imagery can, here lent the added potency of motion and the semblance, however unreal it may be judged, of life. I won't go so far as to say that moment alone is worth the price of admission—ten bucks should still buy more value than that—but it does go to show what might have been done with this property had someone other than Messrs. Schamus, France, and Turman been handed control over it.

And, of course, someone other than Mr. Lee.

I've been told that when Ang Lee was approached by studio people to direct *The Hulk*, he responded that he didn't know if he could make a good comic-book movie, but he did know how to make a good Greek tragedy. Unfortunately, he made neither and perhaps the fact that he thought he knew how to make a Greek tragedy should have disqualified him for the job. Even the Hulk, among the darkest of the *Marvel* heroes, has about him an innate silliness, a humorous aspect (he's a green muscle freak who's capable of bouncing like Super-Super Mario from the bottom of a well to the top of Mt. Everest, for God's sakes!) that Lee apparently failed to notice, a quality that demands something less declamatory than the Classical treatment. There is about Lee's movie an unmistakable whiff of pomposity, and that attitude, along with the characterlessness of the dialogue, doomed *The Hulk* to be not so much a smash as a dull, disjointed thump. It turns out that what was needed to transform Bruce Banner into a monstrous green symbol of the beast within was not a tragedian, but someone who—though they might be conversant with the mechanisms of Greek tragedy— knew a little more than did Lee about Saturday-morning serials.

ADVENTURE IS THE NEW BOREDOM

Van Helsing
Release Date: *May 7th, 2004*
Director: *Stephen Sommers*
Screenwriter: *Stephen Sommers*
Starring: *Hugh Jackman, Kate Beckinsale, Richard Roxburgh,*
Elena Anaya
Distributor: *Universal*
Review Date: *May 15, 2004*

B-MOVIE POSTER COPY AND TAG LINES have always held great appeal
for me. Tacky cinematic haiku such as "See the Valley of Tree-tall
Spiders! See the Fire Monster of the Lava Lake!" (*The Lost
Continent*) and "Die with a little dignity!" from the Thomas Ian
Griffith cop flick *Excessive Force* seem to promise a dram of
panache in what otherwise is likely to be a fairly pedestrian viewing
experience, and even when that dram is not forthcoming (nary a
single tree-tall spider, for instance, was to be found in *The Lost
Continent*), the imagery and atmospherics invoked by the copy act
to compensate somewhat for the film's failures. Conversely, an
uninspired tag line attached to a film, a tag line such as, let's say,
"Adventure Has a New Name," tends to lower one's expectations. I
mean, how many times over the past twenty-five years has
Hollywood decided that adventure had a new name? Must be at

least a dozen, maybe more. And in almost every instance, a more appropriate tag line would have been something on the order of, "Merchandising has a new name," or "Adventure has a new hangnail."

Which brings us to *Van Helsing*, that being the newest new name for Adventure.

We're in an age, cinematically speaking, in which special effects have evolved into a form of pornography, when the design of a good many movies is merely a series of money shots linked by scenes that (for the most part) crudely seek to build the audience's anticipation. On occasion this structure succeeds in supporting a serviceable entertainment, but more often than not it results in abominations like *The League of Extraordinary Gentlemen*, films whose plots are minimally stated justifications for the chaos of explosions, gothic transformations, unfunny one-liners, and ineptly managed CGI that follows. Given the intellectually impoverished condition of our film industry and the current state of the human consciousness American-style, it's not so astonishing that the studios would seek to make B-movies with nine-figure budgets, but it does strain credulity a bit for them to create Ed Wood movies costing upward of 150 million dollars. That, however, appears to be the trend, and this makes the task of critical assessment increasingly difficult, because—God knows—quite a few critics are already grading on the curve, and a more generous curve would, in my view, eliminate all systems based on stars or numbers (as in, "I give *Van Helsing* one star for not impairing my ability to procreate"), and bring into play a scale whose upper end would be signaled by a satisfied belch and whose lower end would be marked by an even less socially acceptable form of gaseous release.

Stephen Sommers, *Van Helsing*'s chief architect, previously directed *The Mummy* and *The Mummy Returns*, two movies that, albeit not very good, have—by contrast to *Van Helsing*—the visionary purity and dramatic scope of *Lawrence of Arabia*. The movies that his latest opus most resembles are that series of venerable Abbott and Costello comedies (*Abbott and Costello Meet the Wolfman*, for one) featuring clusters of the classic Hollywood monsters. True, the Abbott and Costello scripts were more clever and more entertaining, and were often funny, something *Van Helsing* never is, be it unintentionally or otherwise; but the acting of Bud, Lou, and their cohorts is on a par with the posturings of Hugh Jackman (Van Helsing), Kate Beckinsale, and company, and the two films have essentially the same irreverent attitude toward horror. Three salient differences deserve mention: first of all, it's doubtful that the Abbott and Costello movies cost one hundredth of *Van Helsing*'s budget in real dollars, and, secondly, they are all but devoid of special effects. The third distinction I would draw is that the Abbott and Costello movies had little in the way of pretension— they knew exactly what they were, fodder for Saturday matinees and audiences of screaming kids throwing popcorn at each other, whereas *Van Helsing* is pretension swelled to mutant pro-portions, the idea of a simple entertainment belted by gamma rays and presented with a kind of bombastic sanctimony as if it were a pronouncement by Goombaba, God of Fun. I half-expected Sommers to put in an on-screen appearance and announce that he himself was Oz.

I'm not quite clear what Sommers intended with *Van Helsing*. I suspect that he is so incompetent at his craft, he believes he has fashioned a coherent, subtle mix of drama and humor, a film wholly unlike the one he delivered. It may be he was dropping Quaaludes throughout the entire shoot and lost his perspective. Another possibility—Sommers has been designing an amusement park attraction based on his *Mummy* films, and he confused the dramatic demands of the two mediums and thus imbued *Van Helsing* with sufficient substance to sustain our interest for a span of a few minutes. Then again, it is perhaps no coincidence that some movies these days are hyped as "rollercoaster rides" and "thrill rides." This may have become the ruling aesthetic in the industry. The problem is that most pictures so advertised are not in the least thrilling and cause you to question whether their director has ever taken such a ride. They lack suspense, their pacing is clumsy, and their stunts are repetitive. In *Van Helsing*, Van and Anna wander about, engaging in joyless, juiceless banter and casting arch looks at one another to imply a romantic attraction that is never fully stated, let alone explored, and every so often, without preamble, as happens to characters in video games, they fall through a floor or are attacked by something or else must escape the sudden onset of peril by means of a Tarzan/Robin Hood swing from a parapet or balcony: Sommers seems to believe that the such swings are a neglected trope and he can't squeeze enough of them in.

Sommers' Van Helsing is not the mysterious elderly fellow of the Stoker novel—he's far too old to be called elderly, having fought against the Romans at Masada and thereafter killed the man who became Dracula back in the 15th century. Dressed in a slouch hat and a black leather duster, he seems a hybrid of Clint Eastwood's stoic Man With No Name and James Bond (as though to bolster this impression, Sommers provides him with a Q-like sidekick, a Vatican science nerd, Friar Carl [David Wenham, *Lord of the Rings*' Faramir], who whips up groovy weapons like super explosives and a Gatling-gun crossbow). Van's last coherent memories prior to a bout of amnesia are those of Masada and all he knows of the missing centuries is that during them he kept on killing God's enemies. According to the covert Vatican order that has since brought him into their fold and uses him as a black ops killer, he is "the left hand of God." There are intimations that he may be an angel and/or the Wandering Jew, but Sommers leaves this enticing tidbit unexploited and unresolved. After killing Mr. Hyde, a cartoonish animation with the voice of Robbie Coltrane, (an event that in its gory risibility turns one's thoughts to *Van Helsing*'s spiritual precursor, the aforementioned *League of Extraordinary Gentlemen*), heaving him from the belfry of the Notre Dame cathedral in Paris, Van Helsing is ordered by his Vatican operator to travel to Transylvania (that's Tron-seel-VAIN-ya, according to the cast) so as to protect Anna Valerius (Beckinsale), the last remaining member of a family who for generations have fought against Dracula. Should she die before Dracula is killed, the entire family will be forced to spend eternity in Purgatory, a fate that—by the time this plot point was revealed—seemed less cruel than the one to which I, in my theater seat, felt consigned. Not only must Van save Anna from the brides of Dracula, three buxom, screeching vampirettes who taunt Anna ("too bad, so sad . . .") as if it were Hell Week in their sorority and alternately appear to have been costumed by a Carpathian outlet for Frederick's of Hollywood and then, upon sprouting batwings and fangs, are magically clothed in pallid body stockings, he must also deal with Dracula's master plan. For no reason I could fathom, Drac (a deliriously campy Richard Roxburgh, who may be inclined to slit his wrists once he sees this performance) believes that by channeling a lightning bolt through the body of the Frankenstein Monster (hiding in the basement of the windmill burned out long ago from beneath him by enraged villagers), he will be able to bring to life his myriad children—they hang in gooey egg sacs throughout his lair and, when born, resemble wriggly, rubbery, pale green baby bat-boys, objects like those you might find dangling from a rearview mirror and that have the capacity to glow in the dark. (This Frankenstein Monster, by the way, is a flabby, whiny version of the creature; he looks to have been hewn from a Humvee-sized chunk of toe jam and has a green glass top to his skull, the better to watch the electricities playing about his brain, and another glass section in his chest, suggesting that during the sewing-together process, Dr. Frankenstein ran out of body parts and was forced to manufacture replacements from an old Tiffany lampshade.) There is also some hoo-ha about Dracula always keeping an antidote to lycanthropy close to hand, because the only thing that can kill the Count is, natch, a werewolf. Keep this in mind, kids, Sommers seems to be saying. It might just be important.

So off go Anna and Van into the wonderful world of CGI, where they spend much of the next two hours standing in front of blue screens and delivering their inert dialogue to balls suspended on strings. Actually, seeing the screens and balls might have been preferable to the FX, though not all of it is horrible. The opening sequence recreating the genesis of the Frankenstein Monster, filmed in black and white, is cheesy fun; the Carpathian village where Van finds Anna is rendered creepily quaint and picturesque; but there are serious low points. When Velkan, Anna's brother, experiences one of his several transformations into a werewolf, he goes through a prolonged bout of impassioned writhing that calls to mind a woefully bad Alvin Ailey routine and then rips away his own skin to release an enormous rabid poodle with a bad perm and foot-long fangs. In spite of the technical limitations of his era, Lon Chaney's transformation into the original Wolfman was far more persuasive, principally because it was more realistic, but also because Chaney was working with an actual script and, though he was no Sean Penn or Jack Nicholson, had considerably more acting ability than does the pretty boy who plays Velkan and will likely soon be appearing in *The Days of Our Lives* as someone named Storm or Ridge or Thorn.

But acting and script and even story are incidental concerns to Sommers. When Van says, "You think I enjoy being the most hated man in Europe?", we are forced to ponder the question—no answer is supplied by the script and no evidence is given to support the premise as stated. For all we know, Van is just being paranoid. We are further induced to ask why, if the Vanster so hates his life, he doesn't tell the Vatican to bugger off and return to his solitary slaughter? Other questions abound. Why does a wooden coach explode into a fireball when it crashes? Why does one of Dracula's brides dissolve into green goo when she is staked, whereas her sisters turn to dust while suffering the same fate? Why are the Tron-seel-VAIN-yan accents so unvaryingly awful? Couldn't the budget fit in a dialogue coach or wasn't it important? And, most bewilderingly, why at film's end does Anna's ghost appear in the sky, a tear rolling down her cheek? Can Sommers believe that we've been emotionally affected by this uncooked stew of incompatible elements? So it would seem. For my part, I choose to think that it is not Anna who manifests in the heavens, but Kate Beckinsale stepping out of character and, giving expression to our consensus wish, silently imploring, Please, Stephen. For the love of God, no sequel!

Fantasy

ONE FROM COLUMN A

Crouching Tiger, Hidden Dragon
Release Date: *December 15, 2000 LA; December 22, 2000*
Limited; January 12, 2001 Limited
Director: *Ang Lee*
Screenwriter: *Hui Ling Wang, Kuo Jung Tsai, James Schamus*
Source Writer: *Du Lu Wang*
Starring: *Michelle Yeoh, Ziyi Zhang, Chang Chen, Yun-Fat Chow,*
Pei Pei Chang
Distributor: *Sony Pictures Classics*
Review Date: *April 13, 2001*

BEFORE *STAR WARS* THERE WAS *Hidden Fortress*, a film by Akira Kurosawa that provided the source material for George Lucas's epic fanboy treat. Thus it's only fair that an Asian epic of sorts, the best pure entertainment in recent years, cops a few Lucasoid licks on its way to becoming a girl-power version of the trilogy. Perhaps it's sheer coincidence that *Crouching Tiger, Hidden Dragon* revolves about the story of a beautiful princess Jen (Ziyi Zhang) manipulated by a Darth Vaderesque female, Jade Fox (Pei Pei Chang); in love with Lo, a rascally outlaw (Chen Chang); tutored by Jedi-like soul warrior Li Mu Bai (Chow Yun Fat); and given Yoda love by Shu Lien (Michelle Yeoh). True, a great many fantasies contain variations on these elements. But there are a number of clues, such as a bar scene with a distinctly *Star Wars*-ish feel, that lead me to believe this is no coincidence. Similarities aside, however, *Crouching Tiger, Hidden Dragon* stands in relation to Lucas' work as man does to the amoeba. Whereas *Star Wars* was all teenage whizbang gosharootie, *Dragon* manages to jam the essence of the original trilogy (minus, thankfully, any reference to club-wielding teddy bears) into slightly less than two hours, and replaces Lucas' juvenile humor with soulfulness and martial artistry taken to the level of ballet. It was director Ang Lee's (*The Ice Storm, Ride with the Devil*) stated intention to create an homage to the B-quality Chinese sword fantasies he watched as a child, films whose cultural niche was similar to that of our 1940s and '50s westerns. This tradition, previously dominated by pictures laden with cheap effects that effected a burlesque of Chinese opera, has undergone a renaissance in recent years with the production of such films as *Storm Riders* and *A Man Called Hero*, big budget Hong Kong releases with special effects that rival those of *The Matrix* and featuring Ekin Chang and Aaron Kwok, a pair of young actors verging on superstar status in the world of Asian cinema. *Riders* tells the story of the emperor of the "Martial Arts World" (veteran Japanese heavy Sonny Chiba), the greatest swordsman of his time, who kills two great warriors and raises their sons as his own. The sons (Kwok and Chang) have a falling out over the affections of the emperor's daughter, but unite in the end to defeat the evil emperor. The story is a marvel of complexity, tracking—in addition to the main thread—the fates of such characters as an oracular monk who pals around with a god disguised as a monkey, and a villager who cuts off his sword arm so it can replace the missing arm of one of the heroes. The magical duels, of which there are many, put to shame anything along these lines done to date by Hollywood—of special note is the final conflict, which takes place in the "Sword Grave," a plot of malignant earth in which the emperor plants the living swords of his numerous victims.

Hero marks a stylistic evolution of the genre, utilizing a non-linear narrative that cuts back and forth between China and America during the mid- and late 19th Century. The storyline of the movie is so complex, it would take a separate review to do it justice; but put succinctly, it is a generational saga involving father-and-son warriors and the resolution in America of enmities that began years before in China, treating of the exploitation of Chinese immigrants both by Americans and by their own people. The set pieces include an attack by magical shadows on the streets of Manhattan, a performance of traditional Chinese dance that masks the rescue of oppressed railroad workers, and a tremendous duel with magic and swords that takes place atop the Statue of Liberty. Until *Crouching Tiger, Hidden Dragon* happened along, this film established the high-water mark for the Chinese version of high fantasy.

Both the aforementioned films are plotted hyperkinetically, with lots of twists and turns and subplots, and characters who often are not what they originally appear to be. *Dragon*, relatively speaking, eschews complexity of this sort and uses two love stories to ground the action of the movie. One of these threads involves the unconsummated love between Li Mu Bai and Shu Lien, both of whom have rejected their personal desires in order to follow the path of duty and honor. The second thread treats of the volatile relationship between the bratty, rebellious Princess Jen and the outlaw Lo. This simplicity of story, so at variance with the convoluted structures of traditional sword flicks, may be the factor that has caused many Asians to dismiss the film as being aimed at a white audience. (Of course, if one accepts this assumption as true, it would logically follow that George Lucas' target audience for *Star Wars* was the Far East.) Another element that separates *Dragon* from its cousins is its loving attention to setting —not since *Lawrence of Arabia* have the story and landscape of a film heavy on action been so thoroughly intertwined (indeed, during *Dragon*'s wonderful desert sequences, Oscar-winning cinematographer Peter Pau incorporates a number of visual quotes from David Lean's masterpiece); however, in *Dragon* there is a great variety of landscape, and setting is used to reflect the characters' moods rather than, as is the case in *Lawrence*, to frame them. Then, too, there is the character of Princess Jen—she seems more contemporary riot girl than Ching Dynasty princess, willing to rebel against her life of privilege in order to seek personal freedom. But what ultimately elevates Dragon to the status of a masterpiece of its genre are the stunning fight sequences, most achieved not through wire work, as is customary in Hong Kong and in American films like *The Matrix*, but with the deft usage of CGI graphics. The initial sequence in which Shu Lien chases the thief who has stolen the magical Jade Sword over the rooftops is likely go down as one the signature moments in the history of the cinema. It is the theft of the Jade Sword by a masked thief that ignites the plot, uniting Li Mu Bai— whose sword it is—and Shu Lien in a hunt for the culprit, who turns out to be Princess Jen. The princess is being manipulated by the wizardly Jade Fox, who craves the sword for herself and is an old enemy of Li Mu Bai, having killed his teacher in the martial arts. Shu Lien strives to lead Jen onto the path of virtue, but following a duel between the two and a flashback sequence that reprises the inception of the love affair between the princess and the outlaw, Jen runs away. The pursuit of the princess and Jade Fox's attempts to shape events so as bring down her old enemy, Li Mu Bai, comprise the remainder of the plot, but at the heart of the movie is the somber resolution of the relationship between Shu Lien and Li Mu Bai, and its effect on Jen, who, when she finally comes to sober maturity by film's end, is then faced with a choice between love and a life of royal duty. In most sword flicks, the acting is generally (to be kind) broad, but the actors in *Dragon*, manage to raise the bar. Chow Yun Fat's screen presence is, as always, possessed of enormous gravitas and Michelle Yeoh, the real star of the film, turns in an astonishingly subtle performance as Li Mu Bai's forlorn love and Jen's mentor. That Julia Roberts, an actress whose talents are best suited to commercials touting aids for vaginal dryness, should win an Oscar while Yeoh is left off the short list is a monumental idiocy of which only the Academy is capable. The mixture of rage, grief (over the death of Li Mu Bai), and compassion that Yeoh wordlessly conveys in her brief confrontation with Jen toward the end of the movie is stunning. I have read a few critiques that describe her acting in *Dragon* as flat, but that, simply put, is ridiculous. The large part of her emotionality is externalized, announced by her actions, her gestures, and that is quite a difficult trick to pull off. For my mind, Yeoh's take on Shu Lien is the most completely realized action performance I've seen for a couple of decades.

Looking back over the list of Hollywood's entries in the field of high fantasy films, a list that inspires shuddery flashbacks to such experiences such as *Ladyhawke, Willow, Dragonheart, Conan The Barbarian, Legend, The Sword and the Sorcerer,* and *Dungeons and Dragons* (wherein the formerly redoubtable Jeremy Irons takes what may wind up being an irredeemable step into cinematic irrelevance), it's hard to come up with even one movie that belongs in the same league with those covered by this review, not to mention others that spring to mind: *Heroic Trio* (also featuring Michelle Yeoh); Wang Kar Wai's existentialist revision of the genre, *Ashes of Time*; Tsui Hark's *Chinese Ghost Story*; and Zu, *Warriors of Moon Mountain,* to name but a few. Neil Jordan's *The Company of Wolves* is a borderline qualifier. And if we extend the parameters of the genre a bit so as to include films like *Time Bandits* and *The Adventures of Baron Munchausen,* then we might add a few contenders; but otherwise the view is bleak. Perhaps the release of Peter Jackson's *Lord of the Rings* will overcome this lack, but it is nonetheless curious that, given their technical and acting resources, and the wealth of source material available, the studios have failed the genre to such a resounding degree. It may be that American filmmakers have no great feel for a tradition that does not mirror their own country's traditions. This said, one wonders why no one has yet tried to make a film from Steven King's *Dark Tower* series, which retells *The Song of Roland* from the standpoint of a mythical gunslinger, a purely American icon.

It's inevitable that *Dragon*, what with its financial success, will spawn imitations ... and then again, maybe not. If the strikes threatened by the Writers and Screen Actors Guilds go forward, the studios will be unable to obey their cretinous instincts for quite some time, and instead of having to watch shabby imitations, we will be afflicted with shelf-sitting films that the tasteless arbiters of Hollywood culture decided were not good enough to distribute. Given the average quality of product in release, this prospect borders on the obscene. Some of these films (most horribly and imminently notable, the racing movie *Driven* starring Sly Stallone) are already coming off the shelves, and God only knows what gems of high fantasy have been gathering dust in studio archives. Could we be in store for another giddy romp with that cheesy crescent-moon-headed devil guy in *Legend 2*? Will *Daughter of Ladyhawke* lay an enormous egg (I like Drew Barrymore for the part—she could pass for Rutger Hauer's outside child)? Might Schwarzenegger return as *Conan the Right Wing Intellectual*? Will Kull kum again? Far better to stay at home and rewatch *Crouching Tiger Hidden Dragon* or any one of a number of other good Asian fantasy flicks than to risk the soul-death brought on by viewing one too many rotten displays of celluloid witch-mages, overgrown iguanas, and urping trolls who resemble Ernest Borgnine emerging from a mud bath. But whether or not the strikes occur, until some consciousness-changing event influences the tendencies of American high fantasy films, the marquee of any theater showing such woeful efforts as we have become accustomed to should not bother listing the title of the movie, but spell out instead the cliché that has been stated explicitly or implicitly in so many less than magnificent literary fantasies: *Abandon Hope All Ye Who Enter Here.*

TERROR IN SUGAR DUMPLING TOWN

Hearts in Atlantis
Release Date: _September 28, 2001_
Director: _Scott Hicks_
Screenwriter: _William Goldman_
Source Writer: _Stephen King_
Starring: _Anthony Hopkins, Anton Yelchin, Hope Davis, Mika Boorem_
Distributor: _Warner Brothers_
Review Date: _October 16, 2001_

FOR THOSE OF US WHO DID NOT have an especially happy childhood, Stephen King's habitual depiction of children as magical creatures (a trope he shares with another mega-Steven—Spielberg) whose innocence and courage are capable of overcoming supernatural monsters and dysfunctional parents alike has grown more than a little tiresome. If we are to believe King, should Planet Earth suffer an alien invasion or a plague of demons, all we need do is muster a group of pure-in-heart pre-pubescent buddies and turn them loose on the bogeymen, who will surely be daunted, quelled, and shamed into non-being by the clear flame of bravery displayed by these diminutive heroes. King might do well to acquaint himself with the horrific fates of children who are faced with serious threats—the odds are his analysis would conclude that when children are confronted with mortal danger, for the most part they die. Still and all, it is a pleasant-enough fantasy to indulge in, and the latest film based on King's work, *Hearts In Atlantis*, is superior to many previous such cinematic translations. This is not to say that it is worth watching, but it is not entirely without virtue.

Cheap sentiment is yet another trope embraced by the two Stevens who bestride the world of popular culture, and *Hearts* is awash with teary moments cued by maudlin strings that encourage us to let down our cynical shields and surrender to the sweetness of the Über-nostalgia conjured up by the film. The story is framed by the return of Robert Garfield (David Morse) to his hometown to attend the funeral of his childhood pal, Sully. There he learns that another friend of his youth, his first love, Carol Gerber (Mika Boorem) has also died, and this causes him to immerse himself in the hour-and-a-half-long flashback to the early1960s that forms the bulk of the movie. The younger Garfield, known as Bobby (Anton Yelchin), is essentially an orphan, his father having died and his mother Elizabeth (Hope Davis) having chosen to cope with the death by more or less abandoning her child and turning her attention to the pursuit of a career in real estate, a course that inspires her to such cruelties as spending money on a career-assisting wardrobe that might have bought her son his long-coveted bike. Into this less-than-joyous circumstance comes a boarder, Ted Brautigan (Anthony Hopkins) who is fleeing from people he refers to as "low men." This term, it turns out, refers to the FBI. Brautigan is a psychic whose ability allows to him to know everything about whomever he touches—he has been recruited or shanghaied (it is not made clear which) by J. Edgar Hoover to help fight the war on Communism, and he has managed to escape his evil masters and lives his life on the run throughout America. He enlists Bobby to read the paper to him and keep on the lookout for the "low men," thus becoming a father figure to the child and arousing both Elizabeth's suspicion and jealousy. He befriends Bobby's friends, in particular Carol, and saves them from the local bully by threatening to reveal that the bully, prone to using terms like "faggot" and "queer," is himself a closet homosexual. On occasion he lapses into fugues during which he senses from afar the imminent arrival of his pursuers. Unfortunately, these fugues are scarcely distinguishable from the remainder of Sir Anthony's somnolent performance. Once a fine actor, he has for several years been mailing in performances that more kindly critics than I have described as "understated," relying on his voice and presence alone. Perhaps these efforts have been commensurate with the quality of the projects he has chosen to grace. But they are projects that, for whatever reason, he has chosen, and as I watched him emote, his patrician features gone vague in a bout of far-seeing, I had the notion that he was not tracking the movements of FBI ferrets but was rather reciting a mantra in which the words "Where's my check?" figured prominently. The one noteworthy performance in *Hearts* is that of Hope Davis. She succeeds in creating a sharply etched portrait of a woman who, in walling herself off from grief and the world of trouble that has resulted from her husband's death, has also walled herself off from everything that might sustain her. Otherwise, the children are suitably appealing; David Morse is suitably grizzled and soulful, etc. etc. . . .

The virtue I described *Hearts* as not being entirely devoid of is chiefly due to the work of William Goldman. Somehow Goldman, an excellent writer in several forms, has managed to cobble two sections of King's meandering ten-hanky salute to the Sixties into a fairly engaging script. There are a few off-key passages—a scene in which Brautigan speaks elegiacally to Bobby of Hall-of-Fame NFL fullback Bronco Nagurski ("The old man kept crawling . . . he scored for us!") contains enough unrefined sugar to cause a kindergarten class to run amok. But overall, Goldman has crafted these weepy materials with far more cleverness than they perhaps deserve, and had the picture adhered more closely to the dark suggestions of the script, *Hearts* might have given the world something more than yet another reason for Roger Ebert to shake like a bowlful of jelly and chortle "I loved this movie!" to his neutered elf of a co-conspirator in bad taste, What's-his-name.

But then Goldman likely had not reckoned on Scott Hicks, a director apparently in the thrall of the two Stevens. In his hands, the seedy little New England town that serves as the setting for the story becomes a kingdom of childhood possibility, full of quaint desirable objects and secret hideaways and sinister adults, where every shaft of sun creates a mystical dazzle and the music of American innocence—mid-Fifties rock n' roll—plays non-stop on all the radios, as if in those days oldies stations existed. Which, of course, they did not. Like his mentors, Hicks attempts to wring a maximum of tears from a minimum of earned emotionality, and he is, to a great degree, successful in this. As I sat in the darkened theater, scribbling on my notepad, writing down words such as "crap" and "hogwash" and "Gaah!", the druggy mixture of sad-eyed kiddies and treacly post-Mantovani symphonic goop and Sir Anthony's mossy, slumbering presence triggered a chemical reaction that, indeed, brought tears to my eyes, and there were moments when, despite my profound disinterest in most of the characters, I set aside my fantasy that the film would degenerate into a horrific surrealism and I would see Sir Anthony dismembered mid-fugue by a rogue elephant, while Bobby, demented by loneliness, ran wild through that little sugar dumpling of a town, slaughtering his enemies with Carol Gerber's bloody shinbone, and instead, possessed by a sort of repulsively generic nostalgia for all those things we have lost, those shining moments from which we failed to snatch a proper measure of joy, or, alack! from which we snatched too much, and now gleam dully like fireflies stored away in a bottle, their dying energies making a dim and woeful light . . . Instead, I found myself hoping that Bobby would someday get his longed-for Schwinn Black Phantom and ride ride ride through days golden and many (as is implied he shall at movie's end) until, of course, he collides with the grinning tooth-covered bus of circumstance and is rendered into kibble-sized bits.

Blame for what is wrong with *Hearts in Atlantis* must ultimately be laid at the feet of Stephen King. For many years King has been far more a sentimentalist than a horror writer; and now, in a time when real horror has been visited upon us in all its gruesome anonymity and grindstone banality, his giant spiders and freakish clowns and wicked man-shaped devils are more comforting than frightening— they seem assurances (false ones) that evil comes wrapped in an otherworldly gloss that will make it readily distinguishable and therefore avoidable. His once-fresh technique of Americanizing the horror novel by a kind of overwrought product placement, laying in incessant references to McDonald's and popular kitchen cleaners and sinus cures and et al, has these days a period feel similar to that you might obtain from coming across a futuristic science fiction story set in 1985. Reading a King novel has become an act of self-consolation, like eating ice cream when depressed. This is not necessarily a bad thing. Whether we have a jones for S'mores or reruns of *Gilligan's Island*, we need our comforts, and King's lapse into dreary sentimentality doubtless synchs with some similar national lapse, a consensus desire to be told a spooky fairy tale that will make the bad man who lives inside all our heads go away. But the fact remains that King's fictions have devolved from pulpy monuments into bland palliatives, and this perhaps speaks to a creative dotage, conjuring an image of the author sitting alone in his gloomy study, fondling a rusty metal top and muttering the word "Rats" or somesuch, and smiling foolishly. I say this as someone who has enjoyed several of King's books, but lately I have all but given up hope for a return to the form displayed in *The Shining* and *Christine*, in both of which he countered sentiment with considerable menace and interesting sociological observance.

Of all the ghastly sugars yielded by *Hearts in Atlantis*, the most unpalatable is the ending in which Elizabeth Garfield, motivated now wholly by jealousy, turns in Brautigan to the FBI, and is almost immediately forgiven by her son, despite the fact that Brautigan has become his father, his mentor, his great friend. This led me to a new and divergent consideration of Bobby's character. Could his relative lack of anguish over Brautigan's fate be attributed to some pathology? I realized that it was possible to view Bobby as a sociopath, that through a scene-by-scene analysis, a case could be made for his having manipulated the entire scenario so as to acquire the money for his bike (he winds up with money that Brautigan has made by means of a sporting wager to fund an escape), and that now, once again the object of his mother's love, his transportation problem solved, and that smelly old dude upstairs out of the way, he sits in his room as satisfied as a spider with a fresh-caught fly. This interpretation adds a gloating air to the final frames in which a smiling Bobby Schwinn's off into an eternal childhood autumn. I suppose, however, it is unlikely that Scott Hicks is sufficiently clever or subversive a manipulator to have intended this, and that this subtle portrait of a child monster was only accidentally achieved.

If you are in the mood for a film about childhood (among other things) and the remarkable resilience of children that earns its emotionality, I recommend that you rent the outstanding Brazilian film *Central Station*. If, on the other hand, you're a little blue and want to feel good about feeling bad, then I imagine you could do worse than *Hearts in Atlantis*. As a makeshift anti-depressant, it is, I should think, every bit the equal of a dozen Oreos or a pint of Rocky Road.

THE TROUBLE WITH HARRY

Harry Potter and the Sorcerer's Stone
Release Date: *November 16, 2001 Nationwide*
Director: *Chris Columbus*
Screenwriter: *Steve Kloves*
Source Writer: *J.K. Rowling*
Starring: *Daniel Radcliffe, Emma Watson, Rupert Grint, Richard Harris, Alan Rickman*
Distributor: *Warner Brothers*
Review Date: *November 23, 2001*

FIRST OF ALL, AS HE IS PORTRAYED IN the movie, if that little marshmallow-hued choirboy Harry Potter went to a real school, he'd spend most of the seventh grade digging his underwear out of his butt crack and drying off his head after being given a swirlie. Even at Hogwarts School for Witchcraft and Wizardry, which is not exactly South Bronx High, it's likely he'd get punked out. The rougher lads would make sport of his tiny wand and generally torment him until, after years of relentless abuse, miserable, embittered, and borderline psychotic, Harry would break into his uncle's gun collection one fine morning and head off to school with a big smile on his face and a pocketful of hollow points and a crazy little song whining in his brain like the buzzing of an LSD-maddened fly.

Scratch one apprentice wizard.

But that, alas, is not the subject of the film, *Harry Potter and the Booger of Fire*, or whatever that puerile mess of hey-nonny-nonny I just saw was called.

For those of you who have been living inside the biosphere the past few years, Harry Potter is a winsome little scut with a brave soul and an ever-so-clever mind in whom a talent for the Great Art has been perceived, so off he goes to Wizard Junior High where he meets a clutch of equally precocious pals, and together they participate in classes run by quaint curmudgeons with vast powers and have oodles of fun and adventures you wouldn't believe unless you were sufficiently diminished to buy into this chump as entertainment and not the acidic brain-eating alien drool/opiate of the masses it truly is.

What's your problem, man?, someone will surely say.

It's not supposed to wreck your soul. It's a charming whimsy, a veritable banana split of special FX and sense of wonder, a film for children of all ages.

The trouble with that term, "children of all ages," is that it's misapplied—it should be used only in the pejorative. The trouble with the world is, in fact, that it is populated not by adults but by children of all ages, and ruled by schoolyard bullies. Despite the primacy of the juvenile in matters political, it's my feeling that the preferences of children of any age, much as they may gladden our hearts, should not be made into a cultural standard, especially any standard that relates to the entertainment industry. Children, after all, can happily entertain themselves by tossing a ball against a wall for hours on end—this scarcely seems to qualify them as arbiters of taste.

The reason kids say those delightfully barmy things they do is because they're essentially idiots, their brains aren't wired yet. If you think your Boopsy is cute when she spews her spaghetti onto the table and arranges the mess with her grubby fingers and then points and says of the incomprehensible shape she has created,

"Noodlebug!" or some other inanity, why is it any less charming when Cletus Mapes, a 47-year-old schizophrenic who's been institutionalized most of his adult life, smears excrement on the wall, steps back, lifts his arms in exultation and screams, "Yama Yama Bonk," over and over until he's given an injection? I mean, there's not much effective difference between unfinished wiring and defective wiring.

(Let me dial back a second, so as to avoid some of the hate mail. I'm a dad myself and I like kids fine. I'm glad they have movies they can relate to—I simply wish there were a few more I could relate to. But with the average reading ability of the American public hovering around fifth grade level, the chances of that are slim.)

The trouble with *Harry Potter and the Gauntlet of Phlegm* is that while it pleases the little snogginses, it represents corporate synergy at its most loathsome: We're talking about an AOL/Time-Warner product accompanied by AOL/Time-Warner websites and links, AOL/Time-Warner action figures, lunch boxes, pencil sets, toy wands, pajamas, card games, magic sets, watches, ad infinitum, all designed to extract as much money as possible from you, you, and especially you. The movie is a soul-less replica of the novel, and the novel...well, every ten or fifteen years someone hits the lottery and comes up with a fad that's perfect for the synergistic process. Tolkien, Dungeons and Dragons, Magicards. Harry Potter. JK Rowling seems like a nice lady, and it's nice she's getting her reward in the here-and-now. But let's face it, as works of fantasy, the Potter books are (to Rowling-ize the critical terminology) medium-grade gristle bore rife with worn-out muggle-tropes and nary a whittlesap of originality, deriving their Libertarian political sub-text from Ayn Rand, lifting bits from—among others—Tolkien, T.H. White, C.S. Lewis, Superman, and the first of the series having an ending that bears an astonishing resemblance to a Dungeons and Dragons adventure called Ghost Tower of Inverness . They are the Same Old Story we have been hearing since long before Bilbo was a pup: the saga of the Chosen One, the little lost prince with a Destiny, the innocent brought forth from anonymity to duel with the Dark Lord, who in this instance is named Voldemort (a Saxonization of Wal-Mart, perhaps?). They do not challenge, illuminate, or enthrall anyone above the mental age of 12. And it is these very qualities, the purity of their mediocrity, their consummate average-ness, their utter lack of originality, that are the underlying reason for their massive popularity and comprise their chief virtue as regards the culture-engulfing purposes of the marketing machine.

A passel of academics, desperate for a moment's recognition of their own average-ness and mediocrity, have taken it upon themselves to analyze the appeal of Harry Potter. One of these poor souls has opined that it is the orphan motif that causes children of all ages to slurp the books up as though they were chocolate-flavored gruel—they speak to the universal feeling of separateness, blah, blah, blah. Another testifies that Harry's girl pal Hermione's passionate defense of oppressed elves reflects Rowling's social activism and distaste for Thatcherism. This sort of analysis, however, is no more useful than it would be were it applied to a package of Jell-O, for the quintessential allure of both the Potter franchise and a bowlful of strawberry gelatin is their bland goodness, their unsubtle flavor, their palliative simplicity, their debased commonality.

In opposition to this statement, I have been sternly told that the Potter books will be read fifty years from now, and this will prove they are more worthwhile than I have declared. To which I respond: I'm not sure they will be read fifty years from now, nor am I sure that in fifty years any readers will be left alive. But if the books do continue to be read in 2051, this will not, to my mind, prove anything more salient than would be proven by the fact that a package of Jell-O stored in a cabinet for fifty years remains edible.

It has been argued that whatever their quality, the Potter books provide our children with a healthy role model.

Really?

If I were one of those aforementioned academics and seeking to cling by my fingertips to the Harry Potter bullet train, I might essay an analysis of Harry Potter in terms of the British class system. Harry's aunt and uncle, who take him in after his parents' death, are distinctly bourgeoisie—despite having money, their prospects are limited working-class prospects. Although they provide Harry with food and shelter, they're portrayed as spiritually and mentally stunted, and—since they refuse to share their wealth with him— mean-spirited. Harry is presented as woefully put-upon by this circumstance, left sad and alone and without resource; yet being possessed of an incredible legacy and unmatched magical powers, he is essentially a child of privilege who truly does not need their money. Putting up with a doltish cousin and penurious foster parents for a few years scarcely seems the Cinderella-ish plight Rowling intends it to appear, considering the Oxford of wizard schools is waiting to bring Harry into the fold. Harry's teachers at Hogwarts—clearly representative of the upper classes—are depicted as bungling and stupid. And Dumbledore, the headmaster of the school, addled yet capable at times of mystical illumination, surely represents the royals, or more precisely, he mirrors the attitude of the educated middle class toward the royals, one informed by derision, resentment, and a kind of reluctant awe. Thus it seems that Harry, who springs from that sub-class, the same from which Rowling herself sprung, could afford a certain disdain for everyone not of his own smallish circle. While he questions and defies authority (an admirable trait indeed), his defiance strikes me as less an act of reasonable rebellion than an assertion of entitlement. He, like many of his sub-class, might be considered an aristocrat without perfect pedigree, more worthy of the estate than those of the blood, yet kept from his proper station by an accident of birth.

Not the role model I'd want for my kids.

It has come to my attention that the Internet abounds with stories of how the Potter books have affected lives and brought children back to reading. Harry Potter Cured My Dyslexia, How Harry Potter Persuaded My Ralphie to Toss His Gameboy, and so forth.

Cool.

But just what will these newly literate souls read?

If AOL/Time-Warner has its way, the Potter industry will—as did the Tolkien industry—spawn infinite imitations, a glut of wizardly books and films that are easy to produce as Twinkies and have a built-in audience of junk-food junkies who cannot get enough of these starchy treats.

I have heard it put forward that thanks to Rowling's exhaustive research, the Potter books are treasure troves of ancient lore, and reading them will lead children to explore mythology and other related topics. Uh-huh. Suggesting that some little deviant will be inspired to study biology by jamming a firecracker up a cat's butt makes every bit as much sense. It could happen, but the chances are slight. Forget all the analysis, all the testimony that Harry Potter can heal the sick and make the blind see. What the Potter franchise offers is escapism pure and simple, and there's nothing wrong with that. We need our escapes. Whatever does it for you—video games, vanilla ice cream, hacky sack, pornography, Harry Potter—it's a good thing if it keeps you sane. There is no need to justify them, or to claim they have magical powers. They comfort, they insulate, they reassure. The trouble I have with such products is that I fear they will soon narrow our choices to such a degree, it will be nearly impossible to find any alternative to the escapist.

An economist of my acquaintance has chided me for promoting this idea. It is her belief that anything that increases the number of readers and/or moviegoers will ultimately increase the audience for all manner of books and films, and thus every form of the literary and cinematic arts will find its niche and thrive. Though this notion is funded by some logic, I feel my economist friend underestimates the power generated by the overarching corporate culture of the New World Order, the pervasive potentials of its mechanisms. Books and movies compete for our time, and that competition is in process of being overwhelmingly won by the AOL/Time-Warners of the world.

As a small evidence in support of my thesis, on the same weekend I saw *Harry Potter and the Bubble of Sputum*, I went to see *The River*, a movie in its first American release by the brilliant and virtually unknown Taiwanese director Tsai Ming-Liang. While *Harry* was showing on six zillion screens across America, featured on the cover of every magazine, the only hint of *The River* playing in town was an ad in the newspaper about the same size as a classified notice of a rummage sale. In order to view it, I had to travel into the hinterlands of Portland, to a tiny repertory house reeking of cat piss, where I sat with seven other people and watched the unreeling of a work of art. Ming-Liang's film tells a story concerning a dysfunctional family in Taipei and gradually reveals not the secret of some specious magical artifact, but the far more intricate and mysterious secrets at the heart of life...and does so by means of a thoroughly original and purely cinematic style of narration. It is a disquieting film and was never intended to achieve the type of mass audience that *Harry Potter* has received. But seven people? On a weekend night in a large American city?

Some niche.

Perhaps in the long view, the fact that high art may be reduced to nearly outlaw status will be invigorating—art tends to flourish under such conditions. But never before has it been faced by such a mighty enemy, one whose repressive techniques are so insidiously effective.

Having reached the end of this column, I see that I have neglected to review *Harry Potter and the Briquette of Doom*. Oh, well. It's been reviewed sufficiently. The gist of the matter is, had

AOL/Time-Warner wanted to make a great movie, they would have handed the project to someone who would vividly magnify the book, someone like Terry Gilliam, say. But their sole interest lay in protecting the franchise, in guaranteeing that it would be accessible to all children of all ages; they did not want to risk that a real director might offend some small portion of the consumer universe, and thus they passed it into the care of Chris Columbus, a cheese cutter of a director, who has produced a tidily shrink-wrapped, pre-sliced, homogenized product fit for mass consumption, but lacking even a glimmer of inspiration.

What's to review?

Instead, I'd rather share with you a dream I had the other night in which I watched the last *Harry Potter* sequel (number thirty-something) entitled *Harry Potter and the Question of Suicide*. Harry, now fiftyish and a failure, having been stripped of his magical powers and dismissed from his position as headmaster at Hogwarts due to certain shameful behavior that has been hushed up for the good of the school, lives in a seedy London slum with his wife, Hermione, who has changed her name to Willow Bitch and runs an escort service specializing in elvish girls. Their child, Harry Jr., a gifted wizard himself, runs with a gang and squanders his talents on the perverse and the trivial. Bitter and despairing, his dreams in tatters, Harry Senior is about to hurl himself into the Thames when he spies a wizened figure balanced on the opposite railing, apparently preparing to do the same. It is Voldemort, his long-since-vanquished enemy who, shorn of his powers, has spent the past 40 years as a cost accountant in Chelsea (one of his clients is Hermione, whom he has been boinking on the side). Shocked at having seen their nemesis in such pitiful straits, the two ex-wizards gravitate toward one another and eventually, their old enmity dissolved, wind up in a pub, where they indulge in doleful reminiscence and drink themselves into literal oblivion—while urinating behind the pub, in a moment of albumen-fueled transcendence attended only by the red-eyed, black-feathered mutant offspring of Harry's pet snowy owl, good and evil, now both eroded into shades of dolorous gray, merge in a splash of bilious light and become Voldepotter, a new Dark Lord of even greater potency than he who preceded him.

And who will save us from this terrible enemy?

Why none other than Harry Potter Jr., of course. Unmindful that dear old dad has become the dominant half of this syncretic ultra-villain, he abandons his profligate ways, enjoins Hermione to marshal her elvish lovelies into a virtuous force of full-breasted Amazon witches, and marches off toward an ultimate oedipal confrontation with Voldepotter.

Critical reaction to the film has been unvaryingly positive:

"...effects a miraculous revitalization of the Potter legacy..."
—*The New York/London Times*

"...while this hybridization of the two great franchises of the late 20th Century, *Star Wars* and *Harry Potter*, may seem on the surface to lack the stamp of originality, such profound unoriginality contrives in this instance a masterstroke that transcends its banal sources to create an uncompromising work of art, offering not only a stunning visual and emotional experience, but also a view of the architectural imperatives of the new creativity...."
—George Wibberly, Ph.D.
Dean of the Harvard School of Harry Potter Studies

"I wet my pants..."
—Roger Ebert

"Yama Yama Bonk!"
—Cletus Mapes
National Public Radio

ONE FILM TO RULE THEM ALL

Lord of the Rings: Fellowship of the Ring
Release Date: *December 19, 2001 Nationwide*
Director: *Peter Jackson*
Screenwriter: *Peter Jackson, Philippa Boyens, Fran Walsh*
Source Writer: *J.R.R. Tolkien*
Starring: *Elijah Wood, Sean Astin, Ian McKellen, Viggo Mortensen, Christopher Lee, Orlando Bloom, Liv Tyler, Cate Blanchett*
Distributor: *New Line Cinema*
Review Date: *December 26, 2001*

IF J.R.R. TOLKIEN WERE TO POP BACK into the world and see what he has wrought, the teeming hordes of witch-mages and pointy-eared folk and the penny-a-dozen Dark Lords that throng the unsavory underbelly of the publishing world, all straight out of the Elves R' Us cut-out catalogue, their derivative adventures puffing out thinly repetitive plots into plump, garishly bedragoned paperbacks whose weight far exceeds the value of the words they contain, then I am dead certain that the old Oxford don would shake his head ruefully, gather eight companions to himself and journey through hosts of bulbous, blackhead-studded geeks and shriveled Potterites and the evil marketers who rule them, until at last, bloody and haggard, his company in disarray, he reached Mount Doom, where he would heave the original manuscript of *The Lord of the Rings* into the destroying fires, thereby ending the Age of Infinite Crap. Tolkien is, of course, not to blame for Terry Brooks, Terry Goodkind, or any of the semi-literate drudges not named Terry who have either ripped him off or tried to dress their undernourished imaginations in cloaks of his design. The *Ring* books were a labor of scholarly playfulness, a meditation—it seems—on European history, testifying to the end of Old World passions and a cultural loss of innocence, and Tolkien could have had no idea that they would spawn such a glut of talentless imitators, and that they in turn would fund the loathsome industry of the fantasy trilogy, an enterprise rank and gross in nature that preys upon the cultivated idiocy of the consumer mentality, delivering paperweight-sized chunks of savory yet substanceless waste to an audience they have trained to thrive on garbage. It's a shame that Tolkien's work has not produced more of a printed legacy, for despite his often annoying obsessions (endless dinner parties, songs, and so forth), his trilogy stands as a landmark work in genre fiction; but at least it appears that now, thanks to Peter Jackson, a worthwhile cinematic legacy may be his.

To anyone who has ever tussled with the problem of how to skeletonize a five-hundred-page novel into a hundred-and-twenty-page screenplay, it should be apparent that Jackson has made the best movie it was possible to make when confronted with a work of such scope and containing so many characters; and it should be apparent to every reader that in doing so he has been absolutely faithful to the spirit of Tolkien's intent. Everyone who has read the books will have their quibbles—the Balrog was not quite right, say, or the troll wasn't how I imagined it—but this is to be expected. My main difficulty with the film was that the back stories of the characters, that of Strider in particular, were given such short shrift (according to those in the know, Jackson takes care of this problem in the second and third parts of the trilogy). But these quibbles aside, the story of Frodo the hobbit and the Fellowship, their quest to carry the One Ring into Mordor and there destroy it, along with the power of the Dark Lord, has been crafted with loving attention to detail into the most visually spectacular movie in the history of the genre. The set pieces of the book are rendered wonderfully well, with Jackson taking CGI effects to the next plane, and the settings, the peaceful hobbit village, Rivendell, Lothlorien, the mines of Moria, Isengard, and all the rest are every bit as splendid as our imaginations have painted them to be. Indeed, the sequence of scenes in Moria surely must be ranked among the most effective long action sequences in cinematic history.

If *Fellowship* were merely visually satisfying, it might be counted a success, but it is accomplished on every level. Good movies begin with the good choices made by producers, and New Line's decision to give a relatively unknown director from New Zealand 270 million dollars to shoot three films at once deserves our applause and perhaps will teach a lesson to Dreamworks, who, wanting to take no risks, handed the *Harry Potter* franchise over to a maintenance man of a director, Chris Columbus, and achieved a predictably uninspired result. Jackson had previously made a cult comedy/horror movie, *Dead Alive*; an animated feature, *Meet the Feebles*; an acclaimed yet thoroughly uncommercial picture, *Heavenly Creatures*, that dealt with a murder committed by two disturbed teenaged girls; and a forgettable Robert Zemeckis-produced Michael J. Fox vehicle, *The Frighteners*. Hardly the resume to inflame the enthusiasm of the bean counters. But in each of these films, Jackson demonstrated a prodigious visual imagination, and in *Creatures*, the movie that gave Kate Winslet her start, he showed his cleverness in handling actors.

Though it is marvelously well-cast (if there were an Oscar for casting, the office responsible for this cast could start clearing shelf space now), *Fellowship* is not an actor's movie, but Jackson has the wisdom to avoid drowning his players in the action, and makes certain they have enough room to establish their characters—he cannot give them a great deal of room, because there is so much story to get through; but he has made certain that the characters of all the Fellowship are there onscreen, though it will take the three movies to present them each in full. Frodo, played with appropriate soulfulness by Elijah Wood, gets the lion's share of the screen time. A chunkily earnest Sean Astin does the dutiful, dog-loyal Sam Gamgee to a turn. Grizzled Ian McKellen as Gandalf and a majestically hirsute Christopher Lee as Saruman convince us that wizards must have behaved just this way. John Rhys-Davies, who has done woeful duty in any number of horrid genre projects, finally is given a quality part as Gimli the Dwarf, and Sean Bean's Boromir is touchingly, pridefully human. Even the most flimsily realized of the company, Legolas the Elf (Orlando Bloom), is sufficiently defined through the action sequences, especially in his quicksilver bow-and-arrow work, though it will be helpful to see, as has been promised, the fleshing out of his relationship with Gimili in *The Two Towers*. But Viggo Mortensen is the actor likely to benefit most from the movie. Casting Mortensen in the role of Strider, the lean, scraggly, somewhat suspect heir-in-exile to the throne of Gondor, instead of going for a more bankable leading man, was a stroke of genius. Mortensen, one of Hollywood's best-kept secrets, is not only physically perfect for the part, but has the skill and presence to develop a complex character without employing much in the way of dialogue. Prior to *Fellowship*, his most substantial role was that of the miscreant brother in Sean Penn's *The Indian Runner*, which was based on a Bruce Springsteen song, "State Trooper." Following this he took featured roles in a few B pictures, the excellent actioner *American Yakuza* among them. It was clear that he had ability, but the studios did not seem to know what to do with him, and since then he has been cast chiefly as a heavy in pictures such as *A Perfect Murder* and *The Prophecy*, wherein he played Satan. As Strider, Mortensen projects immense depth and presence, deftly externalizing his performance, and I think the studios may now recognize that looking a little seedy and dangerous is not such a bad thing for a leading man, and that the role will have a similar effect on Mortensen's career as the role of Han Solo had on Harrison Ford's.

But in the end this is Peter Jackson's movie, his opportunity to shine, and he delivers the best genre flick since Kubrick's *2001*, and one of the best action movies ever. *Star Wars*? Forget it. Lucas' fan boy orgy was purely kindergarten stuff, finger-painting by contrast to the artfulness and power of *Fellowship*, and sinks lower in my estimation with each abysmally juvenile sequel. Jackson claims to have read *Lord of the Rings* dozens of times, and this shows not only in his faithfulness to the books, but in the touches he has added, which seem entirely of a piece with the products of Tolkien's imagination. The caverns beneath Isengard, for example, wherein he depicts the births of an army of Orcs from pods, lending the creatures an insectile aspect that expands Tolkien's original intent. And that is the salient difference between Columbus' dreary management of the *Potter* franchise and Jackson's painstaking direction of *Fellowship*. To Columbus it was a gig, to Jackson it was a love affair upon which he focused his own imagination, caring enough about the books not only to recreate them, but to expand and illuminate the text. Every scene in the movie resonates with his affection for the materials and his desire to infuse it with something of himself. The magical duel between Saruman and Gandalf; Gandalf's fireworks; the banshee wails and relentlessness of the Nazgul; the immense crumbling stairs of Moria; the hellish terrain of Isengard; the image of the warrior Sauron that opens the film amidst a battle that must have realized the wet dreams of Tolkien freaks everywhere; the Escher-on-Ecstasy atmosphere of Lothlorien; etc., etc. All these instances reflect both Tolkien and Jackson, the imprints of their sensibilities blending perfectly.

My fear after seeing the movie, after recognizing how well it would do, was that a spew of fantasy crap would soon be voided from the orifices of the Hollywood beast, and that we would be forced to confront the awful specter of hastily achieved film versions of such immortal classics as *The Sword of Shannara* and remakes such as *Dragonheart 3*. But now I think—at least I hope—that *Fellowship* may have raised the bar too high, that having seen the real thing, the audience will find that sitting through another lame-ass fake has all the appeal and odorous stimulation of being pissed on by the family dog. It may be that we will see abominations like *The Sword of Shannara* on film, but if we do, while they may prove as noxious as the novels that bred them, it's my feeling that they will at least be well mounted. Perhaps this confidence is misplaced. It's possible that Hollywood will misapprehend what has been done with *Fellowship* and start cranking out sausage for the mass market, not comprehending that the mass palate has now been given a taste for filet mignon. But with the second and third sections of the *Ring* trilogy due out in the next two years, it's probable that shoddy imitations will not generate much in the way of consumer response—not, at least, until the memory of the Jackson trilogy has faded, and that most assuredly will not be for a very long time.

SIGNING OFF

Signs
Release Date: *August 2, 2002.*
Director: *M. Night Shyamalan*
Screenwriter: *M. Night Shyamalan*
Starring: *Mel Gibson, Joaquin Phoenix, Cherry Jones, Roy Culkin*
Distributor: *Touchstone Pictures*
Review Date: *August 11, 2002*

Uzumaki
Release Date: *2002*
Director: *Higuchinksy*
Screenwriter: *Junji Ito*
Source Writer: *Junji Ito*
Starring: *Eriko Hatsune, Fhi Fan, Ren Osugi, Hinako Saeki*
Review Date: *August 11, 2002*

IN JOSEPH CONRAD'S *HEART OF DARKNESS*, the dying words spoken by the evil Kurtz are, "The horror! The horror!" Cesar Vallejo, the brilliant Peruvian poet, ends one of his most powerful poems, "The Starving Man's Rack," with the words, "This is horror." Though the two authors are referring respectively to a spiritual bottomland and abject poverty, both are talking about essentially the same thing: the inescapable. That is the basic element of effective horror, be it fiction or film—the thing we cannot elude, no matter how desperately we try. The inevitable. The irresistible. Monster, disaster, occult shadow. Andromeda Strain or Bubba with a chainsaw. Whatever the horror evoked may be, it must have the aura of inescapability in order to be frightening, thus making it all the more gratifying when an escape succeeds.

It's unclear from listening to M. Night Shyamalan talk about his latest film, *Signs*, whether he intended to make a horror movie—he stresses the film's purported theme, faith and the nature of human spirituality. Whatever his intention, *Signs* has been advertised as a horror movie ("Don't See It Alone"); it indulges in the conventions of the genre (sudden shocks, fleeting glimpses, ominous camera angles, et al); and it borrows its set-up and core structure from one of the most famous of all horror movies, George Romero's *Night of the Living Dead*. In both *Dead* and *Signs* a group of people are trapped—hopelessly, it appears—inside a Pennsylvania farmhouse, while outside, evil creatures are attempting to break in and kill them, creatures whose incidence is not localized but part of a worldwide crisis. The salient difference between the films is that the zombies of *Dead*—though brain-dead—succeed in killing almost everyone in the house; whereas in *Signs*, though capable of crossing interstellar space in a massive fleet that parks itself above over 400 cities and of creating enormous crop circles on every continent to guide their pilots, the aliens are incapable of breaking into a root cellar. They simply cannot solve the problem presented by an ax wedged beneath a doorknob.

Inescapable?

I think not.

In addition, the sole alien who manages a confrontation with the beleaguered family is beaten into submission with a baseball bat wielded by Joaquin Phoenix, cast here as former minor leaguer, Morgan Hess, the brother of Father Graham Hess (Mel Gibson). The bat slots nicely into Shyamalan's thematic structure yet scarcely qualifies as the weapon of choice when one is trying to dispatch a technologically advanced being who, along with his fellows, is harvesting humans for—apparently—food. Nor does it strike me as plausible that such creatures might successfully be locked in a pantry, or that Iranian peasants would be the ones who discover that aliens dissolve in water, as if their flesh were constituted of freeze-dried soup. And it's downright stupid to think that a baby monitor would be able to tune in communications from alien ships.

Despite these and various other humungous logical gaffes, there are a few things to praise about *Signs*. The idea of portraying an alien invasion by focusing on one small corner of it makes a nice change from such overblown cosmic scopefests as *Independence Day*. The editing is excellent, as is the cinematography. The acting . . . well, forget the acting. Mel Gibson used to be an ordinarily inept actor who looked good to women from the rear; now he's become a terrible actor who is starting to acquire (both front and rear, I suppose) the baffled, wrinkled countenance of an incontinent bloodhound. But it is as a horror movie that Signs must ultimately be judged, and as such it flunks every test.

Once Shyamalan isolates Father Hess, his brother, and two cute 'n spunky kids in the cellar, we expect to see alien incursion after alien incursion, walls giving way, weird ooze seeping up through the concrete, mechanical probes, each menace more chilling than the last, fended off by extremes of human ingenuity and valor. All we get is a rattled door, the sound of glass breaking upstairs, footsteps, and alien fingers groping through a ventilation grate. You may not fall asleep, but neither will you jump out of your skin. The characters, however, do fall asleep, taking long naps during the assault on their home—this dissuades us from any notion that their straits are dire. The director tosses in a potentially fatal asthma attack in an effort to raise the stakes, but that speaks poorly of his imagination. *Signs* is the third Hollywood film this year, the second this summer, in which a child in the throes of a severe asthma attack inspires a parent to make a risky move in order to fetch medication. In a Stephen King novel the child would die—that's how you raise the stakes; but Shyamalan has not learned or has chosen ignore this lesson. Rather than seeking to generate more tension, he dissipates it by incorporating into his climactic scene one of a series of flashbacks that explains how Father Hess lost his faith (the death of his wife in a freakish auto accident being the inciting event), a reverie that also provides him with the clue that helps save his family, thus causing him—surprise! surprise!—to regain his faith. The New Age prattle served up by the good reverend is sugary and glutinous enough to stop Deepak Chopra's heart, and whenever the pace slows to permit a character to preach the script's everything-happens-for-a-reason claptrap, energy dribbles from the film.

After a promising beginning, Shyamalan's last two pictures demonstrate that either his talent is in decline or that unsatisfied with millions, he has decided to pursue the billions available to those who pander to the basest of cultural imperatives. In an age when politics and the movie industry—indeed, every marketable portion of society—have been joined in grotesque alchemical wedlock, who knows what heights he may achieve, what worlds he may conquer. One day the word Shyamalan may be branded on all our foreheads. It is for certain, judging by the predictability, the simplistic morality, the heavy-handed manipulation of *Signs*, that he's at least on his way to fulfilling the prediction recently made of him, to wit, that he will be the new Spielberg.

(Here a brief prayer may be in order.)

In the good ol' USA the horror genre keeps lurching along with the same-old same-old. Creature features, dumb devil movies, sentimental ghost stories, and teenage freak-outs, the majority of these films being of a quality suitable for evisceration on *Mystery Science Theater*. *Jeepers Creepers*, *The House on Haunted Hill*, and *13 Ghosts* (a William Castle remake! Who'd a'thunk it?) celebrate the enduring Hollywood axiom that one can never get enough of attractive boys and girls lusting after each other and getting variously eaten, torn apart, and scared out of their thongs. *End of Days*, *Lost Souls*, and the unbelievably dimwitted *Bless the Child*, whose protagonists are saved in part due to a marathon prayerfest performed by a group of nuns, perpetrate the Catholic comic-book version of the struggle 'twixt good an evil: Balrog-like demons; ultra-suave guys who dress in black and start fires by snapping their fingers; Vatican hit squads; exorcists by the gaggle. And then there is the woeful legacy left by the single outstanding American ghost story of the past few years, Shyamalan's *The Sixth Sense*: whipped dogs like *What Lies Beneath* and *Dragonfly*, in which, slowed by glacial box office temperatures, Kevin Costner shows signs of sinking from public view into his own personal La Brea Tar Pit. There seems scant hope of anything vital happening in the immediate future. A remake of the excellent Japanese horror movie, *Ring*, is due out soon, but since it is directed by Gore Verbinski, the man responsible for *The Mexican* (the worst picture in the careers of both Brad Pitt and Julia Roberts . . . which is a hell of a statement), and stars a cast of unknowns, usually signaling an ensemble of hunks and hunkettes who once did a guest shot on *Dawson's Creek* or *Felicity*, one cannot be optimistic. So the horrorhead who is searching for quality must look elsewhere for gratification, and the direction that appears to offer the best chance for this is Far East.

The Asian horror movie reached its popular peak with *Ring*, a complex ghost story involving a psychic ghost and a cursed videotape containing disturbing imagery that visits a terrifying death upon whoever watches it exactly seven days after the viewing. *Ring* broke box-office records in Asia, generating a good sequel (*Ring II*) and a pretty fair prequel (*Ring Zero*). In the wake of this trilogy has come a flurry of horror films, some of the gross-out variety, like the zombie movie *Versus* and its more stylish genre sister *Junk*. But there have been a good many films produced in Asia during the last decade, particularly in Thailand, Japan, and Korea, that have strived for originality. One of the most intriguing is *Uzumaki*, which is currently making the rounds of film festivals and is likely to receive a general release sometime in near future.

Uzumaki means "vortex." In context of the film, vortex refers to every type of spiral form. As the story begins, the schoolgirl heroine, Eriko, comes upon her best friend's father engrossed in videotaping a snail—he has, according to her friend, Fhi Fhan, become obsessed with the spiral in all its incarnations. Over the space of some several weeks everyone in the small rural town where Eriko lives either is possessed by this obsession or becomes victim to a product of it. The most popular girl in Eriko's school begins to wear her hair teased into ornate spirals; another classmate falls to his death down the shaft of a spiral staircase; Eriko's father, a potter, turns a spiral pot for Fhi Fhan's father and falls prey to the obsession. Before too long, as Eriko and Fhi Fhan attempt to unravel the cause of all this, the consequences of the obsession grow still more bizarre. Fhi Fhan's father mutilates himself and contrives an anatomical spiral of his innards before giving up the ghost; crematory smoke forms an enormous sky-filling spiral at the center of which the faces of a newly dead husband and wife are seen; a reporter covering the story drives into a tunnel that proves to be the mouth of an endless spiral; two of Eriko's classmates are transformed into giant snails with spiral shells and take to crawling up and down the side of the high school. Fhi Fhan himself eventually twists himself into a living pretzel. Finally only Eriko is left.

Uzumaki's director, Akihiro Higuchinsky, a Ukranian-born Japanese hitherfore unknown to me, blends these materials into a unique black comedy, a cross between H.P. Lovecraft, *Heathers*, and French surrealism, without eschewing the staples of the horror genre—shocks, creepiness, tension, and, of course, the inescapable . . .

It occurs to me that I have both underestimated the fearful potentials of *Signs*—and been far too strict in my definition of the inescapable. I mean, short of death and taxes what can be more Orwellianly, inescapably dread than a system that ingests a talented artist, grinds him around, and excretes a purveyor of a product so slickly packaged, it causes the public to salivate uncontrollably at the prospect of having their brains oiled with bland toxicity and massaged to the consistency of Play-Doh.

"The horror! The horror!"

M. Night Shyamalan knows all about it.

And if Mister Kurtz were alive today, he might not need to stray so far from home to find his spiritual bottomland.

ONWARD CHRISTIAN MOVIES

Left Behind
Release Date: *February 2, 2001 Limited*
Director: *Victor Sarin*
Screenwriter: *Alan McElroy, Paul Lalonde, Joe Goodman*
Starring: *Kirk Cameron, Brad Johnson, Chelsea Noble, Clarence Gilyard,Jr.*
Distributor: *Cloud Ten Pictures*
Review Date: *January 25, 2003*

Left Behind II: Tribulation Force
Release Date: *December 31st, 2002*
Director: *Bill Corcoran*
Screenwriter: *Paul Lalonde, John Patus*
Starring: *Kirk Cameron, Brad Johnson, Chelsea Noble, Clarence Gilyard,Jr.*
Distributor: *Cloud Ten Pictures*
Review Date: *January 25, 2003*

WHEN STRIPPED OF ITS RELIGIOUS CONTEXT, analyzed in terms of its narrative content alone, *The Holy Bible* contains some of the richest and most spectacularly mounted fantasy tales ever conceived. That they have been elevated to the status of myth, of spiritual text, and— by some—of absolute literal truth does not diminish this fact. It might be said that *The Bible* is, indeed, the source material for all Western fantasy writing. Certainly one can perceive the seeds of the modern disaster novel in the story of Noah and the Arc, and the tale of Christ Himself, that of a child humbly born who is called to a great purpose and difficult ordeal and terrible sacrifice, may be seen as the archetypal model of the moral quest, a plot that in one way or another informs all high fantasy, from Tolkien on. The stories of Moses, of Ezekiel and the wheel . . . these and a number of others each have generated entire sub-genres of fantasy literature.

The *Bible*'s influence on film has been somewhat less profound. In Hollywood the religious picture has evolved from sweetly faithful films such as *Song of Bernadette* to historical epics like *The Robe*, DeMille's *The Bible*, and *Ben Hur*, movies that accentuate the action elements and either play down or bowdlerize the spiritual aspects of the stories; and thereafter to an endless stream of horror movies, beginning with William Friedkin's *The Exorcist* and proceeding on through ever more feeble imitations and variations on the theme. Along the way, of course, there have been films that broke these molds, including several biopics about Christ, most of them risible, notably the horrid *King of Kings*, which the late writer and critic James Agee suggested should be retitled *I Was a Teenage Jesus*. A number of movies have appropriated some element of Biblical lore to further plot, the most accomplished being Steven Spielberg's campy actioner *Raiders of the Lost Ark*. The most intriguing of all these pictures, a film that is actually about a portion of *The Bible* and thus the most pertinent to this review, is Michael Tolkin's *The Rapture*, which tells the story of Sharon (Mimi Rogers), a hedonistic, sexually promiscuous woman who finds salvation in the days preceding the Rapture, the day when God looses the riders of the Apocalypse and calls the faithful home to heaven, causing people all over the word to vanish. Tolkin's take on this portion of scripture presents a rather bleak view of divinity, portraying God as a willful, cruel master who ultimately demands of Sharon the Abraham-like act of murdering her young daughter, an act she subsequently regrets to such an extent that she rejects God and so dooms herself to eternal torment. *The Rapture* should have at the very least associational interest to devotees of science fiction and fantasy in that it offers David Duchovny's best film work to date—Duchovny plays Patrick, Sharon's lover and, eventually, husband. Albeit intellectually imprecise and flawed in execution, it is nonetheless a very watchable film concerning *The Book of Revelations*, an artifact that—whether or not one strips away all religious context—might be classified as The Greatest Horror Story Ever Told.

The Apocalypse, the Rapture, and the entirety of *The Book of Revelations* have provided the subject matter for a great many Christian novels. By far the most successful of these is the *Left Behind* series, which as of this date numbers ten volumes, with more on the horizon. Created by a writer, Jerry Jenkins, in tandem with a fundamentalist expert on *The Bible*, the Reverend Timothy LeHaye, purporting to adhere strictly in its fictional progress to prophecies contained within *The Book of Revelations*, the series has thus far sold in excess of fifty million copies worldwide and recently has spawned two movies, *Left Behind* and *Left Behind II: Tribulation Force*, both starring Kirk Cameron, late of the alleged television comedy *Growing Pains*, in the role of Buck Johnson, a TV journalist (he works for GNN) who might be described as "literally crusading." As is the case with its evil (to fundamentalist sensibilities) twin, the *Harry Potter* books, the *Left Behind* series is a phenomenon whose massive appeal beggars legitimate explanation. Both projects are marginally written, though J.K. Rowling has gained sufficient artistic cachet so as to be awarded one of the genre's many bowling trophies. Both treat of subjects that have been handled far more compellingly, more charmingly. Both rely upon conventional fantasy structures and break no new ground as regards level of invention. LeHaye-and-Jenkins' books are somewhat more standardized and more primitive than Rowling's. Reading them, one gets the idea that the authors are obeying rules set forward by some august institution such as the Famous Writers School: No sentences longer than four inches unless they comprise a list, and so forth. Nevertheless they both thrive in the same simplistic, mega-accessible, commercially viable atmosphere and so demand to be judged by equivalent critical standards. A significant difference may perhaps be perceived in the fact that whereas the Rowling books are primarily aimed at children, the target audience for the *Left Behind* series is the Christian reader.

The film producers of these two franchises have taken widely divergent roads in creating and marketing their products. Preceded by trumpet blasts of Internet buzz and other pre- and post-production unofficial publicity, heralded by gazillions of television and print ads, funded with mega-budgets, cast with top-notch character actors, the Potter films gloriously burst forth on thousands of screens across the nation, accompanied by a deluge of official products and tie-ins. The *Left Behind* movies present themselves more humbly: cut-rate budgets and a cast of non- and used-to-be entities; advertising limited mostly to word of mouth generated by the books; given a limited release and sold as cheaply priced DVDs and videos. There is no doubt that the *Potter* movies, albeit bland as mayonnaise, are better in every respect. The *Left Behind* movies, however, strike me as more interesting in that they are so clearly propagandist in nature—I'm speaking here of propaganda in the best sense of the word. Like the propaganda films of the 1940s that encouraged patriotism, faith in God and country, and constant striving against the Axis menace, the *Left Behind* movies encourage moral behavior, faith in God, and constant striving against the menace of the Anti-Christ. They are billboards for a cause. All art, of course, is propagandist and coercive by nature. We are a simple species. Authors, filmmaker, artists, they are all trying to sell a message to an audience, one that, no matter how complex, can ultimately be reduced to a slogan.

The producers of *Left Behind 2: Tribulation Force* have dressed their message in such thin cinematic cloth, they have managed to turn post-Rapture earth into a rather mundane environment. True, there are riots and conflicts, people grieving their mysteriously disappeared loved ones, etc., but this is all portrayed so flatly, it has no great dramatic weight. The sole special effect of note is that the face of the Anti-Christ, Nicolae Carpathia—played as a fuming and rather inept tight-ass, a kind of Biblical Colonel Klink, by Gordon Currie—morphs into faintly hideous aspect. Yet this may be a case in which ineptitude achieves an artful purpose. As I watched I realized that the post-Rapture was being presented in a way that emulated the way a great many of us view the events that surround us—as history televised by CNN (GNN), with interviews and news footage leavened here and there with commercials for the basic Christian message conceived as playlets involving continuing characters. Be it intentional or by happy accident, that format, despite the atrocious acting, the awful dialogue, came to inspire in me the almost drugged fascination one achieves when watching a white Bronco drive slowly along the freeway or cranes digging through the rubble of the World Trade Center. And this made the future history of *Revelations*, the fantastic tapestry of plagues and apparitions both glorious and monstrous, seem ominously plausible.

The time following the Rapture is known as the Tribulation and the force of the title, numbering four, a nurse, a pilot, a preacher, and the aforementioned journalist, set out, assisted by angelic beings, to make the world aware that Nicolae Carpathia is the Anti-Christ and that his ascendancy to the head of a world government has been foretold by Biblical prophecy. The nurse gives comfort to the dying and goes after Buck in homespun, wholesome fashion that puts those of us addicted to the TV land Channel in mind of Betsy's flirtations on *Father Knows Best*. The preacher instructs the other members of the force as to biblical prophecy; the pilot becomes Carpathia's personal pilot; and Buck the journalist infiltrates Carpathia's inner circle, a task that appears no more difficult than

Col. Hogan tricking Schultz into giving him the keys to the Stalag gate—again, this is redolent of Forties propaganda flicks, which portrayed Axis leaders as bungling and clownish. Buck's overarching purpose is to reach the Wailing Wall in Jerusalem, where God's Witnesses have manifested: two men who, according to prophecy, will wake 144,000 witnesses to stand against Carpathia. The Wall is heavily guarded, but Buck, aided by an angelic being who warbles "Amazing Grace" in such an ethereal fashion that the guards become enthralled, manages to videotape the Witnesses as they speak God's Truth. When the guards break free of the spell and attack, the Witnesses incinerate them by breathing fire from their mouths.

Will Buck get the Word out? Will the Tribulation Force survive the outlawing of religious practice initiated by Carpathia? You'll have to see *Left Behind 3* to find out ... or read the books, which, now numbering eleven, have led their audience to the brink of Armageddon, the bombing of the ancient city of Petra where a multitude has gathered to await the Glorious Appearing, and the declaration by Carpathia that he is God.

If the *Left Behind* series were done as a Hollywood project, we might have Brad Pitt as Buck, George Clooney as the hunky pilot, Morgan Freeman as the preacher, maybe Clair Danes as the nurse, and there would be a multiplicity of pyrotechnic miracles and CGI monstrosities, with video games and perhaps even action figures to follow. Buy, the message would say, not—as it does in the movies that have been made—Believe. That's the salient difference between the two. Film used as a marketing tool or as—in evangelical terms—a mission tool. Both purposes might be better served if *Revelations* were not treated as a tool at all, but as what it most is: a story with the mythic potency that accrues to all great fantasy. We carry in our cells the story of Apocalypse, a story of monsters, plagues, a great decline, and a war of salvation. The story seems to ridge up the very spine of our history, replicating itself over and over again in miniature. Viewed either as a literal or a metaphorical text,

Revelations wields an undeniable power over us and commands our fascination, whether or not we are believers. Thus, though the *Left Behind* movies are somewhat effective, by attempting to make their central myth too ordinarily credible, by neutering the fantastic and grotesque elements thereof, they must in the end be seen only for what they intend to be: ingenuous and rather crude manipulations of a towering legend.

APPARENTLY, HE'S STILL IN THE BUILDING

Bubba Ho-tep
Release Date: *September, 2003 Portland and Seattle*
Director: *Don Coscarelli*
Screenwriter: *Don Coscarelli, Joe R. Lansdale*
Source Writer: *Joe R. Lansdale*
Starring: *Bruce Campbell, Ossie Davis, Bob Ivy, Reggie Bannister*
Distributor: *Vitagraph Films*
Review Date: *November 23, 2001*

THOUGH MOST PROMINENT FANTASY AND science fiction movies typically cost upward of a hundred million to make, the genre has always seemed best served by films unencumbered by huge budgets. Many of these "little" films have brought a fresh sensibility to their subjects, movies such as *The Quiet Earth*, *Donnie Darko*, and Jean Luc Godard's noirish satire *Alphaville*, a movie whose worth is something about which few agree and yet is usually compared, whether favorably or negatively, to pictures made decades after it was shot, this testifying to the fact that it presaged both cyberpunk and the cinematic legacy of Philip K. Dick, while simultaneously glancing back at the work of Huxley and Orwell. *Alphaville* had such a low budget, its special effects were handled by means of a voiceover—secret agent Lemmy Caution narrates an interstellar voyage as he drives his Citroen across the Seine, and, because of the film's metaphorical density, we are more than tempted to disbelieve our eyes and accept what he says as true, that we are crossing the galaxies rather than a stretch of dirty water and that the lights in the sky are not the lights of a bridge but astronomical objects.

Not all low-budget genre pictures, of course, either aim or reach so high. Even more central to the genre tradition are movies like those directed by John Carpenter and his apparent lineal successor, David Twohy (*Pitch Black, The Arrival, Below*). I would argue that apart from a smattering of films such as *2001: A Space Odyssey*, *Star Wars*, and Jackson's *Lord of the Rings* trilogy, not only the most significant films, but the most entertaining films, set with the genre limits have been B-pictures . . . and I intend "entertaining" in both the sense of well-crafted stories and just plain fun. One need only contrast classic genre films with their more expensive remakes to see that budget constrictions have little to do with the quality of the product. True, in some instances the remakes have been better; but more often than not they have fallen flat, and even when they do not so fall, when the remake has proven superior to its original, this has been due to better scripts, direction, and acting, and not because of enhanced production values or any other big-ticket item. Indeed, the best remakes of classic genre films have themselves been B-pictures—Carpenter's *The Thing*, Ferrara's *Invasion of the Body Snatchers*, et al—whereas the worst—Coppola's *Dracula*, a bloated operatic nightmare of the sort that usually follows the ingestion of too much spicy food, though less well-conceived than most; *Independence Day* (not technically a remake, but heavily derived from *Earth Vs. The Flying Saucers*); *Godzilla*; any of the *King Kong* rehashes; etc. etc;—have generally been promoted as blockbusters. In light of these inept monstrosities, when Hollywood talks about plans to remake *War of the Worlds* and *Forbidden Planet*, it becomes necessary to suppress a shudder.

I doubt that anyone will essay a remake of *Bubba Ho-tep*, a low-budget genre picture that passed though the theaters as quickly as Einstein through Kindergarten . . . though given the eccentricity of studio decision-making, one can never be sure about these matters. Whatever the case, director Don Coscarelli, the man responsible (perhaps "culpable" might be a more suitable word choice) for the *Phantasm* series, has made a B-picture that falls into the category of just plain fun and will almost surely develop something of a following on DVD due to the cultish nature of its materials and the cult status of its lead actor, Bruce Campbell. Based on a story by Joe R. Lansdale (an attractive book, by the way, containing both the story and screenplay, along with stills from the movie, is available from Nightshade Books), *Bubba Ho-tep* poses the notion that Elvis Presley (Campbell) did not die in a bathroom at Graceland, but lived on into his seventies and is now experiencing a kind of decaying pre-death in a seedy, abusively neglectful East Texas nursing home. Through flashbacks and the King's voiceover (as effective a device to create suspension of belief as the voiceover in *Alphaville*), we learn that years before, having grown weary of fame, the real Elvis traded places with the world's best Elvis imitator. The two men wrote a contract establishing that the real Elvis could reclaim his rightful status whenever he wished, but the contract was destroyed when a barbecue grill exploded and blew up the imposter's trailer (into which the real Elvis had moved). After his replacement's highly publicized and ignominious death, Elvis makes his way through the world, not altogether unhappily, earning a livelihood by imitating himself until he breaks his hip in a fall from the stage. Now, afflicted with a penile cancer and forced to get about on a walker, he has given up on life. Paunchy, his trademark sideburns and pompadour gone gray, he passes his days limping about the halls of the nursing home, clad in robe and pajamas, and watching his old movies on a black-and-white TV. The other residents of the home are equally deracinated, abandoned by their families, living joylessly and without hope. Included among their number is one John F. Kennedy (Ossie Davis), who claims to be the former president of the United States transformed into an Afro-American by means of surgery and skin dye, this at the behest of his mortal enemy, Lyndon Baines Johnson. It seems that Elvis does not entirely believe the old man is JFK, but he treats him with the respect due a president (the respect due a good one, at any rate), and this serves to reinforce the sweetness of the relationship that develops between the two men.

After several of the residents die under mysterious circumstances, and after Elvis himself is attacked by a flying scarab beetle the size of small dog, he begins to be re-energized by the awareness that some terrible menace is afoot in the nursing home. He joins forces with JFK and learns from him that an ancient Egyptian mummy is loose in the area. Through a succession of telepathic visions and some doddering detective work, Elvis discovers that the mummy was stolen by a couple of good ol' boys from a traveling exhibition of Egyptian artifacts. While making their escape, the good ol' boys ran their vehicle off the road during a heavy downpour and into the river that flows past the nursing home. They died in the crash, but the mummy lived and since that time it has survived by making night raids on the nursing home, deriving sustenance by sucking the souls out of the occupants. For some reason glossed over by the movie, perhaps as a byproduct of the digested souls of the good ol' boys, the mummy appears dressed in cowboy hat and boots and writes hieroglyphic graffiti in the bathroom stalls whereon he voids himself of soul-residue—thus, *Bubba Ho-tep.*

Having read this far, it should be clear that I am not talking about a straight horror flick here. "Gonzo" is a modifier that has been applied to much of Lansdale's fantasy/horror work and it certainly applies to *Bubba Ho-tep.* The movie is more farcical than suspenseful, more comic than dramatic in its pretensions. What horror element there is lies not so much with its improbable boogeyman as with its depiction of the nursing home as a wastebasket for living human remains. Yet while the script is threadbare in patches, and at times the budget (or lack thereof) shows, especially in the realization of the mummy, *Bubba Ho-tep* is nonetheless successful in what it attempts, and this is chiefly due to Bruce Campbell.

Campbell is best known for his recurring role as the wise-cracking, cartoonishly post-modern hero, Ash, in Sam Raimi's *Evil Dead* movies, and gained some mainstream exposure as the star of the short-lived TV steampunk western series, *Brisco County, Jr.* , roles that displayed his considerable comedic skills but provided him with no opportunity to demonstrate that he had range. Folks, he's got range. In *Bubba Ho-tep*, his "aging" of Elvis' various mannerisms is wonderfully managed, particularly his hilarious take on the King's hillbilly kung fu moves; but instead of delivering a mere impression of the septuagenarian Elvis, still sporting big hair and wraparound glasses, he gives us a nicely-observed portrait of a man who, though reduced by age and disappointment, is possessed by a shadow of the macho self-parodying persona that he adopted along his road to fame. It clings to him like a ghostly cape, even as he stands in the front yard of the nursing home, leaning on his walker, craning his neck to see off along the street. He seems himself not to know exactly how much of the persona was a put-on, but it is this persona that he must re-adopt in order to function as a man once again. At the end of the film, like Batman slipping into his costume, Elvis dons a white leather rhinestone-studded jumpsuit and cape, fully stepping into his old role preparatory to a final battle with the mummy; yet it was unnecessary for Coscarelli to incorporate that detail into his script, because Campbell has already achieved the effect by means of his actor's craft. As Elvis seeks out information about the mummy, Campbell shows us a man reclaiming his lost dignity and pride. He encourages us to think of Elvis Presley in a more complicated way than we usually might—as a man of parts, someone who may have become lost in the Chinese boxes he constructed to sustain his personality against the stresses of fame—and he succeeds with a surprising degree of subtlety in illuminating the process of an individual who is trying to re-learn how to play himself. In the midst of all the over-the-top situations and Hee-Hawish redneck foliage and deep-fried dialogue ("I felt my pecker flutter once, like a pigeon having a heart attack...."), Campbell's performance is unexpectedly moving and authentic in feeling, imbuing the absurd plot with a passion and substance it would not otherwise have had.

Coscarelli, whose previous directorial efforts have displayed little concern for character, instills the movie with a leisurely pace that reflects the dreadful slowness of life at the nursing home and gives Campbell and Davis room to develop their roles. Some of his work with the movie's ultra-low-budget special effects is also worth mentioning. That dog-sized scarab beetle, for instance. When it first appears, you're expecting to catch sight of a wind-up key somewhere on its body; but by the time Elvis has finished with it, thanks to Coscarelli's camera, to an expertise doubtless gained from photographing the flying killer spheres in the *Phantasm* flicks, this ludicrous prop has generated a suitable measure of menace. But Coscarelli's best move clearly was casting Bruce Campbell as his lead and doing whatever he did—whether reining him in or giving him his head—to extract this performance. Was it a fluke? The result of the director's sleight-of-hand? Or has there always been a gifted actor trapped inside Bruce Campbell and waiting to get out? I wonder if any studio is willing to take a chance and find out. Probably not. However, at the end of the credits there's a tag that appears to promise a sequel. If Coscarelli manages to get it made, despite my loathing for the very concept of sequels, I'll stand in line to see if he and Campbell can do it again, because *Bubba Ho-tep* has no CGI monsters, no Brads, no Toms, no Bennifers, no refugees from *Dawson's Creek* or *Roswell* desirous of being real live actors, nothing but an outrageous story and a well-drawn main character, and ... Well, all I've got to say about that is, "Thank you, ladies and gentlemen. Thank you very much."

KING ME

Lord of the Rings: Return of the King
Release Date: *December 17, 2003 Nationwide*
Director: *Peter Jackson*
Screenwriter: *Peter Jackson, Philippa Boyens, Fran Walsh,*
Barry Osbourne, Stephen Sinclair
Source Writer: *J.R.R. Tolkien*
Starring: *Elijah Wood, Sean Astin, Ian McKellen, Viggo*
Mortensen, Christopher Lee, Orlando Bloom, John Rhys-Davies
Distributor: *New Line Cinema*
Review Date: *January 6, 2004*

FIRST, THE OBVIOUS: *THE RETURN OF THE KING* is a suitably grand, albeit flawed, finale to what is bar-none, hands-down, and by-a-country-mile the finest high fantasy movie ever made. One question that arises from this verity is: Does that make it a great film or merely the winner of a beauty contest for goats?

On first glance, the imperfections of the film appear as monumental as its length. The endless pontifications, for one. Was the sound bite an invention of Middle Earth? So it would appear, for every time a big moment looms, nothing will do but that someone steps forward to announce its advent with a pithy, faux-Shakespearean and patently unnecessary pronouncement. When, for example, Legolas is given to intone, "There is a sleepless malice in the West," the only appropriate response I could think of, considering the circumstance (not long before the final battle), was, "Duh!" With the exception of Viggo Mortensen, who underplays his role to good advantage, the actors are less acting than posing in costume—at times it feels almost as if we've been invited to a medieval vogue party. The so-last-century British perception of and fixation upon class, most obviously evidenced by the bond between Frodo and Sam, is framed in an especially hideous manner when Frodo the hobbit aristocrat tells his doting gentleman's gentleman that he could not possibly carry the Ring of Power, that it would destroy him, a patent insult to which Sam, obeying the doughty regulations of his kind, responds by saying that he may not be able to carry the Ring, but he can by God carry the young master, whereupon he picks up the enervated Frodo and goes serfing up the slopes of Mount Doom. This relationship came to seem so cloyingly god-awful, I half-expected a scene in which Sam, on his knees, tongue lolling, receives a *Snausage* from Frodo's hand. While these and other imperfections are faithful to flaws in the source material, Jackson has always claimed that he needed to make the material work as a movie, and it strikes me that some minor adjustments in tone might have enhanced the process.

A number of Jackson's own authorial choices are no less dismaying. The editing (a strength of the first two films) is inconsistent, as is the CGI, and cutting Saruman from the final third of the trilogy was not a terrific idea—without Christopher Lee to put a human face on evil, we are left with the Sauron's-flaming-eye dealie, which comes to acquire all the menace of one of those decorative electronic *objets du* excess income that can be ordered from yuppie catalogues. (I would hazard a guess that you might already be able to order a palantir with flaming eye effect from one company or another.) Surely some of the lugubrious farewells at the end of the movie could have been trimmed or left out altogether in order to remedy this omission. The white-light scene-fades upon which Jackson relies in *Return* imbue the film with a New Age taint that serves to leach the impact of its natural pagan coloration, and Howard Shore's score hits new depths of drear sappiness, especially with those incessant Celtic keenings. Will the person who's been torturing Enya or Lorenna McKennit or whoever that is . . . Could they just stop? Some of us need a break, okay? Give the lady a Xanax.

Against all the above we can set the spectacular portions of the movie: the sequence that displays the lighting of the beacons that summon the Riders of Rohan to the aid of Gondor; the stair of Minas Morgul; Shelob's tunnel; and, of course, the battles, in particular the siege of Minas Tirith. Those are the scenes that remain in memory—the majority of the rest fades from mind or has the feel of sideshow material, like the ineptly scripted handling of Denethor, the steward of Gondor, and his parenting difficulties, which seems to have been inserted into the overarching story for no other purpose than to lay on a little Greek tragedy. All this makes me wonder exactly how we should view both *Return* and the entire trilogy. Obviously, a final judgment won't be possible until the extended version of *Return* is released and one can watch the three films in close sequence; but since *Lord of the Rings* is basically a story of war, it might be interesting to contrast the *Ring* trilogy with another ten-plus-hour film trilogy that treats of the same subject— I'm speaking of Masaki Kobayashi's *The Human Condition*.

Kobayashi was a pacifist who was forced into the army and served in Manchuria prior to WW II; he refused all promotion and was beaten frequently for resisting orders. His trilogy, one of the unquestioned masterpieces of world cinema, engages war's despair and the debasing effect it visits upon everyone whom it touches. On the other hand, Tolkien (I prefer to use him instead of Jackson as the comparative, since he was the true author of the piece), served briefly in France during WW I, was wounded by shrapnel, and— invalided—spent the next couple of years standing guard on

Britain's sea wall, a tour of duty during which he wrote the first tales of his mythic chronicle. While *Lord of the Rings* cannot be described as pro-war, it supports the moral rightness of war under certain circumstances, celebrates heroism, exalts the psychic attrition of combat by dealing with it in terms of fell wounds and the like, and confronts death in terms of meeting it nobly or with ignominy. That Tolkien chose to translate his war agony into epic fantasy, whereas Kobayashi strove for a brutal naturalism and limited his canvas to war's destruction of a single soldier, speaks to the cultural differences between the two men and likely to personal differences as well. I suspect Tolkien's Christian faith and the fact that he lost friends in the war yet did not witness their deaths made it possible for him to view death as a transfiguration of the sort emblematized by the white place to which Frodo, Gandalf, Bilbo, and the elves are voyaging at the end of *Return*.

A more apt comparison can be made between *Lord of the Rings* and Richard Wagner's tetralogy of operas, *The Ring of the Nibelung*. Both are cultural landmarks, if not towering works of art, giving voice to the social temper of the times in which they were produced. The similarities between Wagner's libretto and Tolkien's text are profound. In both, a Ring of Power—one that curses its bearer—is at issue; an immortal surrenders her immortality for love; friend kills friend (brother kills brother) to possess the Ring; a broken weapon is reforged; the Ring is returned to its origin; the gods (elves) renounce the world, and mankind is left to seek its own destiny; etc., etc., etc. It might be said that Tolkien reforged Wagner's story and used it for a different purpose. But while these similarities are of moment to those who care to debate the German composer's influence (or lack thereof) upon the Oxford philologist, the question posed is, How should we view Peter Jackson's trilogy?, and there is a similarity yet unmentioned between the two Rings that bears more closely upon this. They each revolve about spectacular set pieces, and the intervals separating those set pieces are filled with padding—silly side plots, incidences of heroic suspense, and literal breaks in narrative that allow for breaths to be taken. Pure connective tissue, much of which seems disposable. A clunky structure that is not untypical of opera. And that, I believe, is how we should judge Peter Jackson's trilogy: as an opera whose arias are battles. (Amazing, if you think about it, that no one has scored an opera using Tolkien as a source.) That's how it works onscreen. If it is to be so judged, then criticisms about the pacing, direction, acting, editing, and so forth, while not entirely irrelevant, are definitely not central to the matter at hand. When we attend an opera, we don't care if the fat lady can act, just so long as she hits the high notes. *The Return of the King* hits all the high notes and sustains them beautifully. Instead of presenting us with the terrible nature of war as did Kobayashi, Tolkien and Jackson have given us war's music, and although those who have experience of war may feel that this music is the translation of bitter actuality into something too glorious, too glamorous, to reflect the agonies of battle, thus creating a kind of moral subterfuge, it is nonetheless stirring.

Late in *The Return of the King*, after Frodo and his mates have returned to the Shire, there is a small moment that makes me hearken back to the *The Fellowship of the Ring*, which stands as the purest cinematic event of the three films, mainly because it contained more effective small moments than did the sequels—moments that permitted character to be defined and gave the project a human scope and poignancy that became lost in all the posturing and spectacle. Frodo, Sam, Merry, and Pippin are sitting at a table in a tavern, silent in the midst of a happy hobbit tumult. Their silence speaks volumes. In it, we feel their separation from the crowd bustling around them, the weight of what they have been through, the strange, magnificent, and horrific sights that they have witnessed. It's a powerfully authentic moment, true to the experience of every soldier who returns from war in a foreign land to discover that he has been alienated from a place that once felt like home, and it's accomplished without a single pompous sound bite. After all the padding, the ill-considered attempts at groundling humor (such as the off-tone dwarf jokes), the inessential suspense bits (Aragorn's brush with the wolves in *The Two Towers*, for example), the less satisfying small moments distorted by pontification, this brief scene shines out. The end of the movie, the tears and smiles and hugs backed by the incessant lament of Enya-or-whomever: these are operatic gestures, sadness as eroticism, emotions so broadly rendered as to be visible to those in the cheap seats, and though they may elicit tears, it's a cheap trick—the tears elicited are Pavlovian, a response to proven stimuli. Those scenes lack all genuineness. They are formal structures, opportunities to reprise the theme music, arias of farewell. They move us, but fail to impose other than a maudlin truth.

I wish Jackson had seen fit to incorporate more small moments like that tavern scene into the last two films, to braid them into the fantasy as he did in *The Fellowship of the Ring*. It would, I believe, have made the trilogy weightier, a film we could reasonably compare with classic war movies such as *The Human Condition*. It would have lent an extra dimension to Tolkien's themes and yet would not have weakened the film's entertainment value. I suppose many will see this as quibbling, and to a degree they are correct, because what Jackson has presented us is worth celebrating simply in terms of his illumination of Tolkien's visuals. That he neglected certain aspects of the story can mainly be chalked up to time constraints and the logistics of making a 360-million-dollar film, and he deserves every reward he receives for his creation. When the Black Tower crumbles and the very land of Mordor collapses and Mount Doom erupts, we are left wishing there was another episode to follow—a sign we have been well-entertained. The trilogy has now gone into the popular culture, standing as an incomparable feat of technical magic, and criticism of the project will seem no more than dust raised by its vast passage. Still and all, a quibble or two are not completely out of order, and I submit, for whatever value it may supply, that *Lord of the Ring*'s hallucinatory content—giant spider, F-16 pterodactyls, super-mega-mastodons, et al—might have been better served with a lighter touch of magic, a few less epic sorrows, and a smattering of sufferings more mundane.

True Life
Adventures

ALMOST...BUT NO CIGAR

Almost Famous
Release Date: *September 15, 2000 Ltd.; September 22, 2000 Wide.*
Director: *Cameron Crowe*
Screenwriter: *Cameron Crowe*
Starring: *Patrick Fugit, Billy Crudup. Kate Hudson, Jason Lee, Frances McDormand*
Distributor: *Dreamworks SKG*
Review Date: *January 2001*

> I got a fortune in my veins,
> policeman's askin' for my name,
> his flashlight's drivin' me insane...
> It glitters!
> He says, 'Hey, man, what you been
>   takin','
> I say, 'Nothin', I'm just fakin','
> He says, 'Son, you're mistaken...'
> I say, 'Gimme a break, huh!
>
> 'See, I ain't holdin' nothin', man,
> 'cept my baby by the hand,
> and we jus' hangin' with the band,
> Hey, all we wanna do is...

'SEE ROCK CITY
'(Oh, yeah! I wanna…)
'SEE ROCK CITY

'SEE ROCK CITY
'(Aw, it's so damn pretty!)
'Before I grow too old to stroll…'

THE LYRICS QUOTED ABOVE STATE WITH some economy my view—and that of most musicians I know—of rock and roll during the 70s. Cameron Crowe's take on the same subject, as expressed in his new film, *Almost Famous*, is somewhat different. Where I saw dope, massive stupidity, women used as drains, psychotic drummers, deviant businessmen, corporate coke whores, suicides, broken lives, and brain damage on a generational scale, Crowe apparently saw a more benign landscape, a happy play land populated by sensitive guitar heroes and intelligent, compassionate teenage groupies—a place where there was minor marijuana use but no powders or injectable potions (unless one counts an overdose on Quaaludes which is played for laughs); where the music was everything and dreams could come true.

The idea behind the film is this: William Miller (Patrick Fugit, an actor who has mastered two whole expressions: a cute smile and an even cuter look of puppy dog bewilderment) is a fifteen-year-old fledgling rock journalist who lands an assignment for *Rolling Stone* and goes on the road with hot new guitar band *Stillwater*—said tour forms the backdrop for a coming-of-age story based on the true-life experiences of director Crowe (*Say Anything, Jerry McGuire*). While on the road, William develops a crush on Penny Lane (Kate Hudson), a groupie who—she claims—is not really a groupie but a "band-aid," a term implying a more elevated status; she, in turn, is infatuated with *Stillwater*'s resident guitar god, Russell Hammond (Billy Crudup). William, too, is infatuated with Russell, albeit in a fanboy sort of way, and this loose triangle, along with the band's internal strife, provides what passes for a dynamic.

Through William's widened, worshipful eyes we are shown (ostensibly) backstage life at big-time rock venues, the secrets of the tour bus, an overdose, band squabbles, the infamous Riot House (International Hyatt House), LA's home-away-from-home to Zeppelin, Bowie, and the entire rock pantheon. None of this, as presented, has more than a superficial connection with how things actually were during the 70s. Crowe is not after gritty, he's after warm and fuzzy, and he delivers those qualities in pillowy buffets of sentiment backed up by a soundtrack heavy on the Elton John/Cat Stevens/Simon and Garfunkel spectrum of soft rock, music poorly suited to the milieu he's purporting to capture, but perfect for the squishy feel-good story he's delivering. When Russell Hammond trades Penny to the Brit band Humble Pie for $50 and a case of beer, he gets all misty-looking—you know he feels awful about the deal, and he'd pull back from it if it wouldn't make him seem like a wimp. And Penny, that plucky sixteen-year-old groupie with the consoling patience of a kindergarten teacher, a boy-toy whose sweetness and purity remain unsullied despite the degradation attendant upon her way of life (it's not really that degrading, according to Crowe)...well, she's a wee bit sad, but she understands. There is minor band dust-up but no sign anywhere of the egos bloated to the point of disease such as have always dominated the landscape of rock and roll. And in the end everyone gets their wish, just like in a fairytale. Miller grows a little, writes his story, and loses his virginity; Penny goes to live in Morocco; and Russell winds up on the cover of Rolling Stone.

Penny is the most problematic figure in the film for me, though none of the characters have the ring of authenticity, not even the cutely bewildered William (except for the scene in which Crowe, in imitation of his rock heroes, sees fit to pad William's briefs so that it appears he's wearing a diaper beneath them). True, a number of groupies emerged from groupiedom more-or-less whole and went on to have successful lives; but I daresay not one of them was as wise and composed and balanced during their teenage years as is Penny. As untouched by the slime through which they had belly-crawled.

There's a song about one particular groupie that includes the following lyrics:

"...she come up to me, open wide,
she said, 'Baby, you're sick, let's get
  acquainted.

I got a gun between my breasts
  that y'oughta see.
If you can get it out without shootin'
  me,
then I'll be yours for tonight,'
she sang between her teeth.
'But please don't attack me
  'less you gotta...'"

The agitated neuroticism of these few lines expresses the quintessential psychology of the groupie, the desire to master those who master them, the use of sex to achieve equal footing with the musician, the contending strains of violence and passivity. There's none of that in Penny. She's just a nice teenage girl with the savoir-faire of Hilary Clinton and the soulfulness of a Renaissance saint who really likes music.

It's not necessary, of course, that a film accurately portray reality for it to be judged successful as an entertainment. Rock and roll may not lend itself to prettification, but hey, if a film such as *Life*

Is Beautiful can treat whimsically of the Holocaust, why not a fairytale set in a rock milieu? And if, as advertised, Cameron Crowe has fashioned a rock and roll fairytale, then it should be critiqued as such...given that it satisfies the requirements of the genre.

But does it?

All fairytales, however sugary their surface, have at their heart some poignant truth. So far as I can tell, all Crowe's movie has to say is that 70s rock and roll was fun, the people involved in it were basically goodhearted, and like that. Hours of close analysis have revealed no cautionary subtext, no leitmotif, no "message" of any sort. Therefore we must conclude that the movie is not a fairytale except as regards its glossing over of reality.

Is it, then, a comedy?

If so, it's not that funny. Which is surprising, given that Crowe has proved himself a consistent writer of clever dialogue. Sentiment, I suppose, clotted his wit in this instance. But there have been several films released during the last two years, most notably *Still Crazy* and *Sugartown*, that reference similar materials and are immeasurably funnier than *Almost Famous*.

The more I pondered this film, the more perplexed I became concerning Crowe's choices, especially the toned-down-to-a-whisper sexuality and drug use. He could have told the same story far more effectively and humorously by keeping in some of the sleaze, so as to contrast the sweetness of his characters—he didn't have to wallow in it, merely add a dash or two of bitters to give his fairytale cast a context that would have caused their actions to seem moral choices formed amidst an infectious immorality. Perhaps, I thought, Crowe was responding to the dictates of commercialism. Saccharine sells in the good ol' US of A, and no one ever lost a buck by giving the public what they want. But then another possibility occurred. A couple of years ago Hollywood began to get the message from Washington, D.C., that if they didn't clean up their act, something might have to be done by way of monitoring the industry. At this point the studios greenlighted a bunch of "positive message" projects and ordered a large number of previously greenlighted scripts to be rewritten and given an uplifting gloss. Among the first of these movies to go into distribution is the forthcoming Kevin Spacey-Helen Hunt-Haley Joel Osment vehicle, *Pay It Forward*, a piece of heartstring-tugging dreck so cloying it would choke a garbage disposal, a minty-fresh mouthwash of a movie that will cause all the bought-and-paid-for, blurb-giving critics to gargle in unison, a synthetic tearjerker that will start ducts flowing in every quarter of the land, a glutinous wad of glup that twenty years from now will be remembered only by archivists.

(Thanks, Tipper. You too, Mrs. Cheney. I can't hardly wait for the heartwarming tsunami of triumph-of-the-human-spirit bullshit that will soon wash away whatever vestiges of creativity remain in the Hollywood brainpan.)

It might be, I told myself, that Crowe's movie was a victim of the same ludicrous and no doubt fleeting attempt at moral renewal that spawned *Pay it Forward*. Certainly, although *Almost Famous* will do big box office and earn several Oscar nominations (director, script, supporting actor), a similar fate awaits it.

Whatever the reason for its shortcomings, *Almost Famous* is in sum almost insubstantial, an exercise in flavorlessness, a veneer without noticeable underpinning, and wastes solid performances by Frances McDormand as William's eccentric mom Elaine, and Phillip Seymour Hoffman as the rock critic Lester Bangs. In a recent TV interview, Cameron Crowe has remarked that he intended the film to be a poem to the people he met when he was fifteen.

Oh...okay.

It's a poem.

Unfortunately for us all, it's a Rod McKuen poem.

CRIME SCENES

The Pledge
Release Date: *January 19, 2001 Nationwide*
Director: *Sean Penn*
Screenwriter: *Jerzy Kromolowski, Mary Olson- Kromolowski, Sean Penn*
Source Writer: *Friedrich Durranmatt*
Starring: *Jack Nicholson, Robin Wright Penn, Benicio Del Toro, Sam Shepard, Helen Mirren*
Distributor: *Warner Brothers*
Review Date: *July 25, 2001*

Sexy Beast
Release Date: *January 19, 2001 Sundance '01; June 22, 2001 Limited.*
Director: *Jonathan Glazer*
Screenwriter: *Louis Mellis, David Scinto*
Starring: *Ian McShane, Juliane White, James Fox, Ben Kinglsey, Ray Winstone*
Distributor: *Fox Searchlight*
Review Date: *July 25, 2001*

EVERY ONCE IN A WHILE HOLLYWOOD screws up and a decent movie gets made. How can this happen, you might ask. Surely a system controlled by bean counters, panderers, two-legged flies, australopithecines, and lawyers so devoid of humanity they haven't taken a leak in years must be incapable of producing even a marginally decent film.

Well, I'll tell you how.

Suppose you're an actor who has the ability to take a character part and do it so well that your performance will add a significant quality to whatever steaming heap of Hollywaste you participate in, enough to cause said heap to grow feet and walk into the theaters with a swagger and earn sufficient good critical mentions to put it in line for the bonus bucks that attend an Oscar nomination. Let's further suppose that you've made enough money and don't care about Oscars and Golden Globes and other such bowling trophies, and have directed a couple of movies and really are only concerned with doing interesting work.

Let's suppose you're Sean Penn.

Had almost anyone else but Penn brought a project based on an old Friedrich Durrenmatt novel to a major studio, they would've been laughed off the lot. But when Penn did exactly this, the studio's response was to say, Yeah, sure thing, Sean. We'll do your movie...if, that is, you sign on to appear in a few of the wads of used Kitty Litter we're preparing to funnel down the throats of the crud-addicted audience we've developed over the past couple of decades. What did Penn do? He said, Okay, and then, instead of turning out your typical half-baked vanity project, he went and snagged Jack Nicholson for the lead, put together a strong supporting cast featuring Sam Shepard, Aaron Eckhardt, and Robin Wright-Penn, then induced actors such as Benicio del Toro, Helen Mirren, Vanessa Redgrave, Tom Noonan, and Harry Dean Stanton, and Mickey Rourke to do small roles, and turned out a little thing called *The Pledge*, which happens to be the best movie released by a major studio in many years.

When *The Pledge* made its all-too-brief circuit of American moviehouses earlier this year, it went almost unnoticed and was dismissed by the majority of the toadying critical establishment as being dreary and too depressing.

Too depressing?

What depresses me and a growing segment of the movie-going audience is the soul-less techno-gunk upon which these punch-and-eberts lavish their slavish approbation. Most of us would give up our popcorn for a year if we could regularly watch high-quality studio films, however depressing their materials. As for "dreary," well, *The Pledge* is anything but dreary.

Jack Nicholson was once among the best film actors in the world. After he played the Joker in *Batman*, however, he entered a period during which he mailed in his performances, letting his smile and sly personal style take the place of craft. But as the retired police lieutenant, Jerry Black, Nicholson does his best work since the 1980s. Though he is an Academy favorite, though his portrayal of the troubled Jerry Black is infinitely more award-worthy than his tic-filled monochromatic Oscar-grabbing role in *As Good As It Gets*, he will almost certainly be neglected come next year's awards season because *The Pledge* is not an "important film", i.e., it didn't make any money. Of course the reason that it made no money is due less to audience dissatisfaction than it is to the fact that the studio gave it an advertising budget of about $5.99 ("We said we'd let you make it, Sean—we didn't say we'd support it"); but such subtleties are bound to be lost on folks who regularly hand out their accolade to mannequins like Julia Roberts.

The film begins on the day of Black's retirement, an event he has been dreading. During his retirement party, the mutilation and murder of a young girl is reported and Black attaches himself to the investigative team assigned to the case. When he learns that no one has yet informed the dead girl's parents, he volunteers for the job, and the mother persuades him to promise that he will find the murderer. Shortly thereafter, a mentally challenged Native American, Toby Wadenah (del Toro), is taken into custody and Detective Stan Krolak (Eckhardt) coerces him not only into confessing but also into believing he actually committed the crime. When Wadenah kills himself, the case is marked closed. But Black knows there is something wrong with the confession, and instead of going gracefully into retirement, he begins his own investigation and soon arrives at the conclusion that a serial killer is operating in the area, preying upon small blond girls in red dresses. Recognizing that the killer is operating within a triangular region of the state map (we are somewhere in the west—Colorado, it appears), Black buys a rundown roadside store/gas station at the heart of the triangle and moves in, hopeful that the killer, who drives a black car, will stop by for a fill-up. Along the way he befriends Lori (Wright-Penn), a barmaid with a young blond daughter who is being abused by her boyfriend. Lori and Black become lovers, and the three become a family. But Black is so obsessed with keeping his promise, he begins to use Lori's daughter as bait, placing a swing set out front of the building where she can be seen at play by every passing car. Eventually the bait attracts its intended prey, and when this happens, Black, who has been in mental decline, begins a downward spiral.

The narrative suppleness of the film is what sets it apart from the usual Hollywood fare. We are led to believe that what we are watching is only another serial killer movie, but as the film progresses we begin to understand that it is most of all a beautifully achieved character study detailing Black's deterioration into alcoholic dementia. The murders, so centrally posed at the film's beginning, prove to be merely the skeleton that supports the story of Black's disintegration, and the shift of focus is done so skillfully, with such economic use of dialogue and camera, it never jars, never pushes us out of the story. Only at the end do we realize what we have watched. The script by Jerry Kromolowski and Mary Olson-Kromolowski never sounds a false note. The cinematography and Penn's direction are deft and atmospheric and—most pertinently—do not obtrude as they layer in the material pertaining to Black's accumulating mental difficulties. Penn has previously made two movies, *The Indian Runner*, a dark and effective piece based on the Bruce Springsteen song "State Trooper," and *The Crossing Guard*, an equally dark but far less effective film in which Penn's creative debt to John Cassavetes shows too clearly. But with this picture he establishes himself as a director of such quality that he will very likely have to get his future funding in foreign lands.

The Pledge is the sort of police/detective/crime movie that Hollywood used to turn out with a fair degree of regularity 20, 30 years ago (small films such as *Remember My Name* and *Straight Time*), but that stands in relation to the industry's current product as does man to the lower invertebrates. Those films, like *The Pledge*, valued story and character above all else, as did the noir films that preceded them. Today, though every studio hack will swear to you that those same values remain paramount, it should be evident to even the casual observer that story and character have been relegated to the same storage facility where the powerbrokers of Hollywood keep Style and Integrity, and as a result of this, the crime film has devolved into a glut of formulaic action pictures in which endomorphic *Terminator* types wreak havoc in the name of all that's good and true, and into equally formulaic films such as Morgan Freeman's *Alex Cross* pictures. Once in a while, something like David Fincher's *Seven* tries to capture lightning in a bottle, but "tries" is the operative word here. In other countries, however, the crime film is still a going concern. Great Britain, for example, has an unrivalled tradition of superior crime movies, starting with Hitchcock's *The 39 Steps*, and peaking, perhaps, with the two movies that made Bob Hoskins a star, *Mona Lisa* and *The Long Good Friday*. Britain's latest entry in the genre, Jonathan Glazer's *Sexy Beast*, may not be quite up to its predecessors, but it is nonetheless a quality picture and features the new Bob Hoskins, Ray Winstone.

Winstone has only been seen in a handful of movies this side of the Atlantic, most prominently Tim Roth's somber tale of incest, *The War Zone*. His spectacular range is best observed in Gary Oldman's flawed but watchable, *Nil By Mouth*, in which he plays a violently abusive husband. He is, like Hoskins, everyman. Paunchy and unprepossessing, baggy-eyed and a bit long in the tooth to be considered a movie star. Of course, Winstone is scarcely a movie star—he is an actor, and despite the fact that Ben Kingsley has drawn most of the film's good press for his powerful albeit one-note performance, *Sexy Beast* is Ray Winstone's movie start to finish.

Gal (Winstone) is a retired mid-level British criminal living in mid-level luxury in a Spanish villa with his wife, whom he loves deeply, and palling around fellow retired criminal Aitch and his wife, Jackie. One morning as he stands beside his swimming pool, a boulder comes crashing down from the hill above the villa, nearly decapitating him and smashing into the pool, causing damage to the tiled bottom. Later that same day, Gal is almost incinerated by his barbecue. Director Jonathan Glazer shows us these events as signs of an impending disaster—that disaster soon manifests in the form of Don Logan (Kingsley), an amphetamine rush of a man who wants Gal to return with him to London to participate in a bank robbery engineered by Teddy Bass (Ian McShane). Logan's reputation is so fearsome that just the mention of his name casts a pall over the moods of the four expatriates, and when he arrives at the villa, their anxiety turns to outright fear. Gal rejects Logan's offer, but Logan refuses to accept this. He continues to harangue his host, to threaten him with the mere possibility of his rage. But after a tense evening redolent of *Who's Afraid of Virginia Woolf*, during which Logan dredges up (among other unsavory bits) the porn-star past of Gal's wife, he leaves for the airport. Once on the plane, however, Logan's rage and frustration with Gal boil over. He causes a scene that results in his removal from the plane and soon he is on his way back to the villa. The resulting violent confrontation concludes with Gal going off to London to do the job and Logan disappearing. Teddy

Bass suspects Gal of being responsible for the disappearance, but Gal claims to know nothing, and the robbery, which targets a bank vault containing a billion-pound treasure, goes forward.

Sexy Beast is a film that treats of evil. Logan's expression of that primal quality is potent enough, but he is a mere precursor to the evil incarnated by Bass, a king of the criminal class and a brutal, conscienceless man who—in his development of the robbery scheme—becomes the lover of the bank president, played by a suitably decadent James Fox. Bass knows that Gal has done something with Logan, and the suspense of the movie is sustained by our expectation that his vengeance is imminent, and that once the robbery is done, Gal will be done for. Whereas Logan is the fist of evil, Bass is its corrupted soul. In the role of Bass, McShane's leathery features seem to have acquired the cold rigor of a basilisk, and he is capable of achieving with a single stare a menace more frightening than that Logan creates by means of all his fulminance and profane temper.

Gal is an essentially good soul whose criminality testifies to the primacy of nurture over nature. He has always been a man who could do what was necessary to live, but now he doubts himself— he's been away from the game too long, and he does not know whether he can successfully resist Logan, and when events dictate that he must participate in the robbery, he is not certain that he can maintain his poise in light of what has happened to Logan. What brings him through is his goodness as it manifests in his love for his wife. The remarkable thing about this is that most of it is not stated in the script, but is externalized by Winstone, externalized so effectively that by expression and gesture alone he manages to convey the complex depth of what appears on the surface to be a rather simple man. Kingsley's performance as Logan, though less complex by script necessity, is nonetheless notable for its molten intensity and is the sort of performance that, despite *Beast*'s low profile, might well earn him a Supporting Actor nomination from the Academy—he has, after all, won before. Seeing him in *Beast* makes you wonder why we haven't seen Kingsley in more substantial roles. Chances are, Hollywood has no idea what to do with him, other than to slot him into projects like *Species*.

For those enamored of Hollywood product, well, then you have a plethora of putrid treats available. *Swordfish*, a film without any perceptible virtue that marks another downward step on John Travolta's career path, following hard upon last summer's Ed Woodesque *Battlefield Earth*. Then there is *The Score*, a bloated waste of Brando, DeNiro, and Edward Norton, three actors in search of a script. But if you enjoy good crime movies, instead of blowing your eight to twelve bucks on raw sewage such as this, you would be far better served to check out *Sexy Beast* or to seek out *The Pledge* at your local Blockbuster. I promise that you will not be disappointed.

ASSASSINS

Our Lady of the Assassins
Release Date: *January 19, 2001 Sundance '01; September 7, 2001*
Limited
Director: *Barbet Schroeder*
Screenwriter: *Fernando Vallejo*
Source Writer: *Fernando Vallejo*
Starring: *Juan David Restepo, German Jaramillo, Anderson*
Ballesteros
Distributor: *Paramount Classics*
Review Date: *September 16, 2001*

SOMEONE IS AIMING A VIDEO CAMERA from ground level up toward a man in a blue shirt, who appears to be having a conversation with someone off-camera. Above him looms the south tower of the World Trade Center. As we watch, what appears to be a large jet plane rendered in shadow comes into view against a cloudless sky and appears to vanish into the side of the tower. An instant later the fireball erupts and the man who is talking turns his head, almost casually, toward the explosion . . .

Reality, we realize now, resembles a bad special effect.

We have been insulated from much painful reality here in the United States, but now we know for certain sure what the rest of the world has known, that terrorism is not so beautifully lit and designed as might be depicted in some blast of digital sound and

Mega-color with a nine figure budget. It is considerably less splendid, much grittier, much simpler, and the heroes do not always survive.

It was the aforementioned video sequence that to a great degree determined my choice of movie the other day. I had no real desire to see any movie, but then again, I needed to remove myself from the vicinity of my TV, from endless replays of the terrorist Super Bowl and the orgy of anchorman and -woman repetition. I decided that I wanted to see something depressing. Comedy, I believed, would fall flat, and action-adventure...well, I'd had a sufficiency of explosions. Perhaps, I thought, a truly depressing film, an engrossing film, would turn my attention away from the tragic circumstances of our lives and briefly dispel the pall of depression that had enveloped me. So it was that I attended a matinee showing of Barbet Schroeder's new foreign-language film, *Our Lady of the Assassins*. This experiment proved only partially successful, but I am here to report, for whatever reason you may choose to see it, that *Assassins* is a very good movie, indeed.

Adapted from the semi-autobiographical novel by Fernando Vallejo, *Assassins* is set in Medellin, Colombia, eight years after the death of Pablo Escobar, the notorious king of the Medellin cartel, a place where successful cocaine shipments to the United States are celebrated with prodigious fireworks displays. Governed by the remnant structure of Escobar's empire, the city is in a state of near-anarchy, a free-fire zone in which children are schooled from an early age in the usage of violence, thereby establishing a terrifying class of youthful street kids to whom killing has become an incidental event, merely an element of the passionless play of violence and death that comprises their milieu. Young men casually murder whoever commits the mildest of slights as they move through this landscape, leaving the bodies untended on the streets and sidewalks. And then they, too, are murdered by rival gang members or family enemies.

Into this most desolate of environments comes Fernando (German Jaramillo), a writer of middle years who has wearied of life and the corruption of the world to the extent that he has returned to die (purportedly) in the city where he once lived as a child. He walks through the streets day and night, offering comment on the ragged lives he observes, contemplating—we are given to believe—his imminent mortality. Along the way he falls in love with a handsome young gangbanger, Alexis (Anderson Ballesteros), one of the violent criminals who flow in an endless stream about him, and they become a couple oddly right for one another—this death-seeking intellectual and the death-dealing boy/man who barely seems to notice the shadow of dread mortality that hovers about him. The two men are pure contraries. Fernando is erudite, a sophisticate who enjoys opera and the classics, and delights in wordplay. Alexis, on the other hand, is a creature who lives only to satisfy his most immediate needs, and is committed to violence, shooting anyone who even appears to be at cross-purposes with him. The soundtrack of his existence is aggressive, characterless rock and roll, a music that sometimes serves him as a chaotic lullaby, provoking dreams of bigger and better guns. As the two wander the city, Alexis' path of incessant slaughter, gunshots and screams orchestrated into a harsh rhythm, becomes a kind of chorus counterpointing Fernando's bleak and often darkly humorous commentaries.

I must admit that I found the constant violence of *Assassins* almost soothing, its debased human-ness far more wholesome than the violence of the shadowy plane aimed at the World Trade Center, and so in this sense, the film did the job I hoped it would, immersing me in a world whose problems were more graspable and visceral than those evolving from the world of organized terrorism. I have no idea how I might have viewed the movie under ordinary circumstances—perhaps it would have numbed me, which is the effect that murder comes to have ultimately on Fernando. Yet while it did take me out of myself, all during the film I had an apprehension that I was sitting in a dark bubble beyond which a terrible brightness ruled, and I could not avoid the tendency to add my own commentaries to those of Fernando—less insightful, perhaps, but no less bleak, grounded in a gallows humor of the kind that often acts to protect me from feelings I would rather not confront, provoked in this instance by the odious preening of various on-camera news reporters as they struck their poses in front of the gargantuan wreckage of the twin towers and the ghastly smoke of five thousand souls, arranged their faces into a telegenic gloom and served up tales of woe and treacly anecdotes, all designed, I suppose, to persuade us of the sensitivity of their affiliated network, and further having, I assume, some more pertinent manipulative intent. Could these professional mourners in their pancake make-up not for one moment stop?, I wondered. Stop their pontificating, their pitiful and irrelevant speculations, their unending statistical noise, their mini-series type ATTACK ON AMERICA graphics and quickly whipped-up theme music for the horror they seemed to be selling us like a brand of patent medicine. Could not they not cease attempting to orchestrate grief into a mourn-by-numbers craft kit, and offer some more dignified programming...maybe even a touch now and again of silence? Could they not allow us to find our own path through the city of grief, to provide our own commentaries, to decide for ourselves how we should feel? Did these overpaid haircuts not understand that their mawkish blather was the most god-awful of distractions and irreverences, every bit as nasty and graceless in their own right as the oft-shown footage of several people on the West Bank celebrating the mass death of innocent Americans? I further recall thinking that whatever good might come from the events in New York; Arlington, and Pennsylvania (I imagine that the chief product of this disaster will be war and death) would be essentially trivial, as in the case of the lifting of Arnold Schwarzenegger's certain-to-be-horrid anti-terrorist flick, *Collateral Damage*, from the fall schedule, though it might be worth the price of admission simply to listen to Arnold attempt to pronounce the title. I decided that the most profound effect upon popular culture would likely be a diminution of the audience for reality television and a deluge of patriotically hued knock-off novels concerned with defending the Land of the Free from sinister plots, something that appears to be in the nature of an afterthought for this and previous Presidential administrations. If, as has been reported, the terrorist attack was causing Hollywood to rethink the content of their films, well, that would be nice, too; but if this is the case, I fear it will be only a phase, a temporary pull-back from the tried-and-true formula of the virtueless action pictures that have become the staple of every movie summer. These bursts of cynicism on my part did not last for long. The movie was powerful enough to reel me back in and involve me again in the vivid progression of Fernando and Alexis through the hellish gutterlands of Medellin.

Barbet Schroeder, who spent his youth in Colombia and has had personal experience of its terrors, brings a powerful intimacy and grittiness to the film, a work far superior to his English-language films, even the much ballyhooed *Reversal of Fortune*. In *Assassins*, he has surpassed the artistry of his early films and created a wonderfully paced and explosive picture (explosive both in terms of its action and its strangely moral heart). Filmed in digital video that is so well-suited for rendering the grimy, blood-stained thoroughfares of Medellin, you can almost smell the brimstone, and utilizing actual street kids as actors, the movie becomes a harrowing document of life on the fringes of the pre-apocalypse, and yet succeeds in conveying through its bloody imagery and the intelligence of its screenplay (also by Fernando Vallejo) a sense of beauty and humanity. Jaramillo's astonishing performance and Vallejo's script slowly reveal rather than state the true character of Fernando, and as the film pounds toward its conclusion, we realize we have been led to understand that though Fernando outwardly derides and belittles all those he observes, he is at heart a deeply romantic soul who is stricken by everything he sees. This sort of complexity is the hallmark of the film. Nothing is truly as it appears, perhaps not even death.

It is films like *Our Lady of the Assassins* that, dismaying and violent though they may be, remind us of what is possible of art in that frequently abused medium. It may not be a timeless movie, but it is a very wise one, one that exposes by example the complexity underlying every human event, the infinite knot of circumstance and time at the heart of every tragedy, instead of glossing over complexity with the simple colors of melodrama as do Hollywood and the network news. I wish I had seen the movie at a time when I was not emotionally corrupted, more oriented to the usual stance of a critic; but having the experience of it I did provided me with a few hours of distance from the moment I inhabit, and for that I remain grateful.

When I returned home, images of the film still playing in my head, I found that Paula Zahn, who had obviously had some touch-up work done on her blond hairdo, and wearing a pained look that put me in mind of a whiney schoolteacher complaining to her principal that she didn't understand the new textbook, was opining for the umpteenth time (upon each occasion utilizing the same constipated expression and affected delivery) that the destruction of the World Trade center, the devastation at the Pentagon and in Pennsylvania, together comprised the greatest man-made disaster in our history . . .as if this mattered, as if it were important that we keep track of the rankings, as if this made the death of five thousand people even more significant. She was responded to by a yea-saying cohort who soberly agreed with her pronouncement and even went so far as to suggest that it might rival in loss of life the Galveston hurricane at the turn of the 20th century, which had resulted in over six thousand deaths.

Wow.

A record.

Paula gave a shake of her head—it was just too much for her to absorb—and then, adopting a subtle variant of her beleaguered expression, she announced that they would be right back. For a time I stared blankly out the window, watching a Serbian Muslim woman who lives nearby hurry across the deserted parking lot, and then, as the theme music for ATTACK ON AMERICA sounded once again, and the signature collage of images, of collapsing towers and weeping women and firemen covered in gypsum dust, began to flicker across the screen, accompanied by sound bites of the President proclaiming his resolve toward vengeance—soul-stirring as all this was, I switched off the set and went to call my son in Brooklyn. He had been scheduled to be married in Greenwich Village on September 15th, and of course the wedding had been postponed. I needed to see how he was doing. When he answered he was standing on his balcony, looking out toward the plume of smoke rising from lower Manhattan. We engaged in a somewhat muted conversation, both of us fatigued in our own way, spiritually unfocused. I told him about the movie I had seen, expressed a number of my reactions to it, inclusive of my dissatisfaction with Ms. Zahn and her equally banal colleagues, and thereafter we discussed rescheduling my cancelled trip to New York. After awhile he told me to hold on for a second, he had to go back inside his apartment. The wind had shifted, he said, and he wanted to avoid the smell of burning metal.

SLEEPLESS IN SOMEPLACE IN ALASKA

Insomnia
Release Date: *May 24, 2002 Nationwide*
Director: *Christopher Nolan*
Screenwriter: *Hillary Seitz*
Source Writer: *Nikolaj Frobenius*
Starring: *Al Pacino, Hilary Swank, Robin Williams, Martin Donavan, Maura Tierney*
Distributor: *Warner Brothers*
Review Date: *June 29, 2002*

IF YOU'RE A HABITUAL READER OF REVIEWS, you're likely going to read several claiming that *Insomnia* is that rarest of cinematic creatures, a remake better than the original. Whether or not you agree with this may depend upon your definition of the word "better." For my part, right up until the last fifteen minutes, I was convinced that director Christopher Nolan had managed to pull off a feat I previously thought impossible, i.e., doing a remake of a quality foreign film that, although not as accomplished as the original, was at least a credible rendering of the materials. But during that final fifteen minutes he succeeds in turning an eccentric, compelling piece of noir into mere melodrama. Given that Nolan's previous films (*Following* and *Memento*) were extremely inventive in structure and design, it seems quite possible that the stock ending of his new movie was forced upon him by producers who did not believe that the audience would be capable of handling ambiguity. Which seems a bit odd, because *Insomnia* is a movie about ambiguity, and for the preceding hour and forty-three minutes, the audience has been drenched in it.

Los Angeles detectives Will Dormer (Al Pacino), a legendary crime solver, a luminary in the police firmament, and his partner Hap (Martin Donovan) are sent to the Alaskan wilderness town of Nightmute to investigate the brutal beating death of a young woman whose body was washed and cleaned by the murderer in order to destroy every last scintilla of physical evidence. The assignment serves also to get the pair out of LA, where both are being harassed by an Internal Affairs investigation of their past cases. Indeed, Hap has already decided to make a deal with IA, one that will imperil Dormer's career, and this creates serious tension between the two men.

It's summer in Alaska, the sun is almost always above the horizon, and Dormer finds himself unable to sleep, his judgment and his general mental state decaying. Nevertheless, he sets a trap to lure the murderer back to the fishing cabin where the victim's body was found. The plan succeeds, but the murderer becomes aware that the police are watching him and flees into the fog. During the ensuing pursuit over rocky ground, Dormer becomes disoriented and inadvertently shoots and kills Hap. Or is the shooting inadvertent? Hap, dying, accuses him of murder and Dormer himself is confused as to what has happened. Local detective Ellie Burr (Hillary Swank), a novice on the job who hero-worships Dormer to the point that one half-expects her to jump and lick his face, or to begin humping his leg, is assigned to investigate Hap's death. At the same time the murderer, a mystery novelist named Walter Finch (Robin Williams), begins calling Dormer on the phone, commiserating with him about his insomnia, telling him that he witnessed Hap's death and is willing to work with Dormer to cover up both their crimes. As Dormer's sleeplessness continues, leaving him prone to flashbacks of memory and hallucinatory breaks, his poor judgments escalate, and he joins, albeit reluctantly, in common purpose with Finch.

The atmospheric Norwegian thriller that serves as Nolan's model, also entitled *Insomnia*, is scene-by-scene almost the same movie for most of its duration. However, there are a number of telling differences between the two. In the Norwegian film the lead detective (Stellan Skarsgard) is a man spiritually crippled by the exigencies of his work and existentially at sea. He has no clear-cut career-oriented motivation for murder as does Will Dormer, and if he did intentionally kill his partner, it was done out of some perverse and momentary impulse. In the Norwegian version, the female detective assigned to the shooting has some admiration for the lead detective, but is in her own right a competent and dedicated public servant. No hint of hero worship here. These distinctions point up the difficulty Hollywood has with telling an honest story. In the view of your average and even not-so-average Hollywood producer, nothing ordinary or small can be considered interesting, and subtle human motivations are deemed too subtle for mass consumption. Their detective has to be a superstar detective, and his motivation for murder has to be—for purposes of generating audience sympathy—the hounding of a good, brave, accomplished man by the weasels of Internal Affairs. Another such difference is brought forth when Dormer begins to defend himself against possible prosecution for murder. He has found a gun—dropped by the murderer—out on the rocky lakeshore where his partner met his fate. He takes the gun, shoots a bullet into a dead dog, and replaces the bullet that was removed from his partner's body with this one. The lead detective in the Norwegian version kills the dog, then removes the bullet, and is far more actively involved in setting up an evidentiary circumstance that will allow him to go unpunished. He is a willing participant along with Finch in the cover-up, every bit as responsible for it, and is no less a manipulator. It is a law of the Hollywood process that while one's protagonist may be troubled, he cannot be a killer of dogs or a man whose ethical compass is other than momentarily out of whack. The American audience, it is felt, simply will not accept a protagonist who, like most of us, is wandering in a moral fog.

Another distinction between the two films is the setting. The Norwegian film utilizes the bleak Arctic tundra, suitable to the bleak materials of the story, whereas the American version offers the lushness of the Alaskan wilderness, waterfalls sluicing down into green gorges, dramatic mountains, gorgeous rocky bays. Once again a Hollywood law—nothing interesting can occur in a place that is not visually spectacular. The majestic setting takes an edge off the grimness of the story, serving to muddy the fact that the citizens of the town, Nightmute, are many of them people who according to the script have hidden themselves away and are running from their pasts. As is Dormer. Though this idea is given lip service in dialog in the American version, it does not resonate with the postcard ambiance and brooding yet glorioso score that accompanies tracking shots of glaciers and foaming rivers, et al. Nor does it synch with the reality of such summer places, towns who derive ninety-eight percent of their income during the summer and whose citizenry, their pockets bulging with tourist loot, spend the winters happily traveling in sunny climes. (Where, by the way, are the tourists in this town? At the height of the tourist season, the place as filmed is almost empty, yet supports what appears to be a luxurious four-star lodge along with other nifty-looking tourist facilities.)

Once a more-than-competent actor, Pacino has devolved over the last fifteen years into a yeller and a scenery-chewer, a caricature of his former self. Praise should be given to Nolan for reigning him in, but a restrained performance is not necessarily a great one, and though Pacino is limited herein to a handful of yells, his customary repertoire of eye-rollings and grunts and dolorous sighs is on full display, and to no good effect. He does not come off at all well by contrast to Stellan Skarsgard's quietly contained and mostly externalized performance in the same role. Robin Williams as Finch is appropriately creepy, but then I find him creepy in every part he has ever attempted—a peculiarly androgynous figure with a namby-pamby voice that at times sounds as if he were speaking through a pair of cotton briefs stretched across his face. The most effective performances in the film are those given by Swank and by Maura Tierney (*Scotland, PA*) as a hotelkeeper, both in rather thankless and truncated roles. Swank's metamorphosis from a cute puppy with a bow around her neck to a thoroughly engaged professional troubled by the growing suspicion that her hero has feet of clay is especially notable.

All this said, for most of its length *Insomnia* is well worth watching due to the cleverness and talent of its director. Nolan manages to overcome the handicaps with which he has been burdened—Pacino, a dumbed-down script by Hillary Seitz, and doubtless the incessant looking-over-his-shoulder presence of his producers—and keeps us involved by means of outstanding camera work and the brilliantly achieved intercutting of Pacino's hallucinations and other such flashy maneuvers. Hopefully, as he gains more power—which is, after all, the only meaningful coin in Hollywood—he'll be able to get rid of the production snoops and make movies in his maturity that fulfill the promise of his youth. For an hour and forty-three minutes, he almost pulls it off. Despite my caveats, there is a lot to like here.

Then comes the ending.

The resolution of the Norwegian film is deft and ambiguous and speaks to the randomness of fate and the awful fragility of the human condition. It is as gray as the fog in which the event that stands central to its plot takes place, and thus is in keeping with the often murkily focused and unsettling resolutions of crises in our own lives. But realism of this sort is not deemed suitable for mass consumption by the lawgivers of the Hollywood film. Hollywood prefers to clobber us with theme and meaning, and so Christopher Nolan's *Insomnia* concludes with a steeped-in-Family-Values, all-loose-ends-secured ending in which every evil is punished, redemption is gained by those who require it, truth and justice are served, and a moral lesson is taught, and whaddya know, this is achieved by means of a full-on blood-spattering shoot-out.

Yippee!

Watching it, I thought of *Death of a Salesman* culminating with Willy Loman dying in a kung-fu battle royale, of *The Grapes of Wrath* climaxing with an army of machete-wielding Okies charging the White House, of Bergman's *The Seventh Seal* remade with heavy special FX and a script by Stephen King, of *Hamlet* closing with a food fight.

That's how clumsy and inappropriate it seemed.

If you're going to take in a thriller this summer, *Insomnia* is probably your best bet. But which *Insomnia*? If you like fifty-million-dollar budgets, terrific production values, and a director whose technique is the cinematic equivalent of early Eddie Van Halen, then go for the theatrical release. But if you're after an experience that will nourish and disturb you, and leave you thinking and not saying—as I did after my exposure to the American version—"Aw, Christ...no!," then you'd be well advised to check out the original. My advice is to see them both. For anyone interested in film, these two movies provide a clear lens through which to focus upon the distinctions between world cinema and our own homegrown, amped-up, and often silly attempts to imitate it.

THELMA AND LUIGI

Heaven
Release Date: *October 4th, 2002 (LA/NY).*
Director: *Tom Tykwer*
Screenwriter: *Krzysztof Kieslowski*
Starring: *Cate Blanchett. Giovanni Ribisi, Stephania Rocca, Remo Girone*
Distributor: *Miramax Films*
Review Date: *November 10, 2002*

NOVEMBER, AND AMERICA HOLDS its breath, awaiting with giddy anticipation the first of the traditional superfreakingawfulalidocious holiday cinematic treats, this being, of course, *Harry Potter and the Bucket of Snouts*, or is it *Harry Potter and the Pork Roast Enema*? Whatever, it's sure to sell tons of *Harry Potter* potty seats (Chamber pots of Secrets?), plastic capes, weed whackers, wands, refrigerator magnets, pregnancy tests, rat poison, Frisbees, whoopee cushions, chainsaws, doggie treats, double AA batteries, pajamas, skateboards, cell phones, nipple rings, et al, and that'll sure make ol' Moloch happy.

In the interim, other films less celebrated compete for the notice of the American public's ADD-afflicted consumerist mentality. Among these is German director Thomas Twyker's latest, *Heaven*. Twyker achieved international attention several years back with the

MTV-inflected *Run Lola Run*, a dazzling display of technique that relates the adventures of a young woman who literally sprints from fade-in to fade-out in an attempt to save her boyfriend's life. Part existentialist video game, part off-beat thriller, though *Lola* was undeniably flashy, displaying a masterful control of camera and pacing and the materials of pop culture, the movie had all the depth of a Brittany Spears lyric, and the general consensus among critics was that Twyker's gift would be judged as suspect until he added a touch of substance to his style. His two follow-ups to *Lola*, the vacuous *Wintersleepers* and *The Princess and the Warrior*, a terminally quirky romance that appeared to have been influenced by the lamentable late-career excesses of Jean Luc Goddard, did nothing to assuage critical doubt. However, both these films continued to offer evidence of Twyker's technical virtuosity and thus there was a modicum of hope that his next project, based on a screenplay by the late great Polish filmmaker Krzysztof Kieslowski (*The Decalogue, Three Colors*) would allow him to handle subject matter of a sufficient weight so as to bring out the best in him. Unfortunately, Twyker's hyperkinetic style poses a pure contrary to Kieslowski's stately sensibility, his classically modulated philosophical and moral concerns, and the result is a curiously inept, thematically murky hybrid.

The last instance of a major director taking on and completing the work of dead master, Steven Spielberg's molestation of Stanley Kubrick's *AI* script, produced one of the most repellent films in recent memory, a pretentious stinkeroo of cosmic proportions. While *Heaven* delivers a few more pleasures than *AI*, its level of pretension is nearly unparalleled—I mean, we're talking not since the worst of Michelangelo Antonioni (*Red Desert*) has such horribly overstated symbolic content been displayed onscreen—and so the project brings little credit either to Twyker or, posthumously, to Kieslowski.

The story goes as follows. Phillipa (Cate Blanchett), a widowed

British schoolteacher living in Turin, Italy, decides to place a bomb in a trashcan at the office belonging to Vendice, Turin's drug kingpin, who is responsible for the death of her husband. A cleaning woman, however, inadvertently carries the bomb onto an elevator, thereby succeeding in killing herself along with a father and his two young daughters. Phillipa confesses to the crime and a police interpreter named—coincidentally—Phillipo (Giovanni Ribisi) becomes infatuated with her and, moved by her story, he helps her to escape from the clutches of the caribineri, who are themselves Vendice's minions and have determined that the murderous schoolteacher must be eliminated before coming to trial, because she knows too much about the druglord's business dealings. (Given the ludicrous ineptitude of the police in their efforts to imprison and then to recapture her, one is forced to assume that either Inspector Clouseau or Roberto Benigni or Meadow Soprano has been put in charge of the pursuit.) Twyker expends a great deal of footage in attempting to justify Phillipa's sociopathic miscreance, hoping to persuade us of her good character by having her tell the police that she not only was seeking vengeance but also was serving the general good by attempting to terminate a villain who had killed thousands of children with his poison—this quite in opposition to the early scenes that show Phillipa making and planting the bomb, operating in a steely, stone-killer mode. The director seems intent not, as would have been interesting and pertinent, on exploring the moral ambiguity of Phillipa's vigilantism, but on transforming her into a romantic figure, a creature of tragic proportions upon whom fate has worked a cruel trick. Had Kieslowski himself directed the film, this transition—albeit perhaps no less dubious—would likely have been handled with some artfulness, layered in and hinted at and otherwise developed in a believable fashion; as things stand, it comes across as clumsy and more than a little perverse. At any rate, love blooms between Phillipa and Phillipo—you might say they Phlip for each other, and they go on the run through scenic Italy. With them goes all hope that the movie can be redeemed.

A considerable portion of the problem with *Heaven* can probably be attributed to the fact that the original script was translated from Polish into French, then French into German, and then German into English before Twyker and one of the films many producers (fifteen in all), Anthony Minghella, perpetrator of the thoroughly unsubtle *The English Patient*, cohabited and together hatched the final version of the shooting script. Doubtless much of Kieslowski's conception was simply translated out of existence. What remains is without question beautifully filmed—Twyker's exceptional cinematographer, Frank Griebe, does a marvelous job of reproducing the voluptuous surface and languorous feel of a Kieslowski picture. But thanks to the absurdity of the action and dialogue, Griebe's work comes to seem scarcely more than mimicry. Blanchett provides a brave and often brilliant performance, but eventually her efforts are overwhelmed by having to speak lines that might have been lifted from a wastebasket belonging to Samuel Beckett's idiot brother. As the dogs of justice—bumbling but relentless in their progress—close in, Phillipa and Phillipo shave their heads and begin to dress in identical clothing. The idea behind this apparently being that we are all the same except for the vowels at the ends of our names, or that the lovers are Adam and Eve, or that unisex fashions will once again be featured on the runways of Milan next spring . . . or something. Finally, as death draws near, the lovers strip to the buff (note to all you *LOTR* geeky boys—Hey, Galadriel nude! Check out the DVD. Awright!) on a sunset-lit Tuscan hillside and consummate their union, thus illustrating Kieslowski's predominant theme—i.e., that even the most flawed among us can achieve transcendence—in terms so unequivocal, so blatantly trumpeted, it's as if Twyker was aiming to make art for the *Jackass* audience, as if the frames were captioned or word balloons were appearing above the heads of Phillipa and Phillipo as they make Philli-pie, saying stuff like, "Do you feel the earth moving, my angel?"

"I don't believe it is the earth, my sweet. It is the firmament."

"The firmament, my love?"

"Yes, my darling . . . the floor of heaven."

Gah!

At this pass, having been drenched, assaulted, and in some cases brain-damaged by a couple of hours (it seemed like much, much more) of such primitively announced symbolism, members of the audience with whom I viewed the film began to laugh.

It is to be hoped that the legacy of *Heaven* will be a reluctance on the part of future filmmakers to complete the unfinished movies of deceased colleagues, but this is undoubtedly a faint hope. Such challenges appeal to the ego and filmmaking is the most ego-fueled of the arts. The likelihood is that such projects will not only proliferate, they will grow increasingly lame as new directors pick up the fallen flags of the Spielbergs and the Scorseses and—God help us—even the Chris Columbuses. Let's suppose (Heaven forefend!) that Chris had dropped dead on the set of *Harry Potter 2*, who then would have stepped forward to carry on his great work? Whoever it might have been, I can just hear the critics praising the director's unimaginative framing, the sublime flatness of the dialogue, his sure-handed way with comic flatulence, the formulaic precision of the storyline. Predictability raised to the elegant. A true homage! The thought of an artist finishing another's work would be deemed abhorrent in any other medium . . .at least this once would have been the case. Now, given the compulsions of the marketplace, we might someday expect to see an unfinished masterpiece by, say, Dom DeLillo, given over to a Michael Chabon or a David Foster Wallace to polish off, redefine, and thereby serve as a kind of literary talk show host. Such projects have, indeed, already been commissioned as regards more commercial novels—witness Terry Bisson's completion of Walter Miller's sequel to *A Canticle for Leibowitz*. Perhaps this sort of morbid collaboration will become the vogue. Authors will sign contracts to write the first three hundred pages of two novels—the literary world going interactive. Perhaps one day we will have museum exhibits of Francis Bacon's sketchbooks rendered in full dimension by Gary Larsen or Peter Max. When that day dawns, it may be that *Heaven* will be looked upon as a progenitor of a significant artistic movement. Until that day arrives, if tempted to see it, take the advice of someone who has done so and run like hell.

TWO OLD FASHIONS

Far From Heaven
Release Date: *November 8th, 2002 (LA/NY)*
Director: *Todd Haynes*
Screenwriter: *Todd Haynes*
Starring: *Julianne Moore, Dennis Quaid, Dennis Haysbert,*
Patricia Clarkson
Review Date: *December 1, 2002*

The Quiet American
Release Date: *November 22nd, 2002 (LA/NY).*
Director: *Phillip Noyce*
Screenwriter: *Christopher Hampton, Robert Schenkkan*
Source Writer: *Graham Greene*
Starring: *Michael Caine, Brendan Fraser, Rade Serbedzija, Do*
Hai Yen
Review Date: *December 1, 2002*

WHEN I WAS IN JUNIOR HIGH, TWO friends and I sneaked a live
chicken into the balcony of a theater in Daytona Beach, Florida
during a promotion billed as a "Women's Matinee." Below us,
hundreds of women were weeping at the sad plight of Lana Turner
in her latest tearjerker. My friends and I covered the chicken with
ketchup and dropped it off the edge of the balcony into the audience,

eliciting shrieks and panicked flight, packs of ketchup-spattered women fleeing the scene while the larger-than-life Ms. Turner continued her overwrought emoting behind them on the screen. The impropriety of this prank is not in question, being offensive to PETA, NOW, the Chicken Rights people, and—I'm sure— Secretaries For A Better Tomorrow; but its motivation is less clear. Doubtless the image of middle-aged women boo-hooing en masse posed a provocation of sorts to my seventh-grade brain; yet I think that even at such a tender age, it was also an inborn distaste for melodrama that goaded me to action. This said, I came to a viewing of Todd Haynes' much-praised melodrama, *Far From Heaven*, with great anticipation.

Haynes, who directed *Safe*, a picture I rank among the ten best American films of the Nineties, is an immensely talented man whose talent lately has been undermined by his obsessions. In his previous movie, *The Velvet Goldmine*, his fascination with glam rock served to corrupt his usually precise artistic sensibility and the result was an indulgent mess of a film that sought to mythologize a dreary, hackneyed plot by imbuing its milieu with homoerotic mystery, questions of identity, and so forth. Now, in *Far From Heaven*, he presents us with what must be considered in part a loving homage to the work of Douglas Sirk, who during the 1950s churned out a succession of lurid, campy, Technicolor tearjerkers (most notably, *All That Heaven Allows*, a Jane Wyman-Rock Hudson vehicle concerning the scandalous romance between a widow and a gardener much younger than she that stands as a direct precursor to *Far From Heaven*). For some un-fathomable reason, perhaps because some academic thought it would be clever to do so, these films have recently been redefined as "important."

Set in New Haven, Connecticut, during the late Fifties, Haynes' film seeks to explore the vanished culture of the suburban aristocracy, the exclusive precinct of country clubs, executives with low golf handicaps, Stepfordesque wives who wore white gloves and cooked like Betty Crocker and did charity work among "the Negroes," a society as structured and fortified and constrained as that of the gentry in the Ante-Bellum South. Julianne Moore plays Cathy Whittaker, the most Stepfordish wife, mother, and hostess of them all, her charity work celebrated in the society pages, leading a superficially perfect life that obscures a terrible flaw in her marriage to Frank Whittaker (Dennis Quaid), one she cannot entirely admit to herself. Frank appears the quintessential successful suburbanite—great golfer, prosperous salesman—but he spends many an evening in downtown New Haven hanging near a movie theater (it's playing *The Three Faces of Eve*), then sneaking into a bar tucked away down an alley where he finds solace in "the love that dare not speak its name." Though he's not fully able to confront the fact, Frank is gay. After Cathy catches him in the embrace of another man, Frank seeks psychiatric help, hoping to cure what he believes must be a disease. Cathy finds a confidante of her own in Raymond Deagan (Dennis Haysbert), a black gardener who has taken over his father's landscaping business and is, in his own fashion, as lonely and disaffected as Cathy. Eventually Frank's struggle to become straight begins to cause him problems at work, and Cathy's burgeoning (albeit innocent) relationship with Raymond sets tongues wagging—to have even a conversation with a black man is a breech of what is thought to be proper behavior by the town gossips (in case the audience fails to grasp the historical significance of this, Haynes runs news breaks concerning the integration of Little Rock's Central High School underneath the action). Before too long, Raymond's daughter is harassed by racists who are offended by his connection with a white woman, Frank reaches a crisis point, Cathy's idyllic life is shattered, and things swiftly build toward a tear-stained ending.

The acting in *Far From Heaven* is first water. Following hard upon his excellent work in *The Rookie*, Quaid continues to reinvigorate his career with a devastating portrait of a man who is part lovesick idiot, part student-body president, and part desolate loser. Haysbert brings an immense Poitier-like gravitas to the role of Raymond, and Moore is simply perfect. Always a luminous figure on the screen, in Haynes' hands she becomes a figure of almost supernatural intensity, an icon in whom cracks of unreality have suddenly manifested. Sitting with a group of other wives, listening to them discuss their husbands' marital demands, realizing that her own husband is never demanding in this way; watching a boy and girl kissing on a bench while waiting for Frank to emerge from his psychiatrist's office: in scene after scene Moore transcends the parameters of her profession, managing to portray not only Cathy Whittaker, a Rockwellian angel shocked by a recognition of life's imperfection, but further to sum up all the actresses who have ever played a similar character, to make of this clichéd role a magical archetype. As the shocks to Cathy's system multiply, layer by layer Moore strips away the artificiality of the character's personality to reveal the frightened woman beneath. There is every chance that she will receive a long-overdue Oscar for this role.

The art direction (Haynes' films are never less than brilliantly mounted) and the gorgeous cinematography initially depict the world of mid-century New Haven done in ochres and ambers and coppers and russets and deep leafy greens, making it appear like a cross between an ad for new cars in the Saturday Evening Post and a mystical forest kingdom. As Cathy's illusion decays and the seasons change, the colors of Haynes' palette dim, foreshadowing a tragedy to come. But for all Haynes' talent and precise control of the cinematic elements, or—more accurately—because of these same qualities, there is a mammoth preciousness about this film that inhibits all its virtues. It's as if we're being shown not a movie but one of those little globes enclosing a miniature scene that swirl with ersatz snow when shaken. We're being asked, it seems, to view this tiny incidence of light and color from the vantage of contemporary expectation, to gaze upon it with an arch superiority, to feel good, I suppose, that we live in a less deceitful age, one in which the sickness of the culture—though it remains untreated—has at least been revealed. We're also being asked to revel in the costumery of the past, to delight in its pretty dysfunction and fakery. Ultimately, what causes the whole of *Far From Heaven* to total less than the sum of its parts is its unappetizing source materials—the awful films of Douglas Sirk—and the cleverness with which it attempts to reinvent the tired form of the melodrama, a reinvention that cannot completely succeed because it is too dotingly in love with the old-fashioned fashion of the form, with its structural and quasi-artistic conventions. One senses that Haynes has an overweening sympathy for his characters, like someone playing with dolls, painting a tragedy in too-lush colors for an audience overly conversant with tragedy's actual colors. He cannot restrain himself from proclaiming his cleverness and sympathy in various unsubtle ways—for instance, during the aforementioned scene wherein Cathy watches a young couple kissing on a bench, when understatement would have better served the dramatic purpose, he crowns her head with an exalted, saintly radiance, a heavy-handedness that acts to reduce what might have been poignant to the campy. The idea itself, of making a great Douglas Sirk movie, is wedded to triviality, and the notion of yet another film dealing with the fraudulence of suburban life, a list that includes such recent unfortunate entries as *Happiness* and the grotesquely pretentious *American Beauty*, borders upon thematic overkill. It's a near certainty that because of the power of its performances and—more significantly—because of Hollywood's embrace of movies that comment upon the glory days of the star system, *Far From Heaven* will receive a Best Picture nomination. Haynes well may deserve the award. It's been a bad year for movies. But my feeling is that the award he wanted to win was not this year's Oscar, but the Best Picture Award for 1956, and that ambition, which pervades the movie, limits the degree to which it can be considered a success.

Another new film that references—albeit somewhat less

devoutly—an old-fashioned type of narrative is Phillip Noyce's (*The Hunt for Red October, Clear and Present Danger*), remake of *The Quiet American*. Noyce's leisurely, understated version is redolent of 1970s filmmaking and hews far more faithfully in style and substance to the Graham Greene novel than did Joseph L. Mankiewicz's 1958 glossy disappointment...though neither explores as deeply as one might hope Greene's basic materials, i.e., the nature of American involvement in creating the circumstances that brought about the Vietnam War. Nevertheless, *American* stands as the best Graham Greene cinematic adaptation since Orson Welles' *The Third Man*, succeeding in evoking the overarching theme of all Greene's novels, the intertwining of coincidence and fate.

Like *Far from Heaven, The Quiet American* is a piece of technical virtuosity and this is in large part due to the efforts of two accomplished men: cinematographer Christopher Doyle, mostly known for his work with Wang Kar-Wai (*Chungking Express, In the Mood for Love*), and editor John Scott (*Sexy Beast*). Utilizing an impressive but always subtly managed array of camera movement and speeds and digital effects, Doyle summons up the lush, steamy, seductive atmosphere of Saigon circa 1952 with such potency, you can almost smell the perfume and the sewage, creating sumptuous images that Scott orchestrates into breathtaking passages of violence and romance. Against this beautifully executed backdrop, Noyce mounts the story of a love triangle that serves as a lens through which we are allowed to view a poorly lit corner of history, the transitional stage between the end of the French-Indochinese War and the beginning of the tragic American misadventure in Vietnam.

At the outset, the body of a young American, Alden Pyle (Brendan Fraser), is found in the river; an elderly, cynical journalist, Thomas Fowler (Michael Caine), is brought in to identify him. Here Noyce drops us into the past, telling the story in flashback, and we begin to learn how both men reached that moment. Pyle, who introduces himself as a doctor attached to the American Economic Mission, first encounters Fowler at breakfast at the Continental Paradise Hotel. In his blatant naïveté, his bumbling, sloganeering manner, Pyle is the perfect emblem of America during those days, giddy with post-war confidence, bluffly anti-communist, and having an aggressively childlike view of history. Fowler has a mistress, a beautiful Vietnamese woman named Phuong, whom he cannot marry because his wife will not grant him a divorce. Phuong (Do Hi Hai Yen) is a naïf whose chief worry is that she will wind up alone, as have so many Vietnamese women with foreign lovers, and when Pyle falls in love with her, he plays upon this fear, perceiving himself—as he does in all things—as righteous, refusing to admit any possibility that he may be errant in his judgments. Pyle is a fool, not evil, but when political goals are at stake—Greene and Noyce are telling us—perhaps the distinction between these two conditions is irrelevant, and as it becomes clear that Pyle is working in the interests of a shadowy force that is neither the French nor the Indochinese, we understand that for all his talk of good works and right action, this bungling, affable soul is an extremely dangerous man.

The political conflict deepens and Fowler's detachment from the turmoil around him takes a hit as he becomes aware of hideous atrocities committed against the civilian population and of the increasing American encouragement of and support for a certain Vietnamese general who poses an alternative to those offered by the colonialists and the communists. Despite their romantic rivalry, he and Pyle have developed a friendship, but eventually he tumbles to the connection between Pyle's American Economic Mission and the general. A terrorist bombing in the heart of Saigon causes Fowler to understand that Pyle is a complicitor in events and he commits to a course of action. The question arises, does he act out of moral concern or he is merely wounded by the fact that he has lost Phuong to the younger American?

Though he has not received due critical attention, Brendan Fraser is beginning to make a case for himself as one of the great supporting actors in the cinema today. In *Gods and Monsters* he provided the solid perch upon which Ian McKellen could deliver his quirky, birdlike performance. It is doubtful that the Oscar would be resting on McKellen's mantle had a less generous and genuine actor been in the subordinate role, and I was astounded when Fraser did not even receive a nomination for Best Supporting Actor. In *The Quiet American* he supplies a similar service for Michael Caine. Everything in Fraser's bulky, bearish delivery appears designed to focus us on Caine's subdued moral struggle, and it's quite possible that the end result will be much the same—an Oscar for Caine and a smattering of off-handed praise for Fraser. Be that as it may, the picture does belong to Caine. His portrait of Fowler must be judged among his most brilliant performances. From the bemused smiles that evidence his earliest reactions to Pyle to the horror he registers when he comprehends the ambiguity of his ultimate motivations, Caine conveys complexities of emotion with exquisitely nuanced gestures and expressions. Simply put, his achievement is remarkable.

As is that of the director.

It appears that Noyce, grown weary of blockbusters, pyrotechnics, CIA superheroes, and ham-sandwich leading men such as Harrison Ford and Val Kilmer, has decided to eschew the demands of commerce and to return to making the smaller, less commercially viable films that marked his early career. Along with *American*, 2002 will see the release of his Australian-set film, *Rabbit Proof Fence*, a story of three aboriginal girls kidnapped to serve as household menials who escape and make their way home across the Outback. *The Quiet American* may not fit the definition of a small film as regards budget and scope, but it is decidedly of questionable commercial potential. It has been sitting on the shelf for a year, obviously held back as a result of the events of 9/11, the thinking being that given the political climate following the destruction of the World Trade Center, Americans might not welcome a movie that portrays our nation's foreign policy in anything other than a glorious light. In a very real sense, the arbiters of taste in this country seem committed to sustaining in the general populace the same childish view of the world that afflicted Alden Pyle, and one wonders if any film that does not treat history in simplistic black-and-white terms will find a mass audience waiting to embrace it. Hopefully this is not the case. Hopefully movies like *The Quiet American*, movies that illuminate and inform and challenge the prevailing hot air blasts emanating from the political process, will be perceived as alternatives to idiocy and not as subversive statements. Hopefully those who see the film may be inspired to question if not to resist the heavy-metal red-white-and-blue cheerleading that may soon lead us into yet another uncertain foreign adventure. But as any number of Graham Greene's characters—men and women who have witnessed too much of the world to be deceived by it—might well have said, "Hope is a splendid thing so long as one does not believe in it."

THE ENVELOPE PLEASE...

Monster
Release Date: *December 24, 2003 Nationwide*
Director: *Patty Jenkins*
Screenwriter: *Patty Jenkins*
Starring: *Charlize Theron, Christina Ricci, Bruce Dern, Lee Tergesen*
Distributor: *New Market*
Review Date: *January 31, 2004*

I USED TO LIVE CLOSE BY THE LANDWARD end of a short dock on a saltwater inlet in Florida and every once in a while my neighbor would catch something off the dock that he couldn't eat—a stingray or some piscine mutant with deformed scales and flesh permeated by mercury—and leave it lying there to rot in the sun. Each time the Oscar nominations are announced, I have a flashback to those whiffs of weird spoilage. This year—whoo-eee!—it's extra pungent. Not that there aren't a number of worthy nominations. To mention a few: Naomi Watts and Benicio del Toro for *21 Grams*; Ben Kingsley and Jennifer Connolly for *House of Sand and Fog*; Peter Jackson for technical wizardry, if nothing else; and it's always good when Sean Penn, hands down the best actor of his generation, gets short-listed, even though on this occasion, it's for the wrong movie. But there are so many terrible nominations in 2004, if the list were actually a fish, it would weigh about a quarter-ton, have melted-looking skin (sort of like Charlize Theron in *Monster*), six or seven inflamed rectums, and a single horrid eye resembling a fried egg the size of a tractor tire.

The Best Picture category is especially putrid (though we should all cheer the omission from the list of Anthony Minghella's British All-Star, Southern-accent-impaired, romance-novel take on the Civil War, *Cold Mountain*). Leaving aside *The Return of the King*, which is less a movie than a three-hour tour of a Tolkien theme park, we have, to begin with, *Lost in Translation*, a not altogether incompetent existentialist parfait that effects a celebration of the soulfulness of two shallow and rather aimless people who are (1) isolated (more like imprisoned, we're supposed to believe) in a Tokyo luxury hotel; (2) suffocating in the grip of privilege; (3) too enervated to do other than indulge in self-pity; (4) terminally bored. The lead performances by Scarlett Johansson and Bill Murray are fine, even admirable, but the script plays like a pastiche of John Updike having a really bad day and, although we are persuaded by director Sofia Coppola's manipulative narration to share the characters' ennui and to mist up when they part—because, golly, they're just like us, you know, only richer—once the credits roll, the entire experience dissipates like a perfumed fart in a hurricane.

Master and Commander: The Far Side of the World is the best of the lot, a big ol' Boy Scout adventure that would have knocked my socks off when I was ten. Rousing PG-rated fun. Then there's *Seabiscuit*, a horse-racing biopic that has as much to do with the sport of kings as a can of Alpo has in common with Secretariat. It surely must have earned its nomination on the basis of the nostalgia factor, since it's almost indistinguishable from every other pile of heartwarming underdog slop we've had poured into our bowls since *Rocky* staggered up off the deck and clobbered Apollo Creed. It's comfort food of a particularly nutritionless variety. An inspirational sermonette expanded to two hours, brought to you courtesy of

Cheez Whiz and the good folks over at the Republican National Committee. Featuring Toby McGuire as a very large jockey and Jeff Bridges reprising his Tucker role as the Eternal Optimistic Spirit of Good-For-You American Commerce. My recommendation? Save your empty popcorn bag and keep it handy for when the violin section starts to soar and *Seabiscuit* comes pounding down the home stretch toward glory hallelujah, with every fiber of his equine being devoted to making America smile again and forget all about that nasty Depression, and this encourages you to think, by God, if that little horsie can overcome the odds, am I gonna let global warming and the Seven Plagues of Osama hamstring my hopes and dreams? Hell, no! So you rush on home, read The Little Engine That Could to the kiddies, then sit out on the back porch with your arm around your sweetheart and watch the evening sun decline though clouds of poison gas, with part of you saying, Lord, that is such a beautiful sight!, and the other part going, Yeah, but suck up too much of that crap, it's bound to make you hurl.

Which is why you need to hang onto that popcorn bag.

Last and most assuredly least, we have the sluggishly flowing, cliché-polluted *Mystic River*, Clint Eastwood's vastly over-praised tale of murder and retribution among the blue-collar Irish criminal class in Boston. Tedious and tensionless, the film is an exemplar of uninspired storytelling, having none of the leanness and vigor of superior Eastwood pictures such as *Unforgiven* and *The Outlaw Josie Wales*. If it were to be discovered that Clint has developed something incurable, I suppose that might explain *River*'s Best Director and Best Picture nominations. A little parting gift from the Academy. But how to explain its three acting nominations? Tim Robbins (Supporting Actor) once again exhibits the emotive range of a Lincoln penny, and Marsha Gay Harden (Supporting Actress) basically pops in for a cameo as Robbins' wife and does a fidgety-flighty thing that never alters its pitch. As for Best Actor nominee Sean Penn's eye-rolling, mane-tossing portrayal of a grieving father bent upon avenging his daughter's murder, it would have been more suited to the title role in the aforementioned *Seabiscuit*. In *21 Grams*, collaborating with talented young director Alejandro Innaritu, Penn's gift is on full display, beautifully nuanced, but here, apparently under orders to go for the overacting record, it's like he's performing in a Mr. Olympia pose-down, flexing every freakish muscle.

River is, plain and simple, a bad movie, and while it utilizes superior source material (Dennis Lehane's novel) and is far more atmospheric than Eastwood's recent crime movies, *Blood Work* and *True Crime*, it's no more spirited or accomplished. Many of the main characters lack a consequential plot function. As cops, Kevin Bacon and Laurence Fishburne do interviews, crack wise, and look despondent. Marsha Gay Harden blithers on to no appreciable effect and, as Penn's wife, Laura Linney seems to have no purpose other than to wear dresses, until the final five minutes when, with nary a hint of foreshadowing, she morphs into Lady MacBeth. The screenplay, itself Oscar-nominated, doesn't telegraph the ending, it trumpets it, and there is ample reason why the film failed to be nominated for best cinematography: attempting to create a feeling of oppression and gloom through the incessant use of blue filters has all the evocative subtlety of a child crayoning a black cloud over Mommy's head to signify that she's sad.

My favorite stinker of a nomination, however, has nothing to do with *Mystic River*, but derives from a movie that will doubtless earn the golden prize for its star.

If a used car salesman tells you the Beamer you're looking at was never driven over seventy, you can bet your body parts that the only time it ever dropped below seventy was when it was pulling into a parking garage. By the same rule, when large numbers of critics fall all over themselves in telling you that Charlize Theron's turn as Aileen Wuornos, the bottom-feeding hooker who serially killed seven of her johns along the blue highways of central Florida, is oh-so-much-more than a mere impression assisted by thirty extra pounds of Charlize and a Halloween Hall of Fame make-up job complete with a full set of snaggly brown teeth, well . . . what you're getting here is the standard-issue wave-your-hands-in-the-air-and-proclaim-the-miracle PR that always attends a beautiful actress donning a fright wig and a prosthetic device or two and laying on the histrionics until everybody shouts, Oscar! Oscar!, because they don't want to listen to her whine if they don't. It's the same-old, same-old. It's Nicole Kidman and her award-winning fake nose. It's Halle Berry impersonating a minimum-wage waitress. It's Hillary Swank disguised as a boy. Theron plays Wournos as she was not long before her execution, an unsightly caricature of a human being given to outbursts of fury and staring at the world through wide, unseeing eyes. The difficulty one has with that portrait is that *Monster* purports to show Wuornos at earlier stages of her life and it's tough to swallow that she was as thoroughly whack during those stages as she was at the end, that her madness didn't evolve from some slightly less dysfunctional state. It's not that Theron is awful—she's about as good as Berry and Kidman and Swank.

Which is to say, she's okay.

But *Monster Ball* and *Boys Don't Cry* were decent movies that supported their lead, and though *The Hours* was spotty at best, Kidman had some heavy-hitters giving her a leg up. *Monster*, on the other hand, is a tepid exploitation rape-and-murder flick that the Lifetime Network would be proud to give its television premiere, maybe leading off their Dangerous Woman Weekend during the May sweeps, where it'll fit in nicely with a couple of dozen less-expensive movies whose heroines are also driven into a life of degradation, pushed to the moral brink, steeped in a soul agony, and finally lash out at the evil men who have debased them, flaunting themselves naked and blood-spattered before our eyes. Such, more-or-less, is the picture Aileen Wuornos painted of her life and, though she changed her story often and ultimately came to recant everything she had said, this is also how director/scripter Patty Jenkins has chosen to depict her. The movie is an appeal for us to understand Wuornos, to feel her pain and acknowledge that she was molded into a monster, as if this would be somehow exculpatory. I suppose the case can be made . . . and I suppose a similar case can be made for most serial killers. That's scarcely a news flash and does nothing to elevate *Monster* above the level dictated by the lame-ass women-as-victims agenda of its script. The irony of the exercise is that Theron, who served as a producer on the project, did all that dog work and went through the whole Oscar-bait makeover thing in order to validate her credentials as a serious actress, to overcome the oppressive Hollywood masters who forced her into debasing hot-babe roles, and once she's completed her ritual transition from teary-eyed catatonic to award-acceptance elation, the chances are good she'll go back to making romantic comedies and devil movies and caper flicks and maybe become the new Bond girl, sinking back into the pack as have Berry and Swank.

I watched the Golden Globes the other night when Ms. Theron rehearsed the spontaneous reaction she'll perform again on Oscar night, because I enjoy observing the emotional rush actors get on seeing a plucky young millionairess cast off the vile chains of stereotyping that always ensnare great beauty and put herself in the way of earning even higher paychecks. My goodness! Meryl Streep was close to tears of joy and pride, and several other ladies were grabbing for their hankies, overborne by thinking about how poor Charlize suffered for her art, the trials she must have undergone in order to reach this blissful moment when she could be jumped into their sorority. (All that ugly fat she had to gain and those horrible teeth they made her wear! Her plight should have been brought to the attention of Amnesty International!) Looking around that glowing room filled with the painted, the dyed, and the surgically enhanced, I asked myself how in the hell could we have become so enamored of these self-absorbed mental defectives, and then, after answering my own question (sinister marketing forces, the dumbing down of the populace as a result of an insidious class war, etc.), it struck me that we shouldn't be passing out golden statues to these Hollywooden stiffs, but rather to those who are making the movie of the world, who energize the forces that have perilously retarded our culture and reduced our common focus to the superficial, who have transformed news into entertainment and vice versa, whose postmodern sensibilities have erased the lines between the fictive and the real.

We should officially anoint the Bush Administration to be a major studio and award them Best Picture, Best Director, Best Every Damn Thing for their thrilling blockbuster Operation Freedom (Best Score to CNN for their stirring theme), whereupon George W, our living national sequel, would rise thunderstruck and gaping from his seat, hands clasped to his head, unable to believe the generosity of the Academy, and then would rush onto the stage to accept the Oscar from Kevin Costner, who's had his forebrain removed so as to free up more hairy scalp to cover his bald spot. George would hold the statue down at his waist for a long moment, unable to tear his eyes away from it, like a boy staring at his first erection.

"My God!" he would say in an awestruck tone; then, with that familiar simian twinkle in his eye, he'd brandish the statue and add: "Talk about your weapon of mass destruction!"

This gets a nice laugh.

George shakes his head in wonderment. "There's so many people . . . I know I'm gonna forget 'em all. Dick Cheney. Dick, you're a mean ol' man! Yes, you are! You scared me sometimes. You really did . . . but I needed it. And John!" He points to John Ashcroft who's sitting down front, cradling the Best Supporting Actor Graven Image in his arms, trying to teach it the Ten Commandments. "You took so much pressure off with that loony-godboy act, John ol' buddy. Dressing up those statues out front of Justice was brilliant improv, man!" He puts a hand on his chest as if to calm his racing heart and blurts out the next few names. "Tom Selleck, Bruce Willis, Chuck Norris . . . Arnold. You made me believe I could swim in this ocean. Weezy Wright, Karl Rove, Paul Wolfowitz. When I talked about making a film in which we actually overthrew an evil empire and killed a buncha people, you didn't start throwing deficit figures at me; you said, W, follow your vision, we'll get you the money. I love you for that." He draws a deep breath, lets it out slow. "The boys over at the CIA. Sure, you took a big hit with Nine-Eleven, but you came back strong! And I'm proud of you. America's proud. And Colin Powell. Your testimony about Iraq's nucular capacity . . ." He grins broadly and winks. "Hey, you almost sold me!"

A big laugh erupts from the audience. George waits until it subsides. He's feeling it now, he's working the crowd. "Thanks to Sol, Rudy, and Sonya over at MCA. Ted Turner, Laura, Jesus, the Illuminati. Of course a huge thank-you has to go to the folks in black ops. I'd mention you boys by name, but that might get me suddenly un-elected, you know what I'm saying?"

A nervous titter ripples across the gathering and once it fades, George adopts a somber face and says, "The largest cast of extras in the history of motion pictures. You gave everything to your roles. Our victory here tonight is most of all your victory. We will never forget your sacrifice."

Cue standing ovation.

Cue Freedom Theme.

Standing in the front row, clapping his enormous hands in a ponderous mechanical rhythm redolent of a wind-up toy that has almost wound down, Governor Schwarzenegger beams. His perfect teeth resemble a row of tombstones in a mouse cemetery. Beside him, the once-beautiful Maria is openly weeping.

Where's that damn popcorn bag?

It's amazing what's happened to the real world, whatever the hell it used to be. Amazing that you can now give pretty much the same speech after winning an election as you do after being handed a small androgynous statue. Amazing that putting on and taking off weight has become a surefire track to the awards stand. Amazing that we can sit in our living rooms and be convinced that we're watching a war on the TV when all we see is an embedded reporter standing by a pile of dirt and telling us that nothing is happening. Amazing that the administration hired a marketing expert (the same who came up with the idea of embeds as a means of pretending to show us the war, as beautiful a sleight-of-hand as has ever been pulled on the American public) to handle their Pentagon briefings. Amazing that coherent story and well-defined character are no longer considered integral to the success of a motion picture . . .not if you've got enough cool CGI. Amazing that singers no longer need to sing well in order to gain fame and fortune; that novels are often written by the pre-literate; that Ben Affleck has a career other than in sales. Amazing that the truth can no longer set us free, because the truth doesn't grab good enough ratings. Amazing that Michael Jackson, Kobe Bryant, or Martha Stewart can lead the evening news. Amazing that yuppies are not an endangered species and that reality shows are not designed to cause their deaths. Amazing, the amount of crap we've been conditioned to swallow; amazing that we still say, "Yum." Amazing that . . .

. . . Well, at the moment I'm sitting on my sofa, glass of vodka in hand, and I'm watching MSNBC. Onscreen, a beautifully tailored Miss America-level brunette in a red sweater that's just a wee bit tight is standing by a display board upon which has been painted the crude representation of a racecourse. Velcroed to the racecourse are five cartoonish figures—the Democratic presidential candidates. They're mounted on red-white-and-blue donkeys. Their photo-real heads are too large for their bodies. A sign affixed to the top of the board reads DEMO DERBY. In the right-hand corner of the screen, there's an inset enclosing a live shot of some doofus wearing black-rimmed glasses and a bad suit. Every so often his mouth moves and, each time that happens, the brunette adjusts the position of one of the candidates' figures, moving it slightly forward or back. This is what currently passes for political analysis. I am not particularly amazed. I find myself becoming interested in the Demo Derby. I am content to watch the brunette reach like a fate onto the board and nudge the candidates in turn. Perhaps, I think, she's the one who's truly in control. Perhaps a spell has been cast and the world has become a magical place in which actors are gods and anchorpersons are their instruments and presidents are showbiz humps and all our troubles can be cured by topical remedies such as Viagra, Propecia, Rogaine, and smart-bomb surgical strikes. Perhaps ignorance has at last been proven to be bliss. Perhaps nothing should be thought of as amazing now that everything has come to smell like Oscar.

WEAPONS OF MASS SEDUCTION

The Passion of the Christ
Release Date: *February 25, 2004*
Director: *Mel Gibson*
Screenwriter: *Ben Fitzgerald, Mel Gibson*
Starring: *James Caviezel, Monica Bellucci, Sergio Robini*
Distributor: *Newmarket Film Group*
Review Date: *May 3, 2004*

The Big Bounce
Release Date: *January 30, 2004*
Director: *George Armitage*
Screenwriter: *Sebastion Gutierrez*
Source Writer: *Elmore Leonard*
Starring: *Owen Wilson, Morgan Freeman, Gary Sinise*
Distributor: *Warner Brothers*
Review Date: *May 3, 2004*

UNABLE TO LOCATE SADDAM HUSSEIN'S stockpiles of nuclear explosives, bacteriological agents, and poison gas, the Bush Administration has launched an offensive against a newly perceived threat to the American way of life. I am speaking, of course, about Janet Jackson's right breast. The moment Ms. Jackson's nipple-shielded love puppy bounded into view during the worldwide television broadcast of the Super Bowl halftime show, the administration, having had a less than successful several months in the War on Terror, announced the War on Impropriety, and shifted its most fearsome and reliable resource, The Army of Bigotry and Repression, into the fray, directing them not only to prevent further breast exposure, but to wage battle against Web porn, MTV, gay marriage, Howard Stern, Triple X motels, and all things that might subvert the American Dream, the cutting edge of which is currently on exhibition in the Middle East, doing God's work on behalf of the world's newest democracy.

Some of us, naturally, were amused. We had become somewhat inured to the depredations of Dubya and his legions of neocon orcs—amusement was a necessary refuge. It was a relief to take a cynical, soi distant view of the black-bone nightmare spell into which the Constitution was being reshaped. And so, as I watched one of our great senators speaking at the congressional hearings attendant upon the Awful Shame visited upon us by Justin and Janet, I found myself laughing uproariously when she declared herself to be vastly relieved that her children had been upstairs during halftime and thus had not been privy to the Horrid Revelation that might have stained their innocence, infected their behavior, and sullied their birthright. What, I wondered, did the Senator think her children were doing upstairs? Listening to Christian rock? It's far more likely that the little dicksenses were exploring their sexuality. And what does the Senator think would happen should her issue (or the issue of anyone else, for that matter) catch a glimpse of a 36-year-old gazonga? Would a juvenile form of stroke ensue? Would our kiddies be desensitized to the point of dysfunction and thereafter, upon seeing any breast, retreat into catatonia? Would their moral compass be so damaged that on reaching puberty they would immediately go breast-hunting with bow and arrow?

There I was, chuckling over these notions, when a particulate haze began to form in the midst of my living room and, before I could react, said haze coalesced into the form of a partially realized breast, a glandular incarnation of monstrous proportions complete with lifelike areola—a puckered, pinkish sunburst some three feet in diameter—that hovered above the floor, bobbling as if afloat upon choppy water. I was alarmed, and I grew increasingly alarmed when the breast, speaking through a mouth formed by the irising of the areola, intoned, "I am the Ghost of Mammaries Past. Follow me!"

With a delightful jiggle, the breast led me toward the kitchen door, bumped it open with a newly stiffened nipple, and I saw not stove and refrigerator and sink, but the bedroom of a nine-year-old tow-headed lad, Jason Pharb, who, having witnessed the unshelling of the Jackson hooter, sat on the edge of his bed, his mind reeling from the shock engendered by that nanosecond of pure tittage. I needed no tour conducted by the Ghost of Mammaries Future to see what lay ahead for young Jason: an embrace of the New Puritanism that inspires him to evolve into the first official neocon child evangel, appearing with such regularity on Scarborough Country, he's virtually made a citizen of that tiny, tedious nation; a celebrity adolescence during which he advocates chemical castration for teenagers in the name of a god he has invented, though his fans believe it's just good ol' Jehovah; fame and fortune follow, and—finally—a night when a maid or a houseguest stumbles upon a secret room in his mansion containing a long white table upon which rest dozens of silvery metal domes—room service food warmers—and beneath each one there lies a grisly relic of the obsession born during that long-ago Super Bowl halftime.

God knows how many pure-hearted American children have been turned down similar paths! The Ghost of Mammaries Present, another Z-cup hallucination, wanted to tell me exactly how many, but I hooked her bra strap (she was a chaste tele-friendly right-wing apparition) over a banister post and made my escape.

It seems more than a little odd that the political Right, their dull sensibilities stirred by the Jackson Nipple Incident and, shortly thereafter, stirred again by Mel Gibson's Whack-a-Savior flick, should choose the entertainment industry as a target upon which to vent their considerable spleen. Granted, Hollywood Babylon is one of their traditional targets, but over the past two decades or thereabouts, it has been something of a straw dog, because during that time the studios have proved themselves to be standard-bearers in the rabid anti-intellectualism that has brought the country to its current pass—though Barbra Streisand, Martin Sheen, and various other Hollywood figures support a leftist agenda, the thrust of the industry has been to employ its potent charms toward instilling in its audience a bedrock stupidity that would allow them to be manipulated by certain tones and colors conjoined with a handful of keywords, that will persuade them to accept without analysis a comic-book-level presentation of current events by the news media, and to endure the theft of their constitutionally guaranteed freedoms, their wages, and the quality of their futures, all the while smiling and nodding when they hear that all this is being done for their own good. It's quite possible that some movies and television shows do tend to encourage the inception of aberrant behavior in America's youth, but it's a dead certainty that these same productions are helping to anaesthetize an ever more manipulable and unquestioning populace, which—as far as the corporate movers and shakers are concerned—is just the ticket. I am not positing the existence of a vast right-wing conspiracy. Like the Left, the Right is not smart enough to be so organized. One need only look to our president and the marginally more clever clods that surround him to recognize that our country is not led by Einsteins, or even by Machiavellis, but by men who share the intellectual and psychological purview of your average assistant manager. Check out the video of the million-dollar-plus birthday party that indicted Tyco CEO Dennis Koslowski threw for his wife in Sardinia—the ludicrous faux-Roman decor (a kitschy Fifties-era take on decadence, complete with waitress nymphs and toga-wearing pool boys) serving as the backdrop for a Jimmy Buffet concert—and it becomes evident from this unimaginative excess that Koslowski and his peers are far from mental giants; they are slightly-smarter-than-average Joes whose ruthlessness and grasping natures have allowed them to master a certain style of acquisitiveness. No less could be said of rats. Judging from this and numerous other incidences of the bumbling arrogance that typifies the new ruling class, no great leap is required to infer that it's not human villainy that has conspired to lobotomize our culture—it is the tide of market forces sweeping across the centuries, a wave building and building until, at last, it seems ready to inundate us. The Right have simply been in a superior position to capitalize on the flood.

Motion pictures were originally perceived to be entertainment, secondarily as a new art form, but propaganda is their most natural use. The movie industry has, more-or-less inadvertently, done for the corpocracy what Leni Riefenstahl did for the Third Reich. Some of Hollywood's biggest hits (films like *Forrest Gump* and *American Beauty* for instance), have—if they do not qualify as straightforward propaganda—given voice to a palliative message that encourages their audience to accept the rule of the ordinary as if it were an eleventh commandment: Thou shall not think, and if thou dost think, thou shall not think analytically. Gump's "Life is just a box of chocolates" makes the same basic statement as Lester Burnham's posthumous reflection ("I wouldn't change a single thing") on his terrible and unfulfilling life. These films and those like them promote the trickle-down theory of happiness, of satisfaction, of accomplishment—we should be satisfied with what we have and not injure ourselves by aspiring too high. The wealthy and the highly placed will take care of us if we just stay the course, ride out the storm, whatever cliché applies. Everything happens for a reason. Things are as they are. If life hands you lemons, make lemonade. It's the American way, okay? They further influence us to identify with weak, hapless figures (in the films mentioned, a mentally challenged man and a disaffected neurotic), whose endurance in the face of tribulation, we are asked to believe, speaks to our innate nobility of spirit or our uniqueness or some other suitable-for-framing sloganized hoo ha, and not, as is actually the case, to our gullibility. It's a stratagem that helps to persuade us that we are powerless. Most studio films about heroes don't celebrate the average person transcending normal expectations, but deal with superheroes, whether costumed like Spiderman or non-costumed types like the governor of California and the Rock; and if they do portray ordinary heroes, those heroes usually die, because the idea of sacrificing oneself for some idiot-with-a-title's latest whim is just dandy with the Guys in the Big Chairs. They have a never-ending need for cannon fodder and they love it when we embrace the thought that it's ennobling to die for a cause—it's the one myth of transcendence of which they approve. Corporate Christianity makes promises to its martyrs that aren't much different than those made by radical Islam—we simply don't have that many virgins to pass around.

Speaking of corporate Christianity, it might be of moment to examine *The Passion of the Christ*, a picture that strikes me as being the *Rocky* of religious movies. Rocky's fistic battle against Apollo Creed was a fight that, in real life, would have been stopped in the first round, or—if it had not been stopped—would likely have terminated with the death of both combatants; correspondingly, had Jesus taken a beating like that portrayed in *Passion*, he wouldn't have managed two steps up Calvary. One of the things that astonishes me about the phenomenon of *Passion* is that you will often hear people marvel at Jesus' resilience in the movie, saying, "I don't know how he kept getting up," having lost track of the reality that it was a motion picture they watched and not an portal opening through the fabric of time onto the event itself. I think this reaction is in part due to the fact that films like *The Passion of the Christ* paint the concept of powerlessness in seductive colors by making it inclusive, a club that wants us for members and whose central figures transform powerlessness into a radiant and alluring virtue, one that may have a confusing effect upon those whose immunities to such appeals are underdeveloped. The pertinent propagandic thrust of *Passion* is not whatever dollop of anti-Semitism it embodies (that's a bonus treat); no, like all good propaganda, it enjoins, it summons, it enlists, it plays upon our central hopes and fears, and although the cause *Passion* espouses is ostensibly a fundamentalist form of Christianity, this is Christianity wedded to a corporate purpose, Christianity in the functional employ of the state. Christianity utilized as secular mind control. Whatever Mel Gibson intended by the film is unimportant. Mainstream movies have become other than what they were intended to be—most flow along a cultural channel dredged by years and years of a ceaselessly digging economic imperative, adding their momentum to the whole; they are every bit the work of the culture as they are of an auteur or a studio. Thus the message of *Passion*—the Christian portion of that message—has been co-opted, its values debased and utilized for the purpose of merchandising. We are, after all, talking about a movie that's on its way to doing half-a-billion at the box office and is responsible for selling who knows what quantity of necklaces and photo books and so on. One might say (and many have) that its success comes as a result of people crying out for movies of this kind, but while there may be some truth to that viewpoint, it is undeniably true that the marketing of the picture, not to mention its structure and focus, have all acted to downgrade Jesus' own message to a sidebar issue and that the success of the film owes every bit as much to its subliminal persuasions. Dependent upon one's point of view, it will be either a depressing or a bleakly comic moment when—years from now—those among us who were seduced into the confession of past crimes by the gestalt surrounding Gibson's movie are in their cells, counting the days to freedom or awaiting execution, cut off from the center of the culture, distanced from its effects, and *The Passion* comes on the small screen, perhaps its network debut. I imagine bewilderment will be the initial reaction, bewilderment funded by the lack of feeling they derive from this second coming, this viewing behind walls that shield them from society's radiations. I imagine their next reaction may be something on the order of, "I screwed my life up over this (epithet)?," followed by an orgy of destruction that earns them thirty days in isolation.

First-run movies that once opened in vast rococo downtown palaces, each new opening an event of sorts, now flicker into being inside characterless little screening rooms in the midst of strip malls, as one with and surrounded by the hamburgers and fish sandwiches and soft drinks and preservative-laced chocolates with which they have merchandising tie-ins. This is entirely appropriate, for most movies are themselves no more than tiny portions of artificial flavor, mildly addictive chemicals, and ersatz food substitutes enclosed in cheap, bright packaging. Watching a film such as, say, *The Big Bounce* in any setting more grand than the egg carton where I experienced it would be akin to breaking out your best china to present a serving of Chicken McNuggets.

The Big Bounce is a perfect example of post-millennial Hollywood banality, a product designed to be acceptable to as many varied palates as possible. Cinematic Cheez Whiz. It has a certain market luster, being based on an Elmore Leonard novel, yet it typifies that most potent of propagandas, propaganda without any message, or rather whose only message is to pacify, to soothe with stress-free, non-threatening non-meaning. It's negligible, leaving no more than a faint, sweet aftertaste. A remake, the original being a terrible 1969 movie starring Ryan O'Neal, it has a cast that includes a young male lead (Owen Wilson) with a good deal of charm, a young model-turned-actress (Sara Foster), and a venerable character actor or three (Morgan Freeman, Harry Dean Stanton,

Willie Nelson). It occupies a place in the tradition of the comic-noir film, a genre that Hollywood has not completely forgotten how to make, and its director, Geoffrey Armitage, has previously made a couple of good films that roughly conform to that genre, *Miami Blues* and *Grosse Pointe Blank*. Lastly and most significantly, its script has that peculiar leached quality symptomatic of having been reworked, tweaked, and re-tweaked by serial hacks until it has become the screenwriting equivalent of a pretty child with a crooked spine, a feebly beating heart and no discernable brain function. It does not essay to challenge our stupor or ruffle our sense of well-being. That it did not succeed at the box office is immaterial—ten minutes after it vanished from the theaters, another similar vacuous two-hour stretch of happy colors and nutritionless dialog was slotted into the multiplexes and had a thirty-million-dollar opening—everything is positioning. If the proles don't fancy their food substitute in a pineapple-colored wrapper, they'll love it in cherry pink.

There is a plot, or rather the remnant of a plot—the original Leonard plot having been deconstructed. Jack Ryan (Wilson) is a drifter who passes his days committing small-time robberies and serving as a construction worker for a real estate developer, Ray Ritchie (Gary Sinise)—he's building a hotel on a section of the North Shore of Hawaii sacred to native Hawaiians. After assaulting his foreman with a baseball bat, Ryan is befriended by Walter Crewes (Freeman), the judge who handles his arraignment. Crewes offers Ryan a job at his resort and there he meets Nancy (Foster), Richie's live-in girlfriend—she has a plan to steal 250K from Ritchie and thinks Ryan's just the guy to help her. Of course there are twists and turns, but such narrative complexity is not essential to *The Big Bounce*. Nor is acting, nor is any other dramatic element traditionally accessible to criticism. This movie is about its attitude, an amiable smarminess—it celebrates amorality, sexual promiscuity, and any number of neocon no-nos. It has approximately as much weight as would a perfumed fart, a pastel gas loosed into several thousand theaters at once, a weapon of mass seduction designed to render us conscious though not alert. If the moral police are looking for a deadly threat to the purity of our nation, *The Big Bounce* and its amoral ilk—movies in which perverts and criminals are treated like charming, quirky, relatively harmless uncles and cousins, objects that inspire amusement, not scorn—should serve to jump their threat levels into the red and send them scurrying for the duct tape, because this bland effluvium of the culture is, like a candy-colored smog, suffocating our thought, polluting our will, and muffling our vital impulses. Yet we hear no Christian outcry, no Congressional bleating, no pundit-launched belches of indignation regarding such movies. Breasts and sex are no big deal to us. The imagery of the breast can be seen everywhere in America and sexuality is the foundation of the vast majority of the ads that are hourly beamed into our consensus cerebral cortex. How many times has a breast slipped free of a tank top or a bra on America's Funniest Home Videos , the nipple obscured by a little blurry patch? Our general reaction to those displays—no less gratuitous, albeit far less frequent than the ten thousand similarly blurred replays of Janet Jackson's passion pillow shown on the local and national news, each repeat delivered by a smirking anchor—was laughter.

Why, then, all the furor in the wake of the Jackson Nipple Incident?

Because when Justin Timberlake ripped away Janet Jackson's bodice, it broke the flow of the programming; it interrupted the message that streams unendingly into our brains from every broadcast source. An unexpected oscillation in the Great Hum, it woke us to the irony of our fate. We sensed a wrongness. Naturally we misinterpreted that feeling—most of us, at any rate—and blamed Jackson, MTV, gay marriage, Howard Stern, et al. We did not stay awake long enough to home in on the actual culprit. The signal was too quickly restored. For an instant we may have understood that we were victims of a greater scourge than that pointed out by Colin Powell's prudish get. Like a lab monkey whose drugs have been cut off, the culture yammered and lashed about until its fear had been channeled into an appropriate response. Soon the tubes will be re-inserted, the drugs will kick back in, the monkey will be pacified, the committees will make their reports, and, gradually, titty bars and porn shops and Howard Stern and everything that has been lumped into the Bushian "... they're evil ..." category along with Saddam and steroids and smart-ass reporters and licorice gummy bears, will once again be blended into the American mix...or maybe not. Maybe this time good will triumph and the culture will go all-the-way Orwellian. It wouldn't take much. We're already an inch away from Anti-Sex Leagues and Two Minute Hates and the Ministry of Truth and Double-Speak.

For the sake of argument, let's say you're awake. Marginally; briefly; but awake nonetheless. Soon you'll switch on the TV or visit the multiplex or pop a game into the Playstation, hook yourself up to some dispenser of corporate juice, and then everything will be fine. Before you do that, however, you might want to take a look around, maybe make a few notes on the reality you're preparing to escape, just on the off-chance case you're trapped for the rest of your days inside a bland pink bubble that enforces a bovine indifference. Here's what you'll see if you do. Global warming? Uh-huh. The ice caps are melting. This April, the mercury hit 100 degrees in LA. Nuclear proliferation? You betcha! Pakistan, India, Iran, North Korea and, coming soon, maybe Al Qaeda. The price of gas is at an all-time high. The economy is teetering on a knife-point. We are at war with zealots intent upon blowing us up either piecemeal or, if Allah permits, in big bunches. Occasionally, following cabinet meetings, John Ashcroft will sit at the piano to accompany Condi Rice as she sings gospel songs. Our president talks to God.

Got the picture? Okay. Now, how about a video? *The Big Bounce*? Cool. Owen Wilson. Mmmm ... He's funny. Sara Foster.

She has terrific breasts. Hawaii looks post-card pretty. All those beaches and palm trees and green hills and everything. Maybe someday you'll go there on vacation. That would be really, really cool. Something's troubling you, but it can't be anything important.

You are getting sleepy . . .

Ravings

LITTLETON FOLLIES

DURING THE DAYS FOLLOWING THE MASSACRE at Columbine High School, I was laid up with back problems, watching through a haze of Vicodin as the media vultured down onto the community of Littleton, Colorado, snapping up every least scrap of emotion and rendering it juiceless, trying to hide their lust for telegenic survivors behind unconvincing masks of piety and woe. Pundits of every imaginable stripe began popping up with the frequency of maggots in a slaughterhouse dumpster, seeking to place blame for the tragedy (according to their political agenda) on video games, the lack of a stringent dress code, violent films, the song stylings of Marilyn Manson, the abandonment of prayer in schools, the availability of automatic weapons, and so on. There were ex-DAs and prominent defense lawyers; psychiatrists with a book to hump; grief counselors; gun enthusiasts; Hollywood producers; religious leaders; politicians by the bushel; and actors. Oh, yeah! How can the nation possibly recalibrate its moral compass without hearing from great intellectuals like. . .Charlton Heston. Ol' Charlton's been my favorite pundit ever since his Gulf War debate on CNN with British journalist Christopher Hitchens, a titanic struggle during which Hitchens challenged Heston to prove his expertise by naming the Gulf states. Charlton did not do the right wing proud; unnerved by his derisive opponent, he managed to name only three.

At any rate, my reaction to this fiesta of punditry came in the form of a Vicodin-induced flash-dream heavily influenced by Gary Larson's late lamented Far Side strip. The dream was basically a single image: an enormous herd of cows, on the outskirts of which two wolves dressed in black trench coats were engaged in picking off a few strays. In the foreground two especially pompous-looking cows were holding converse, and one was saying to the other, "I blame it all on the moral decay of the culture."

That appears to be the consensus of the pundits, that the moral decline of the American culture was the primary causal agent driving Eric Harris and Dylan Klebold over the edge. I have something of a problem with that conclusion. . .though I might feel better about it if the word "decline" were changed to "sickness" or "vacancy" or some such. The concept of the moral decline presupposes the existence of its opposite, but when, pray tell, was our culture ever in a state of moral ascendancy? Certainly not in my lifetime. I suppose we were on the right side in WWII, but a war fought in defense of life and liberty hardly qualifies as a moral Everest. How about the Depression? The Roaring Twenties? The period of Westward expansion, with its slaughter of Native Americans and rampant lawlessness? The Civil War era? Slavery Days? Go all the way back to the beginning of the nation, back to the Declaration of Independence—a document that, no matter its worth, was drafted in large part by slave-owning tax evaders with undeniably self-serving motives—and you'll be hard pressed to find a period that wasn't marked by the same brutality, base motives, and indifference to suffering that flourish in our times. There may well have been a stronger sense of family and community in the past, and that may have helped restrain some of the darker urgings of human nature, but video games are hardly the cause of its erosion. Population explosion, the technologies of rapid travel and communications—indeed, all myriad incidences of cultural evolution—have put the days of quilting bees and barn-raisings behind us for good. And, in any case, however much those forces have transformed the world around us, they have not had any significant effect upon our essential natures. We remain the same hoping, grasping, desperate creatures that we have always been, capable of the same sins and virtues, both admirable and despicable. Our culture is merely a symptom of our human truth. It does not define us—we define it.

What, I wonder, were your high school days like? I attended Seabreeze High in Daytona Beach, Florida during the 60s, period which—though currently viewed with some nostalgia through the media lens—was basically a time of casual destruction (both in a personal and geopolitical sense) and vapid excess. The student body of Seabreeze was mostly white, mostly middle to upper-middle class, with a few black kids, even fewer Hispanics. Cliques abounded. Jocks were at the top of the food chain, geeks and people of color at the bottom. Bullying, taunting, and physical abuse were commonplace. I recall sitting in the cafeteria, watching as jocks entertained themselves by rolling dimes down a long table toward a group of Jewish students, betting on which one would make a grab for the coins. I recall beatings, racist attacks, sexual assaults, etc., etc., many of which were reported to the administration, which did nothing about them. Then as now, the basic job of a high school administrator was to maintain the status quo, to be a kind of Darwinian hall monitor, overseeing the survival of the fittest. If a few geeks and blacks and Latinos took a physical and/or psychological beating along the way, well, that's just the way it crumbled, right? Conformity was rewarded. Non-conformity was bad. . .maybe even evil. In essence, Seabreeze was a Tek-9 and a smattering of pipe bomb technology short of being Columbine South.

Judging by my experience, and by those of others, it doesn't seem that the nature of the pressures upon high school students have changed that much over the years. And I don't believe that video games and gory films and shock rock have done all that much to amp up the blood and thunder of childish fantasies. The flood of dark imagery washing over us through the Internet and movies may have had an exacerbating effect on kids with violent tendencies, but my own boyhood fantasies, conceived in a Doom-free environment, were thoroughly vicious, vindictive, and mean-spirited to a fault. The main influence on them was a physically abusive father whose easy way with belts, electrical cords, tree branches, and whatever else fell to hand bred in me a lust for brutality that resulted in hundreds of fights and inspired me to carry a knife well into my adult years. That I failed to kill someone—or be killed—was a matter of sheer luck. It's like Henry Jenkins (an MIT professor and expert on popular culture who recently testified at the Congressional hearings inspired by the Columbine massacre) has said: "Reality trumps media images every time. We can shut down a video game if it is ugly, hurtful, or displeasing, but many teens are required to return day after day to schools where they are ridiculed and taunted and sometimes physically abused by their classmates."

Jenkins' statement echoes the suicide note left by Eric Harris, which reads as follows:

"By now, it's over. If you are reading this, my mission is complete. . .Your children who have ridiculed me, who have chosen not to accept me, who have treated my like I was not worth their time are dead. THEY ARE FUCKING DEAD...Surely you will blame it on the clothes I wear, the music I listen to, or the way I choose to present myself, but no. Do not hide behind my choices. You need to face the fact that this comes as a result of YOUR CHOICES. . .

Parents and teachers, you fucked up. You have taught these kids not to accept what is different. YOU ARE IN THE WRONG. I have taken their lives and my own—but it was your doing. Teachers, parents, LET THIS MASSACRE BE ON YOUR SHOULDERS UNTIL THE DAY YOU DIE."

To my knowledge, Harris's note has been reprinted only once before, that in the Rocky Mountain News, and considering the high profile of the story, this at first struck me as odd. On second though, however, I realized that the explanation of the massacre offered by Harris and Professor Jenkins, the notion that, "Reality trumps media images every time," was not what the media or the politicians wanted to hear. It's much sexier, much more facile, to point at a spot of decay on a leper's cheek and shout, "Unclean!" than it is to work quietly and diligently on finding a cure. And so, knowing that such simplistic reactions would play to the groundlings and do good things for their polls, the leaders of our nation, almost as one, rose with evangelic intensity to denounce video shooter games and Marilyn Manson (who has far more Alice Cooper than Kurt Cobain in him) and Hollywood gore, going so far as to draw idiotic distinctions between morally uplifting carnage (Saving Private Ryan and Clear and Present Danger = Gooood!) and the kind of blood and guts that undermines the truefine spirit of our nation's youth (Casino and Scream = Baaaad!).

I'm always amazed by the tolerance of the American public for the sort of Bad Breath Committee on Armchair Disarmament and/or Quasi-Spiritual Reform such as is now playing to SRO audiences in Washington, D.C. Maybe it's comforting somehow, all that pompous bluster and flatulence echoing through the marble halls. Maybe it has the soothing effect of a mantra. But this particular version of the old standard has been made especially nauseating in my view thanks to the gloomy, rhinoceros-like presence of William Bennett, the nation's self-appointed moral policeman, a man to delights in referring to his days of public service when he was—as he likes to call himself—"drug czar." (And what a bang-up job he did solving that crisis, huh, folks?) Bennett, who has discovered that one can make quite a nice living by being a professional prude, often delivers his neo-Puritan cant with a lugubrious spite that has caused me to wonder at times if this blue-serge-suited tub of goo isn't really Sheriff Andy's Aunt Bea made up to play Cotton Mather in Mayberry's annual Segregation Day Festival. During the current hearings, it has been Bennett's role to show edited clips from films such as The Basketball Diaries and Scream, intoning lines such as "Have we seen enough? Is that enough for you?", while women hide their eyes and senators shake their heads ruefully, as though unmanned by the recognition that this vile pornography could have been produced in the Land of the Free. It is a proceeding reminiscent in its emotional falsity and specious political intensity of that revival-like declaration-of-war scene in the Marx Brothers' Duck Soup. Watching on C-SPAN, I kept expecting one of the senators (Lieberman, perhaps) to put on blackface, drop to his knees in the aisle and offer up a soliloquy beginning with the words, "Lawsy, Lawsy, what's we gwine do now?" backed up by a chorus of his colleagues humming "Swing Low, Sweet Chariot," with every now and then a shouted "Amen!"

The chances that anything salient in the way of reform will emerge from this Congressional minstrel show, or from the so-called "moral summit" sponsored by the White House, are slim and none, and—to quote Don King—slim just left town. Professor Jenkins reports that one senator put forward the notion that what was needed was not gun control, but (heh heh heh) "goth control," thereby displaying a near-total ignorance of the Goth subculture, and ignoring the fact that neither Harris nor Klebold was a Goth. Other senators enjoyed making homophobic jokes about Marilyn Manson, the "is it a he or she" kind of thing. Jenkins notes that these comments were likely similar to those leveled at Klebold and Harris in the halls of Columbine. By implication, Jenkins suggests that the senators themselves may once have been successful high school kids, clique-dwellers who lorded it over their less fortunate peers, and that—most pertinently—embedded in the traditions they strive to maintain through the legislative process is something akin to the high school hierarchy of jocks and geeks. It's not a difficult leap to make. The poet Allen Ginsberg once described America as "the vast high school," and viewed in light of the petty self-absorption of national concerns, the shallowness of out focus on glittering celebrity and trendiness, the unrelenting banality of our leaders, the image has come to seem increasingly apt.

Over the past twenty years I've watched American presidents go to war in places like Panama, Somalia, Iraq, Grenada, et al., employing billions of dollars' worth of explosives and other forms of technology against countries with marginal capacities for self-defense. As regrettable as these exercises may have been in their own right, they have been made even more so by the media's treatment of them. It's not the war coverage itself I'm speaking about—it's the base motivation that commentators have ascribed to the presidents involved. George Bush needed to prove he wasn't a wimp. Reagan had to distract attention from the Iran-Contra scandal. Clinton bombed Iraq to get the nation's mind off his infidelities. Whether or not these assertions are accurate is certainly relevant to the subject at hand, but even more relevant is the way in which the assertions were made—off-handedly, blithely, sometimes jokingly, as if the act of bombing a civilian population or of killing more than 4,000 Panamanians in order to arrest a man who had not yet been charged with a crime were, more or less, pranks. Reprehensible, but pranks nonetheless, and to be expected from a president under heavy domestic pressures. This pervasive and almost fondly shaped image of the American president as a roguish bully with a pocketful of testosterone, tough-talking but always ready with a quip, like across between David Letterman and Teddy Roosevelt on steroids, an image recast again and again by Chairman Channel Twenty-Five—this has surely had at least as much subversive effect upon the nation's moral climate as have video games and slasher flicks. Like the man said: Reality trumps media images every time.

Whatever went wrong in the heads of Eric Harris and Dylan

Klebold cannot be explained by their attraction to shooter games or death metal, or by any of the simplistic answers put forward by the pundits. One cannot logically blame the sickness of the culture for a specific act of violence, and then claim that if one or two elements of that culture were excised all will be well. The culture is too large, too interpenetrating, to respond to such primitive surgery. We may certainly examine the question of whether popular culture is having a deleterious effect upon the citizenry or not, but we need to approach the matter calmly, deliberately, and without recourse to political agenda. Unfortunately, given the current national temperature, such a rational approach is probably impossible. If it were possible, however, I firmly believe we would discover that whatever has gone wrong with our culture has been going wrong for a long, long time, and that only recently have the symptoms of the affliction grown sufficiently pronounced to provoke our alarm. And I bet we would find that the causes of youth violence in cases like Littleton have a lot more to do with serotonin deficiencies, pre- and post-natal care, early childhood experiences and nutrition, the over-prescription of antidepressants, parental dysfunction, lack of mentoring, and similar socio-biological factors than they do with all the really cool causes du jour like black lipstick, gypsy curses, and The Evil That Is N'SYNC.

But the sad truth is, now that dead have been buried and the funerals broadcast to the world, the story of the Columbine massacre is heading for the back pages. I suppose we can expect the usual blahblahblah to be modified by sanctimonious calls to set political differences aside and focus on the problem. We expect symposia to be held, grants to be handed out, presidential task forces to be mounted. We can expect civil lawsuits, a few last tabloid surprises, and commissions to report to Congress as part of what will be called a "rigorous national dialogue." But can we expect any vital change? Any steps taken to create a healthier high school environment, or a healthier cultural climate in general?

I doubt it.

And if that's the case, if we let this moment pass without substantive reaction. . .well, to paraphrase Eric Harris, let the next massacre be on our shoulders until the day we die.

*Originally published by **Event Horizon**.*

BRIGHT LIGHT CITY GONNA KNOCK ME OUT: MIKE TYSON AND THE NEVADA BOXING COMMISSION

CAN ANYBODY TELL ME WHY the mean lady from *The Weakest Link* was sitting in with the Nevada Boxing Commission on January 29th? Her hair wasn't as red as it appears on network TV, but I could have sworn it was her. Sure looked to me like she was dying to get all gussied up in black vinyl and give Mike Tyson a pants-down spanking.

Maybe what Iron Mike needs is a little Victorian discipline.

Who knows? A couple of weeks on a short leash trailing behind Mistress Ayoub or Agwe or whatever the mean lady's name was, might be the most effective training he ever had. Maybe French-kissing her high-heel sneaker every night before curling up at the foot of her bed would put him in touch with his feminine side.

Scary thought, that.

Frankly I don't care if I ever see Mike Tyson fight again, because he's become a bore, but the exercise in sanctimony performed by that august body, the Nevada Boxing Commission, was much more of an atrocity than Tyson's quasi-rumble with Lennox Lewis and friends before the press in New York City. There was Dr. Flip

Homansky, ring doctor to the stars, doing his Sensitive Nineties Guy impression and evoking memories of Nancy Reagan by saying with a look of pale regret writ large upon his face, "It was just time that someone said. No."

Gosh, Flip.

That statement's right up there in its simple-minded perspective with, "Can't we all just get along?"

(I think Wink Martindale with a fake goatee should play you in the movie.)

Then there was Bailey, the new guy on the commission, with his brow-furrowed ultra-sincerity and that I-really-want-to-understand-you-Mike spiel—the man's apparently watched way too many Richard Dreyfus flicks.

Tyson himself, appearing old and tired (make that very old and very tired), overweight and sad, promised solemnly to be a good boy and never do it again. "It" being anything that the *Weakest Link* lady might disapprove of, which—judging by her clenched demeanor—probably included the thinking of impure thoughts.

And his droning gray eminence of a lawyer doing that logically-evasive-yet-somehow-forthcoming lawyer thing we've all come to loathe and love courtesy of *LA Law, Law and Order, The Practice,* and the Clinton administration . . . that was sweet, huh? Even his suit looked like it had died of boredom.

It was, in sum, a lounge act from hell, far less entertaining than the usual lame dance number featuring bare-chested gay guys armed with teensy whips chasing around half-naked hookers pretending to be ponies to some marshmallow disco tune, while a seventy-year-old Jewish comedian wearing a sombrero tells sixty-year-old fart jokes.

But no doubt it played in Peoria.

And this, the applause emanating subsequently from the heartland, helps to convince me that the commission's vote to deny Mike Tyson a boxing license in the state of Nevada—more pertinently, in the suddenly family-oriented enchanted kingdom of Las Vegas—was in essence a marketing decision.

Since the tragedy of last September 11, our country's self-image has been transformed from a brawling, confusing *menage a* 300 million into a red, white, and blue poster for noble enterprise and enduring freedom, with pre-pretzel George W. playing the fife, head wrapped in a bloody bandage, and ol' Enron-loving Dick Cheney waving a tattered battle flag, leading a parade of soldiers, paperboys, waitresses, factory workers, farmers, et al, black and brown and white together, all with shining countenances and all fervently committed to spreading the gospel of the American Dream to the ends of the earth. Even junkies and armed robbers, poltroons and deviants of every stamp, are now given to sporting flag pins and pasting anti-Osama stickers on their bumpers. But while the war on terrorism is a commitment worthy of our passion, the fallout from the war effort is strictly commercial. Patriotism is once again box office. Morality sells. Simple values are in vogue. No matter what your belief as to how deep a hold these values and passions have on the American public, it's plain that profit-taking and exploitation are, as always, also in vogue. Thus it is my fervent and deeply held belief that the Nevada Boxing Commission, after receiving counsel from various and sundry millionaires with vested interests in the outcome of their deliberations, recognized that the quick hit of 200 million that would be generated by Tyson vs. Lewis was small potatoes by contrast to the long-term gains that might be accrued by consolidating Las Vegas' image as oasis of family fun, and that this, not any semblance of a moral consideration, informed their decision. And it was apparent from watching the commission in action that this decision had been made long before their ludicrous dog-and-pony show.

Perhaps they acted with some reluctance. Two hundred million in hand is a great temptation. But they did so realizing that they could not afford to swim against the tide of generic media-sponsored virtue that is washing shore-to-shore, and were therefore forced to have faith that this tide will continue to run long enough for their judgment to show a profit. Given the public's short attention span, it's unlikely that their faith will be rewarded.

Though the four members of the commission who voted against the issuance of a license to Tyson have assured us that their decision was based not upon the dust-up with Lewis in New York, but upon their concerns over Tyson's pattern of behavior during the past year, this is patently false. Nary a whisper of said concern was heard prior to the press conference. Everyone knew a license would be issued. But after the press conference, once the media had freshly demonized Tyson, portraying him as a creature of darkness, yet another insane adherent of Islam, the members of the commission were on the tube night and day, expressing their angst over the vast moral dilemma with which they had been confronted.

And now, out there in the hinterlands, solid middle-of-the-road citizens are saying to themselves, Y'know, now they kicked that no-good expletive deleted outa the place, maybe it's time I took granny and the kids to Las Vegas for some good ol' All-American Keno and craps.

At least such is the commission's hope.

There is no doubt that to a great degree Mike Tyson brought all this down on himself, that he enabled the commission's hypocrisy by his continued malfeasance. Surely he and his advisors understood the tenor of the times; surely they understood that Tyson's image was such that even the slightest misstep would create a media furor and cause him to be cast in the worst possible light. If, as has been suggested, the display of testosterone by Tyson, Lewis, his bodyguards, hairdresser, dogwalker and best friend Pete at the press conference was a staged event, Tyson's advisors should have kept its dire potentials in mind and never have bought into it, knowing the volatility of the circumstance. I have no personal knowledge of Tyson, and as stated, I don't care if I ever see him fight again, because his shtick has become tiresome and he's no longer much of a fighter. (Then neither do I care if I ever see Lennox Lewis or any other of the current crop of heavyweights fight again, for more-or-less the same reasons.) Whether he is man or man-beast is beyond my capacity to determine--I am not so prescient or well-grounded in the study of psychology as are, it would seem, those journalists who assess the measure of his soul on a daily basis. Obviously Tyson has problems, but many athletes have had disturbing histories and, rightly or wrongly, have been granted leniency under the law and the absolution of the media. But Tyson has never warranted this tender treatment. He is the Bad Man from the Streets and, as such, plays into the stereotypes that fund a reflexive judgment on the part of the fools who command the bully pulpits along press row.

It's quite possible that Tyson is a terminal asshole who is dangerous to himself and others, but that fact, if true, should not occlude the ultimately more salient fact that those who sit in judgment upon him, be they members of the Nevada Boxing Commission or gentlemen of the press or ravers on call-in shows, are for the most part motivated to damn him not because he is who he is, but because they are who they are. Whether they are purely cynical in their stance or are giving voice to a morality they glean from television and have learned to parrot, or be they the so-called opinion-makers who preach only what they believe their audience can accept, only what they want to hear, Tyson has become for them all a kind of pornography. They can't wait for him to fuel their arousal, to provoke an incident that will allow them to vent their crypto-sexual outrage. He is the target of a national focus that longs for him to perpetrate a final tragic act, a murder or a self-immolation of some sort, and being at the center of this million-eyed stare, perhaps he will be prompted to satisfy that longing. For it is clear that whatever the extent of his personal darkness, the nature of his culpability, the quality of his rage and duplicity, he is tormented by this focus, challenged and even goaded by it. Perhaps one day soon he will provide us with the profound yet fleeting gratification of seeing his celebrity displayed post-mortem in all its bloody and broken hubris on the cover of a dozen tabloids. The demon whom we have exhorted and exalted, whom we have licensed to play out his creaturely life before our eyes, now brought low not by his actions alone, but also by the radiation of our distaste for this charmed and charmless icon that we have partially created out of our need for demons, for figures that have the power to eat our sin, to absorb our own darkness and shape it into a form that we feel comfortable in condemning.

What the Nevada Boxing Commission did on January 29th is, in the end, irrelevant. The fight will or will not take place. Tyson will likely die horribly or diminish into a pitiable state. September 11th will fade into history and be remembered on national occasions with speeches and shows of grief, both actual and contrived. And scarcely anyone will be left to wonder why the mean lady from The Weakest Link sat in on the licensing hearing. But the commission's actions are valuable in one regard. Irrelevant and fundamentally meaningless though they are, their very insignificance, the smallness of their scope, succeeded in sharpening the general focus to such a degree, it had the effect of a flash bulb going off, allowing us to take a snapshot of the culture that mostly illuminates not the state of Mike Tyson's soul, but the state of the national consciousness, spots and all. In the image of the tired, declined athlete, the aging bad-boy monster surrounded by his bland mouthpieces and wishing for his Zoloft; in the serial blah blah blah of the commissioners; in the prurient glee of the media; in the shabbiness of the entire business; anyone who wanted to look closely enough could see the operations of the forces that employ us to their ends, the reactive nature of our morality, the deprived condition of our spirits, the randomness of our days. For that alone, even in its hypocrisy and sanctimony, the commission and that bright light city whose imperatives they serve should be congratulated. The sport of boxing can hold its head high-

-it has joined the great parade and now can proudly go oompah, oompah, oompah with all the rest of the Uncle-Sam-come-latelys. And the image cultivated by the resort, the idea promoted that it is home to larger-than-life figures in their decline remains intact. Gone are Elvis and Frank, but hey, Iron Mike lives on in the desert.

For a while, anyway.

Viva Las Vegas.

LUCIUS SHEPARD has been one of the most honored writers in science fiction, fantasy, horror and beyond, winning each of the World Fantasy Award, Hugo, Nebula and International Horror Guild Awards.

His recent publications include *Two Trains Running*, *Louisiana Breakdown, Aztechs, Floater, Trujillo* (a collection of short works from P.S. Publishing), *The Handbook of American Prayer* (a novel) and *Viator* (a novel from Night Shade Books).

Shepard regularly reviews films for both *Electric Story* and the *Magazine of Fantasy and Science Fiction*.

Born in Virginia and raised in Florida, Shepard has lived in the Midwest, New England, New York and most recently the West Coast. His travels throughout the world are reflected in the exotic settings of much of his work, especially Latin America. He currently lives near a strip mall in Vancouver, Washington.

Polyphony 1
Edited by Deborah Layne and Jay Lake
First volume in the critically acclaimed slipstream/cross-genre series with stories from Maureen McHugh, Andy Duncan, Carol Emshwiller, Lucius Shepard and others.

All-Star Zeppelin Adventure Stories
Edited by David Moles and Jay Lake
Original zeppelin stories by David Brin, Jim Van Pelt, Leslie What, and others; featuring a reprint of the zeppelin classic, *"You Could Go Home Again"* by Howard Waldrop.

American Sorrows:
Stories by Jay Lake
Four longer works by the 2004 John W. Campbell Award winner; includes his Hugo nominated novelette, "Into the Gardens of Sweet Night."

Greetings From Lake Wu
Jay Lake and Frank Wu
Collection of stories by Jay Lake with original illustrations by Frank Wu.

Paradise Passed: A Novel by Jerry Oltion
The crew of a colony ship must choose between a ready-made paradise and one they create themselves.

Twenty Questions
Jerry Oltion
Twenty brilliant works by the Nebula Award-winning author of "Abandon in Place."

Dream Factories and Radio Pictures
Howard Waldrop
Waldrop's stories about early film and television reprinted in one volume.

Thirteen Ways to Water
Bruce Holland Rogers
This collection by the Nebula and World Fantasy Award winning author spans a period of ten years and brings together several award winning stories.

Order on the web at:
http://www.wheatlandpress.com

www.ingramcontent.com/pod-product-compliance
Lightning Source LLC
Chambersburg PA
CBHW031241090426
42742CB00007B/264